Big Data Technologies and Analytics

Big Data Technologies and Analytics

AI, IoT and Blockchain Technology

Aparna Kumari

Department of Computer Science and Engineering
Institute of Technology, Nirma University
Ahmedabad, Gujarat

WILEY

Published by John Wiley & Sons, Inc., Hoboken, New Jersey.

Library of Congress Cataloging-in-Publication Data has been applied for:

Print ISBN: 9781394280278
ePub ISBN: 9781394280285
ePDF ISBN: 9781394280292
oBook ISBN: 9781394280308

Cover Design: Wiley
Cover Image: Andriy Onufriyenko/Getty Images

Dedicated to my mother, whose unwavering support has shaped every word on these pages.

–Dr Aparna Kumari

Table of Contents

Acknowledgments

First and foremost, we would like to thank the almighty God, who gave us the courage and strength to overcome all the obstacles and complete this endeavor.

I would like to express my sincerest thanks to my parents and my little kids, Dev and Varen, for being good babies in the past few months and making it possible for me to complete what I have started. Their unconditional love, constant support, and motivation have made me capable of accomplishing various milestones in my life. I feel blessed to always have them by my side. I sincerely acknowledge my brother for his constant encouragement and motivation, which inspired me to pursue and complete this book. I am fully indebted to Prof. Sudeep Tanwar for his enthusiasm, wisdom, understanding, patience, and encouragement and for pushing me farther than I thought I could go.

I also wish to express my sincere gratitude to the authorities of Nirma University for providing me with all the necessary resources and facilities to complete my work. I wish to express my heartfelt appreciation to collaborators, mentors, and peers whose support has been integral to my journey.

The chain of gratitude will definitely be incomplete if I forget to thank my complete family, specifically my younger sisters and sisters-in-law, for their total love, support, and encouragement in every phase of my life. Finally, I want to express our gratitude to one and all who supported us directly or indirectly during this journey of knowledge.

Thank you.
Dr Aparna Kumari

About the Companion Website

This book is accompanied by a companion website.

www.wiley.com\go\kumaribigdatatechnologies1

This website includes:

- Free supplementary material for Big Data Processing using MapReduce.

1

Introduction to Big Data Analytics

LEARNING OBJECTIVES

- Define data and its classification into structured, semi-structured, and unstructured formats.
- Learn about the different types of data analytics, including descriptive, diagnostic, predictive, and prescriptive, and their applications.
- Trace the development of data analytics from early statistical methods to modern big data techniques.
- Grasp the concept of big data and its five V's (volume, velocity, variety, veracity, and value).
- Explore how big data analytics can be used to address global challenges and promote sustainable development.

1.1 Introduction

In today's digital age, data is being generated at an unprecedented rate, fueled by the proliferation of technological advancements and the increasing interconnectivity of devices, systems, and people. From social media interactions to financial transactions, and sensor data to scientific experiments, the world produces a torrent of information that is both a challenge and an opportunity. *Data is facts or numbers that can be used for analysis, reasoning, or decision-making.* This explosion of data has given rise to the field of data analytics, a discipline that promises to unlock valuable insights, drive innovation, and enable organizations to gain a competitive edge. Small data, which predates the big data era, focuses on certainty. It involves well-defined data sources and stable composition and context, with minimal changes. However, big data introduces complexity. This complexity involves dealing with multiple and often unknown datasets, a rapidly increasing volume of data, the speed at which it is generated and needs to be processed, and the diverse types of data being produced, whether internal or external, behavioral or social. *Big data refers to massive and intricate datasets that are too large or complex to be handled by conventional data processing tools. It is characterized by its volume, velocity, variety, veracity, and value.* Big data analytics is a multidisciplinary field that combines various techniques and technologies to analyze and extract meaningful information from large and complex datasets. It involves the application of statistical methods, machine learning algorithms, and data mining techniques to uncover patterns, trends, and relationships within the data. Transforming raw data into actionable insights has become essential to modern business operations, enabling data-driven decision-making across industries. Figure 1.1 illustrates the five Vs of big data: volume, velocity, variety, veracity, and value. Each of these dimensions is explored in greater detail in the subsequent sections of this chapter.

The evolution of big data analytics spans several decades, tracing its roots back to the early days of computing and scientific research. The advent of computers and relational databases in the 1970s revolutionized data management, laying the foundation for subsequent advancements in data analytics. The proliferation of the Internet and e-commerce in the 1990s facilitated the collection of data from online interactions, driving developments in web analytics and business intelligence (BI). The concept of big data analytics gained prominence in the early twenty-first century with the exponential growth of data volume, velocity, and variety. This led to the development of distributed computing frameworks like Hadoop and Apache Spark, enabling organizations to process and analyze massive datasets efficiently. The convergence of big data with machine learning, artificial intelligence (AI), and cloud computing further expanded its capabilities,

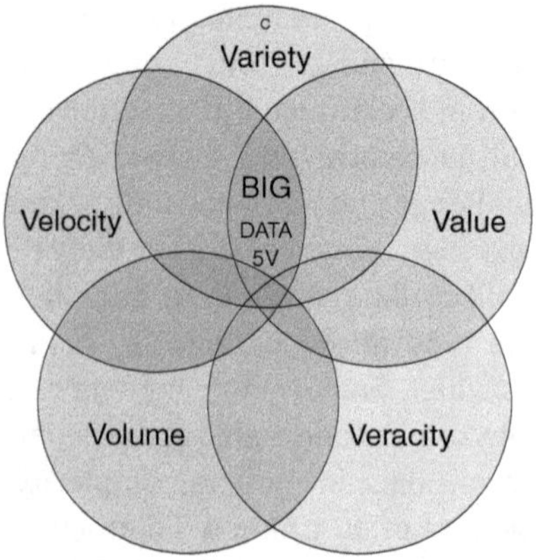

Figure 1.1 Different Vs of big data.

facilitating predictive analytics, anomaly detection, and decision support systems. The practical applications of big data analytics are vast, extending to sectors such as health care, finance, retail, manufacturing, and transportation. By harnessing the power of data analytics, organizations can gain profound insights into customer behavior, streamline supply chain processes, expedite product development, and identify untapped revenue streams. Moreover, big data analytics plays a pivotal role in tackling global issues like climate change, resource management, and sustainable development.

This chapter aims to provide a comprehensive introduction to big data analytics, serving as a foundation for students, researchers, and professionals. It begins by defining data and its various classifications, establishing a solid understanding of the diverse nature of information generated across industries. The chapter then explores the different types of data analytics, including descriptive, predictive, prescriptive, and diagnostic analytics, highlighting their respective applications and methodologies. Central to the discussion is the concept of big data, which encapsulates the challenges and opportunities presented by the massive volume, velocity, and variety of data generated. The chapter examines the defining characteristics of big data, including volume, velocity, variety, veracity, and value, providing a comprehensive understanding of this phenomenon and its implications for data-driven decision-making. Significantly, the chapter underscores the vital role of big data analytics in fostering a sustainable society. It showcases how this discipline can be applied in areas such as environmental sustainability, social sustainability, and economic sustainability. By leveraging the power of data analytics, organizations and governments can tackle intricate challenges, foster innovation, and pave the way for a more sustainable future. As technology continues to evolve, the trajectory of big data analytics promises continued innovation and transformative impact across industries. Through its comprehensive coverage of key concepts, historical context, and the potential impact of big data analytics, this chapter is an invaluable resource for students, researchers, and professionals seeking to navigate the rapidly evolving landscape of data-driven decision-making and sustainable development.

1.1.1 Motivation

This chapter is driven by the revolutionary potential of big data analytics to address urgent social issues and promote sustainable development. By examining key concepts, the historical evolution of big data analytics, and practical applications, it aims to provide readers with the knowledge and insights necessary to navigate the complexities of the data-driven landscape, spur innovation, and pave the way for a more resilient, equitable, and sustainable future.

1.1.2 Chapter Contributions

- This chapter provides an overview of big data and its significance in modern industries and research.
- It highlights the categorization of data based on structure (structured, semi-structured, unstructured), source, and processing methods.
- It includes an explanation of different types of data analytics, including descriptive, diagnostic, predictive, and prescriptive analytics.
- It discusses characteristics of big data (5V's: volume, velocity, variety, veracity, and value) and associated challenges.
- The chapter shows the progression of data analytics from traditional data processing to big data analytics.
- It describes the applications of big data analytics in energy efficiency, health care, smart cities, and resource optimization for a sustainable future.

1.1.3 Organization of the Chapter

The remainder of the paper is structured as follows: Section 1.2 presents a detailed discussion on data and its classification. Then, Section 1.3 discusses the historical evolution of the big data era. Section 1.4 covers the understanding of big data. Section 1.5 presents big data analytics and its types, and Section 1.6 covers the importance of big data analytics. Then, Section 1.7 presents the role of big data analytics in sustainable society with respect to the United Nations' SDGs. Table 1.1 shows a detailed comparative analysis of the existing work in the domain of big data analytics with the Internet of Things (IoT).

1.2 Data and Its Classification

In the realm of data science and analytics, understanding the fundamental concept of data and its classification is paramount. Data, in its essence, refers to raw facts, observations, or symbols representing information. These raw elements may take various forms, including numbers, text, images, audio, video, or any other format that can be processed by a computer or analyzed by humans. The significance of data lies in its potential to convey meaning, provide insights, and drive

Table 1.1 Comparative analysis of the existing work.

Authors	Year	Title	Summary	Pros	Cons
Eugene Siow, Thanassis Tiropanis, and Wendy Hall	2018	Analytics for the Internet of Things: A Survey	This survey reviews the application of data analytics across IoT domains, providing a categorization of analytic approaches and proposing a layered taxonomy from IoT data to analytics	Offers a comprehensive taxonomy and insights into the appropriateness of analytical techniques for IoT data	Being a survey, it may lack in-depth analysis of specific applications or case studies
Mehdi Mohammadi, Ala Al-Fuqaha, Sameh Sorour, and Mohsen Guizani	2018	Deep Learning for IoT Big Data and Streaming Analytics	This paper provides a thorough overview of using deep learning techniques to facilitate analytics and learning in the IoT domain, discussing IoT data characteristics and the potential of emerging deep learning (DL) techniques	Highlights the promises and challenges of deep learning in IoT data analytics, offering a comprehensive background on different DL architectures and algorithms	Focuses primarily on deep learning, potentially overlooking other relevant machine learning approaches

(Continued)

Table 1.1 (Continued)

Authors	Year	Title	Summary	Pros	Cons
Muhammad Habib ur Rehman, Ibrar Yaqoob, Khaled Salah, Muhammad Imran, Prem Prakash Jayaraman, and Charith Perera	2019	The Role of Big Data Analytics in Industrial Internet of Things (IIoT)	This study investigates recent big data analytics technologies, algorithms, and techniques that can lead to the development of intelligent IIoT systems, presenting a taxonomy based on important parameters	Provides a detailed taxonomy and discusses frameworks and case studies of enterprises benefiting from big data analytics in IIoT	May not cover the most recent advancements in the rapidly evolving field of IIoT
Erwin Adi, Adnan Anwar, Zubair Baig, Sherali Zeadally	2020	Machine Learning and Data Analytics for the IoT	This paper critically reviews how IoT-generated data are processed for machine learning analysis, highlighting current challenges and proposing a framework for adaptive learning among IoT applications	Offers a framework to enable IoT applications to adaptively learn from others, discussing key factors impacting future intelligent applications for the IoT	The proposed framework may require further validation through practical implementation and testing
Abu Fuad Ahmad, Md Shohel Sayeed, Choo Peng Tan, and Kim Geok Tan	2021	A Review on IoT with Big Data Analytics	This review discusses the integration of IoT and big data analytics, exploring various applications and highlighting the benefits and challenges of this convergence	Provides insights into the applications of IoT with big data analytics, discussing benefits and challenges	May lack detailed technical analysis or case studies demonstrating practical implementations

Authors	Year	Title	Summary	Pros	Cons
Acharya, S. and Chellappan, S.	2022	*Big Data and Analytics* (2nd ed.)	This book provides a comprehensive overview of big data concepts, tools, and analytics techniques. It covers topics such as Hadoop, data mining, and machine learning	—In-depth coverage of big data concepts —Practical examples and exercises for hands-on learning —Covers both basic and advanced analytics topics	—Can be complex for beginners without prior technical knowledge —Focuses more on theory, with fewer real-world case studies
Aroraa, G., Lele, C. and Jindal, M.	2022	*Data Analytics: Principles, Tools, and Practices: A Complete Guide for Advanced Data Analytics Using the Latest Trends, Tools, and Technologies* (English Edition)	This book offers a comprehensive guide to advanced data analytics using the latest trends and technologies, covering principles, tools, and practical applications	—Detailed coverage of advanced data analytics tools and technologies —Suitable for practitioners and students looking to delve into advanced topics —Clear explanations	—May not be beginner-friendly —Limited focus on foundational topics, requiring prior knowledge of data analytics concepts
Selmy H.A., Mohamed H.K., and Medhat W.	2024	*Big Data Analytics Deep Learning Techniques and Applications: A Survey*	This paper explores the latest advancements in big data analytics, focusing on new techniques and their applications	—Offers insights into cutting-edge developments in the field. —Focuses on practical applications and emerging technologies	—May require a deep understanding of big data and related fields. —The scope might be narrow for readers interested in a broader range of topics

informed decision-making across diverse domains. Data comprises a few characteristics, these are:

- Composition: Data composition refers to the organization of data, including its sources, level of detail, types, and whether it is static or provided in real-time streams.
- Condition: The condition of data pertains to its current state, such as whether it is ready for analysis as is or if it needs to be cleaned and refined for further improvement and enrichment.
- Context: The context of data involves understanding where the data was generated, the reasons behind its generation, its sensitivity, and any associated events or circumstances.

Typically, we can answer questions about why data was created, its origin and timing, how we intend to use it, and what questions it can address. Next, good data is accurate, complete, consistent, relevant, timely, valid, unique, secure, accessible, and understandable, while bad data lacks one or more of these qualities. Here are some key qualities that good data should possess:

- **Accuracy:** Data should be correct and free of errors.
- **Completeness:** Data should be whole and not have missing parts.
- **Consistency:** Data should be uniform and not contradictory.
- **Relevance:** Data should be pertinent to the specific task or analysis.
- **Timeliness:** Data should be current and accessible when needed.
- **Validity:** Data should be sound and adhere to established rules.
- **Uniqueness:** Data should be distinct and not have duplicates.
- **Security:** Data should be safeguarded from unauthorized access.
- **Accessibility:** Data should be obtainable and easily retrievable.
- **Understandability:** Data should be clear and interpretable.

Data can be classified into various types based on different criteria, including its structure, source, and usage.

1.2.1 Classification Based on Structure

One common classification categorizes data into three main types, as shown in Figure 1.2 and also described here:

1. **Structured Data:** Structured data refers to information organized in a predefined format, typically represented in tabular form with rows and columns. Examples of structured data include databases, spreadsheets, and relational data stored in tables. Structured data is characterized by its uniformity, making it easy to store, retrieve, and analyze using traditional database management systems. Approximately 10% of an organization's data is in this format.

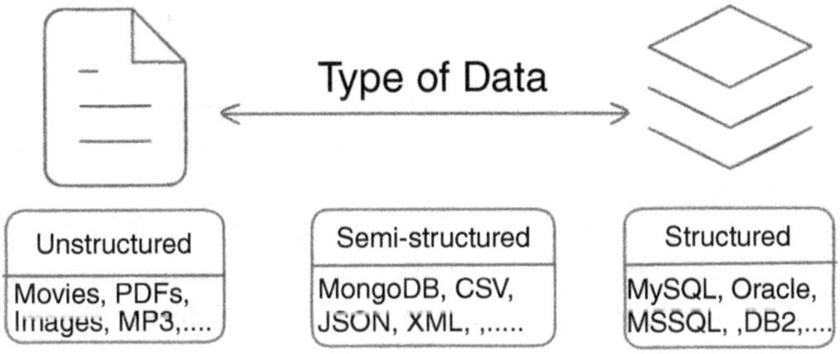

Figure 1.2 Types of data.

2. **Unstructured Data:** Unstructured data lacks a specific format or organizational structure, often comprising textual content, multimedia files, social media posts, and sensor data. Unlike structured data, unstructured data does not adhere to a predefined schema, posing challenges for storage, processing, and analysis. However, advancements in natural language processing, image recognition, and other technologies enable organizations to extract insights from unstructured data sources. Approximately 80% of an organization's data falls into this category, including memos, chat messages, PowerPoint presentations, images, videos, letters, research papers, white papers, email content, and similar types of documents.
3. **Semi-structured Data:** Semi-structured data lies somewhere between structured and unstructured data, possessing some organizational elements but not adhering strictly to a predefined schema. Examples of semi-structured data include XML files, JSON documents, and log files. While semi-structured data may exhibit some level of organization, it offers flexibility in representing complex relationships and hierarchical structures. Approximately 10% of an organization's data is in this format.

1.2.2 Classification Based on Source and Usage

In addition to structural classification, data can also be categorized based on its source and usage:

1. **Internal Data:** Internal data originates from sources within an organization, such as transactional systems, customer databases, and operational records. Internal data often pertains to organizational activities, processes, and interactions, providing insights into business operations and performance metrics.
2. **External Data:** External data encompasses information sourced from external sources beyond the organization's boundaries, including market research reports, social media feeds, public datasets, and third-party data providers. External data supplements internal data sources, offering broader insights into market trends, customer behaviors, and industry benchmarks.

3. **Transactional Data:** Transactional data records specific transactions or interactions between entities, such as sales transactions, financial transactions, and customer interactions. Transactional data is characterized by its high volume, velocity, and granularity, making it valuable for operational analysis and decision-making.
4. **Analytical Data:** Analytical data is aggregated, summarized, or transformed for analytical purposes, typically used for reporting, visualization, and BI. Analytical data may encompass aggregated metrics, KPIs, and derived attributes calculated from raw transactional or operational data.

1.3 Historical Evolution of the Big Data Era

Small data, which predates the big data era, focuses on certainty. It involves well-defined data sources and stable composition and context, with minimal changes. Typically, we can answer questions about why data was created, its origin and timing, how we intend to use it, and what questions it can address. However, big data introduces complexity. This complexity involves dealing with multiple and often unknown datasets, a rapidly increasing volume of data, the speed at which it is generated and needs to be processed, and the diverse types of data being produced, whether internal or external, behavioral or social.

Before the 1970s, the era was dominated by mainframes, where data was mostly primitive and structured. The 1980s and 1990s saw the development of relational databases, marking a period of data-intensive applications. With the advent of the World Wide Web (WWW) and the Internet of Things (IoT), there has been a surge in the generation of structured, unstructured, and multimedia data and the evolution of big data, as shown in Table 1.2.

Table 1.2 Evolution of the big data era.

Era	Time frame	Characteristics	Key developments
Mainframe era	Pre-1970s	Primitive and structured data	Mainframes, early databases
Relational era	1980s–1990s	Data-intensive applications, structured data	Emergence of relational databases, SQL
Early web era	1990s–2000s	Growth of web data, beginning of unstructured data	Rise of the World Wide Web (WWW), early data warehousing
Big data era	2000s–present	Explosion of structured, unstructured, and multimedia data	Proliferation of IoT, social media, and advanced analytics tools

1.4 Understanding Big Data

Big data consists of information assets that are characterized by high velocity and a wide variety, requiring cost-effective and innovative processing methods to improve insights and decision-making. It refers to datasets that are usually too large and complex for traditional database software tools to handle. Essentially, big data encompasses any data that surpasses the capacity of conventional human and technical infrastructure for storage, processing, and analysis. It is defined by its massive volume, rapid generation, and diverse types. Figure 1.1 illustrates the five V's of big data: volume, velocity, variety, veracity, and value.

- **Volume**: Volume can range from terabytes to petabytes, and even up to zettabytes.
- **Velocity**: Velocity refers to the speed at which data is generated in real time. We have progressed from basic desktop applications, such as payroll systems, to applications that handle real-time data processing.
- **Variety**: Data comes in different forms: structured, semi-structured, and unstructured. Structured data is organized and stored in databases. Semi-structured data includes formats like HTML, XML, email, and CSV files. Unstructured data encompasses a range of formats such as PowerPoint presentations, images, videos, research papers, white papers, and the body of emails.
- **Veracity** refers to the reliability and accuracy of data, addressing inconsistencies, biases, and uncertainties to ensure trustworthy insights.
- **Value** represents the meaningful impact derived from big data, emphasizing its ability to generate actionable intelligence and drive informed decision-making.

Definition of Big Data: According to the Gartner Glossary, big data refers to information assets characterized by high volume, high velocity, and/or high variety. These assets require cost-effective and innovative processing methods to provide improved insights and support better decision-making. Further, we can also refer to it as "big data is high-volume, high-velocity, and high-variety information assets," which refers to extremely large datasets that may include a mix of structured, semi-structured, and unstructured data. These datasets require rapid storage, preparation, processing, and analysis that could lead to various challenges.

1.4.1 Challenges with Big Data

Key challenges associated with big data are outlined below, focusing primarily on issues related to data integration, quality assurance, and real-time analytics

i. **Data Volume**: Data is growing exponentially, and this trend is expected to continue. Key questions include the following: Will all this data be useful for analysis, should we work with the entire dataset or just a part of the dataset, or how can we differentiate valuable knowledge from irrelevant information?
ii. **Data Retention**: Determining how long to retain data can be challenging. Some data might be needed for long-term decisions, while other data may become irrelevant quickly.
iii. **Storage**: Cloud computing offers a cost-effective, flexible solution for managing big data infrastructure, including the ability to easily scale and adjust resources. However, this also raises questions about the decision to host big data solutions outside of the enterprise.
iv. **Visualization**: Big data often exceeds the capacity of traditional database tools. Data visualization, a growing field, is crucial for understanding and interpreting large datasets, yet there are few experts in this area.
v. **Skilled Professionals**: Organizations require highly skilled data scientists to develop, manage, and operate applications that generate insights from big data.
vi. **Other Challenges**: Additional challenges include the capture, storage, search, analysis, transfer, and security of big data.

1.5 Big Data Analytics and Its Types

In the era of digital transformation, the exponential growth of data has given rise to a new field called big data analytics. This discipline combines various techniques and technologies to analyze and extract meaningful insights from large and complex datasets. Big data analytics has emerged as a powerful tool for organizations seeking to gain a competitive edge by leveraging the wealth of information at their disposal. At its core, big data analytics involves the application of statistical methods, machine learning algorithms, and data mining techniques to uncover patterns, trends, and relationships within vast amounts of data. This process of transforming raw data into actionable insights has become an essential component of modern business operations, enabling data-driven decision-making across industries. Big data analytics can be broadly categorized into four main types, each serving a distinct purpose and addressing specific analytical needs, as shown in Figure 1.3 and also described in the following text.

1. **Descriptive Analytics**: Descriptive analytics is concerned with summarizing and describing historical data to understand what happened in the past. It involves techniques such as data mining, statistical analysis, and

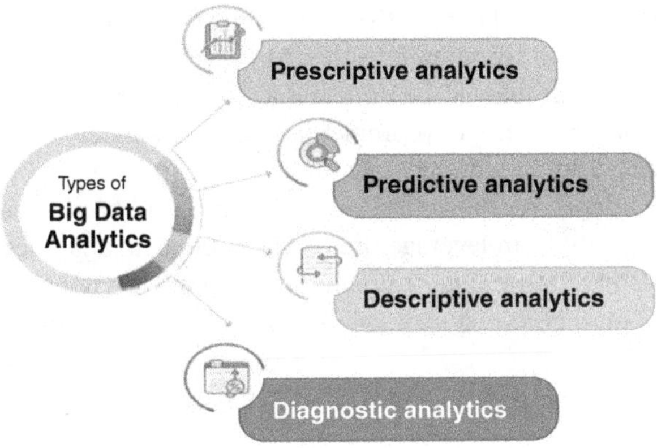

Figure 1.3 Type of big data analytics.

data visualization to identify patterns and trends within the data. Descriptive analytics provides a comprehensive view of past events, enabling organizations to gain insights into consumer behavior, market trends, and operational performance.

2. **Predictive Analytics:** Predictive analytics utilizes historical data, statistical models, and machine learning techniques to identify patterns and make predictions about future events or behaviors. By analyzing past data and identifying relationships between various factors, predictive analytics can forecast future outcomes, enabling organizations to make informed decisions and take proactive measures.
3. **Prescriptive Analytics:** Building upon the insights gained from predictive analytics, prescriptive analytics goes a step further by providing recommendations or prescriptions on the best course of action to take based on the predicted outcomes. This type of analytics combines optimization techniques, business rules, and machine learning algorithms to suggest optimal solutions or strategies for achieving desired outcomes.
4. **Diagnostic Analytics:** Diagnostic analytics aims to understand the root causes behind specific events or patterns by analyzing historical data and identifying relationships between various factors. It involves techniques such as data mining, regression analysis, and exploratory data analysis to uncover the underlying reasons for certain outcomes or behaviors. Diagnostic analytics is particularly valuable in troubleshooting and problem-solving scenarios, enabling organizations to identify and address the root causes of issues.

These four types of big data analytics are interconnected and often employed in a complementary manner. For instance, descriptive analytics may be used to gain insights into past performance, while predictive analytics can forecast future trends, and prescriptive analytics can recommend actions to optimize outcomes. Diagnostic analytics can then be employed to understand the reasons behind any deviations or anomalies observed. Effective implementation of big data analytics requires a combination of advanced analytical tools, powerful computing resources, and skilled professionals. As the volume, velocity, and variety of data continue to grow, organizations that can leverage the power of big data analytics will gain a significant competitive advantage, enabling them to make informed decisions, drive innovation, and achieve sustainable growth in an increasingly data-driven world.

1.6 Importance of Big Data Analytics

Having more data for analysis improves the accuracy of our insights and increases our confidence in the decisions we make based on these findings. Greater analytical precision can significantly enhance operational efficiency, lower costs and time requirements, and lead to the development of new products and services, as well as the optimization of existing ones.

1.6.1 Traditional Data Warehouse Environment

Operational or transactional data, collected from sources such as enterprise resource planning (ERP) systems, customer relationship management (CRM) systems, legacy systems, and various third-party applications, often comes in different formats. This data undergoes a process called extraction, transformation, and loading (ETL), where it is integrated, cleaned, transformed, and standardized. After transformation, the data is loaded into either an enterprise data warehouse (at the organizational level) or data marts (specific to business units or processes). BI and analytics tools are then employed to facilitate decision-making through methods such as ad-hoc queries, SQL, enterprise dashboards, data mining, and online analytical processing.

Figure 1.4 illustrates a structured process best suited to help solve data-driven problems in a traditional system using the Data Science Life Cycle. The cycle begins with identifying problems and understanding the business context, followed by dipsticks for detecting, gathering, and fitting useful data from different sources. Efficient data collection and organization permit raw data to become sterile and useful while making it ready for analysis. So, it is only in the next phase called data modeling, when the true power of predictive or descriptive modeling is harnessed in the contemporary statistical approaches or simply leverages

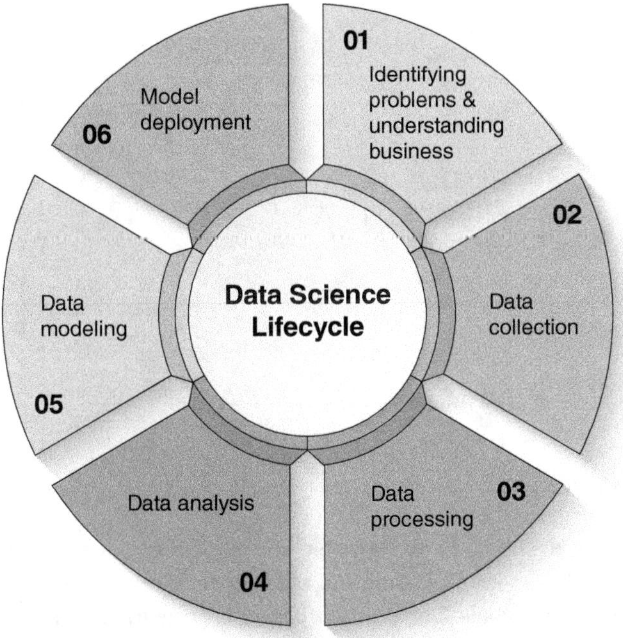

Figure 1.4 Data science life cycle.

the incipient true power of machine learning. Finally, the last mile is model deployment, where systems manage the operational complexities, real-world adjustments, and regulatory compliance required for successful adoption. The continuous loop ensures that the data-driven solutions fulfill the business need.

1.6.2 Big Data Analytics Life Cycle

Figure 1.5 posits the big data analytics life cycle as a structured means by which large-scale data can be analyzed for informed decision-making. The life cycle starts off with data collection, where large quantities of data are scooped from diverse heads, such as sensors, logs, and social networks. In the data storage and management stage, the data is first organized and then stored within systems that facilitate both scalability and access and dependability. In raw data handling and processing, raw data gets cleaned, transformed, and prepared for various analyses. Finally, in the data analysis phase, data is taken through advanced techniques that consist of machine learning and statistical methods, aimed entirely at extracting patterns and insights. All results can then be presented in the form of data

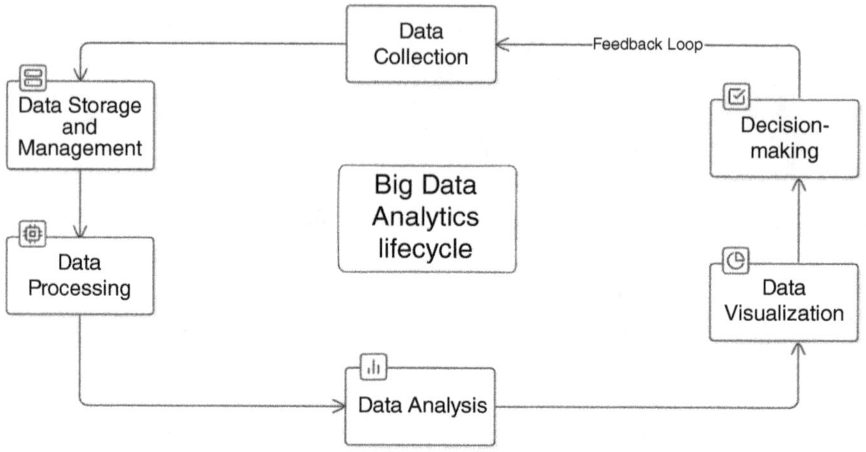

Figure 1.5 Big data analytics life cycle.

visualization-something like dashboards, bar graphs, and pie charts for gaining better intuition. Ultimately, these sets of information assist in decision-making for pursuit of strategic or operational goals. The entire process also integrates continuous feedback to further inform data collection and analytics, feeding back for an ongoing improvement pathway that is continuously adaptive.

1.6.3 BI on Traditional Data Versus Big Data Analytics

This comparison highlights the evolution of BI from traditional structured data processing to modern big data-driven analytics, enabling deeper insights and real-time decision-making. Here's a tabular comparison of BI on traditional data versus big data analytics in Table 1.3.

1.7 The Role of Big Data Analytics in Sustainable Society

In an era marked by unprecedented environmental challenges, resource constraints, and the pressing need for sustainable development, big data analytics has emerged as a powerful tool to drive positive change and foster a more sustainable future. By harnessing the power of data-driven insights, organizations and governments can develop innovative solutions, optimize processes, and make informed decisions that contribute to environmental, social, and economic sustainability, aligning with the United Nations' Sustainable Development Goals

Table 1.3 Traditional data BI versus big data analytics.

Aspect	Traditional data BI	Big data analytics
Data type	Structured (relational databases, spreadsheets)	Structured, semi-structured, and unstructured (databases, logs, social media, and IoT)
Data volume	Limited (MBs to GBs)	Massive (TBs to PBs and beyond)
Data velocity	Batch processing, periodic updates	Real-time or near-real-time processing
Data variety	Primarily structured data	Diverse formats (text, images, videos, IoT sensor data)
Data veracity	High accuracy with well-defined data sources	Requires advanced techniques to handle inconsistencies and noise
Data value	Limited insights, mainly historical analysis	High-value insights, enabling predictive and prescriptive analytics
Processing speed	Relatively slow, dependent on predefined queries	High-speed processing with AI/ML-driven insights
Scalability	Limited by traditional storage and computing resources	Highly scalable with cloud and distributed computing
Analytics approach	Descriptive and diagnostic analytics	Predictive and prescriptive analytics with AI/ML integration
Storage	Relational databases (SQL-based)	Distributed storage (Hadoop, NoSQL, Data Lakes)
Technology stack	Traditional BI tools (Excel, SQL, Tableau)	Advanced tools (Hadoop, Spark, Kafka, AI/ML frameworks)
Decision-making	Based on historical trends and reports	Real-time insights with proactive recommendations
Cost efficiency	Higher costs for scaling and storage	Cost-effective with cloud and open-source big data solutions
Use cases	Financial reports, sales forecasting	Customer sentiment analysis, predictive maintenance, and real-time fraud detection

(SDGs), particularly SDG 7 (Affordable and Clean Energy), SDG 11 (Sustainable Cities and Communities), SDG 12 (Responsible Consumption and Production), and SDG 13 (Climate Action), and so on. The potential applications of big data analytics in promoting a sustainable society are vast and multifaceted. In the realm of environmental sustainability, big data analytics plays a vital role in addressing

Figure 1.6 Role of big data analytics.

critical issues such as climate change, resource management, and ecosystem preservation, as shown in Figure 1.6 and further described in the following list:

1. **Climate Change Analysis and Modeling (SDG 13 and SDG 15):** Big data analytics can be leveraged to analyze vast amounts of climate data, including atmospheric measurements, satellite imagery, and weather patterns. By processing and modeling this data, researchers and policymakers can gain a deeper understanding of climate dynamics, identify trends and anomalies, and develop accurate forecasting models. These insights can inform mitigation strategies, adaptation measures, and environmental policies aimed at reducing greenhouse gas emissions and minimizing the impacts of climate change, directly supporting the United Nations' Sustainable Development Goals (SDGs), particularly SDG 13 (Climate Action) and SDG 15 (Life on Land). By integrating data-driven approaches, stakeholders can make more informed decisions that contribute to a more resilient and sustainable future.

2. **Resource Management and Optimization (SDG 6, SDG 7, and SDG 12)**: Efficient resource management is crucial for achieving sustainability goals. Big data analytics can be applied to optimize the use of natural resources such as water, energy, and raw materials. By analyzing data from various sources, including sensor networks, smart grids, and industrial processes, organizations can identify inefficiencies, reduce waste, and implement data-driven strategies for resource conservation and sustainable consumption, aligning with SDG 6 (Clean Water and Sanitation), SDG 7 (Affordable and Clean Energy), and SDG 12 (Responsible Consumption and Production).
3. **Ecosystem Monitoring and Conservation (SDG 14, SDG 15)**: Preserving fragile ecosystems and biodiversity is a critical component of environmental sustainability. Big data analytics can be used to monitor and assess the health of ecosystems by combining data from remote sensing technologies, field observations, and citizen science initiatives. This information can guide conservation efforts, inform land-use planning, and support policies aimed at protecting vulnerable habitats and species, contributing to SDG 14 (Life Below Water) and SDG 15 (Life on Land).

   Beyond environmental sustainability, big data analytics also plays a pivotal role in social and economic sustainability. In the realm of social sustainability, big data analytics can contribute to improved health care, education, and urban planning.
4. **Health care and Public Health (SDG 3)**: By analyzing large health-care datasets, including electronic medical records, genomic data, and population health statistics, big data analytics can enable personalized medicine, early disease detection, and more effective public health interventions. These insights can lead to improved patient outcomes, reduced health-care costs, and the development of targeted prevention strategies for promoting overall societal well-being, aligning with SDG 3 (Good Health and Well-being).
5. **Education and Skill Development (SDG 4)**: Big data analytics can be applied to analyze student performance data, learning patterns, and educational trends. This information can inform the development of personalized learning approaches, identify areas for curriculum enhancement, and support data-driven policies aimed at promoting inclusive and equitable access to quality education, fostering human capital development, and driving social progress, supporting SDG 4 (Quality Education).

   In the domain of economic sustainability, big data analytics can contribute to supply chain optimization, risk management, and innovation.
6. **Supply Chain Optimization (SDG 9, SDG 12)**: By analyzing data from various sources, including logistics, inventory management, and consumer behavior, big data analytics can optimize supply chain processes, reduce waste, and enhance overall productivity. This can lead to cost savings,

increased efficiency, and a reduced environmental footprint, contributing to both economic and environmental sustainability, in alignment with SDG 9 (Industry, Innovation, and Infrastructure) and SDG 12 (Responsible Consumption and Production).

7. **Risk Management and Fraud Detection (SDG 8, SDG 16)**: Big data analytics can be used to analyze large datasets from financial transactions, customer behavior, and cybersecurity threats. This information can enable better risk assessment, fraud detection, and prevention strategies, promoting financial stability and consumer trust, which are essential components of a sustainable economy. These efforts align with SDG 8 (Decent Work and Economic Growth) and SDG 16 (Peace, Justice, and Strong Institutions).
8. **Innovation and Product Development (SDG 9, SDG 12)**: By analyzing customer data, market trends, and emerging technologies, big data analytics can drive innovation, identify new business opportunities, and support the development of sustainable products and services. This can foster economic growth while minimizing environmental impacts and promoting social responsibility, aligning with SDG 9 (Industry, Innovation, and Infrastructure) and SDG 12 (Responsible Consumption and Production).

To fully realize the potential of big data analytics in fostering a sustainable society, it is crucial to address challenges such as data quality, privacy concerns, and the ethical use of data. Collaboration among stakeholders, including governments, businesses, academia, and civil society organizations, is essential to develop responsible and transparent data practices that prioritize sustainability goals. As the world grapples with the complexities of sustainable development, big data analytics emerges as a powerful tool for driving positive change. Emerging technologies like edge computing and blockchain are expected to augment big data analytics. Next, ethical issues in big data analytics are crucial because data misuse can lead to privacy violations, biased decision-making, and potential harm to individuals or groups. Ensuring ethical use fosters trust and prevents exploitation of sensitive information.

AI enhances big data analytics by providing advanced algorithms for data processing, real-time analytics, and predictive modeling, making the analysis more efficient and insightful. Interdisciplinary cooperation brings together diverse expertise, fostering innovation, solving complex problems, and improving the accuracy and relevance of data-driven insights across various sectors like health care, finance, and urban planning. By leveraging the wealth of data available and extracting actionable insights, organizations and governments can make informed decisions, optimize processes, and develop innovative solutions that promote environmental stewardship, social equity, and economic resilience, paving the way for a more sustainable and prosperous future for all.

1.8 Conclusion

Investigating big data analytics demonstrates how crucial it is in forming modern civilization. The capacity to mine enormous amounts of data for insightful information has become essential as we work through the complexity of a world that is ever more and more interconnected. Big data analytics has many uses, ranging from environmental conservation to health care, and it has the potential to spur innovation, efficiency, and sustainability in various fields. In this study, we have highlighted its alignment with the United Nations' SDGs, showcasing how it contributes to environmental, social, and economic sustainability. However, as we proceed, we must remember ethical issues and ensure data management is done responsibly. We may minimize potential dangers and obstacles while optimizing the advantages of big data analytics by adhering to the principles of responsibility, openness, and privacy. Developments in AI, machine learning, and data processing technologies will likely drive the further evolution of big data analytics. The potential for augmenting the capabilities and influence of big data analytics by integrating cutting-edge technologies like edge computing, blockchain, and quantum computing is enormous. Cross-sector alliances and interdisciplinary cooperation will also be essential for tackling complex societal issues and opening up fresh avenues for innovation. We can fully utilize big data analytics to create a more sustainable, fair, and resilient future for future generations if we embrace these future directions.

Practice Set

A Multiple Choice Questions (MCQ)

1 What is the primary role of big data analytics in modern civilization?
- a Entertainment
- b Forming modern civilization
- c Managing finances
- d Simplifying communication

2 Which field is NOT mentioned as having potential benefits from big data analytics?
- a Environmental conservation
- b Health care
- c Agriculture
- d Financial trading

3 What is a key concern when using big data analytics, according to the chapter?
  a Cost of technology
  b Ethical issues
  c Data speed
  d Hardware limitations

4 Which technology is NOT listed as potentially augmenting big data analytics?
  a Edge computing
  b Blockchain
  c Quantum computing
  d Virtual reality

5 What principle is emphasized for managing data responsibly?
  a Secrecy
  b Privacy
  c Exclusivity
  d Transparency

6 Which emerging technology is expected to drive the evolution of big data analytics?
  a Cloud computing
  b Artificial intelligence
  c Internet of Things
  d 5G networks

7 How can interdisciplinary cooperation contribute to big data analytics?
  a By increasing data storage
  b By opening new avenues for innovation
  c By improving data security
  d By reducing data costs

8 What does the chapter suggest is crucial for minimizing potential dangers in big data analytics?
  a Advanced algorithms
  b Strict regulations
  c Responsible management
  d High-speed Internet

9 Which of the following is a potential benefit of big data analytics, as mentioned in the chapter?
- **a** Decreased decision-making accuracy due to limited data analysis
- **b** Improved decision-making through data-driven insights
- **c** Increased manual processing of business data
- **d** Reduced ability to identify customer trends

10 What is the potential impact of integrating quantum computing with big data analytics?
- **a** Decreased processing speed
- **b** Enhanced capabilities and influence
- **c** Limited data analysis
- **d** Increased data storage requirements

B Fill-in-the-Blanks

11 Big data analytics has applications in various fields such as __________, health care, and environmental conservation.

12 One of the principles for responsible data management mentioned in the chapter is __________.

13 Emerging technologies like edge computing and __________ are expected to augment big data analytics.

14 The chapter emphasizes that cross-sector alliances and __________ cooperation will be essential for tackling complex societal issues.

15 To fully utilize big data analytics for a sustainable future, we need to embrace future __________.

C Short Answer Questions

16 What are some of the potential uses of big data analytics according to the chapter?

17 Explain the importance of ethical issues in big data analytics.

18 How can big data analytics contribute to environmental conservation?

19 What role does artificial intelligence play in the evolution of big data analytics?

20 Describe how interdisciplinary cooperation can benefit big data analytics.

D Long Answer Questions

21 Discuss the potential benefits and challenges of integrating blockchain technology with big data analytics.

22 Analyze the impact of responsible data management on the effectiveness of big data analytics.

23 Evaluate how emerging technologies like edge computing and quantum computing can transform big data analytics.

24 Explore the implications of big data analytics for creating a more sustainable and fair future.

25 Assess the role of cross-sector alliances in advancing big data analytics and addressing complex societal issues.

Further Readings

Abu-Salih, B., Wongthongtham, P., Zhu, D., Chan, K.Y. and Rudra, A., 2021. Introduction to big data technology. In: *Social Big Data Analytics: Practices, Techniques, and Applications*, pp. 15–59. Springer.

Abu-Salih, B., Wongthongtham, P., Zhu, D., Chan, K.Y. and Rudra, A., 2021. *Social Big Data Analytics*. Singapore: Springer.

Acharya, S. and Chellappan, S., 2022. *Big Data and Analytics* (2nd ed.). Wiley.

Ahsaan, S.U. and Mourya, A.K., 2019. Big data analytics: challenges and technologies. *Annals of the Faculty of Engineering Hunedoara*, 17(4), pp. 75–79.

Aroraa, G., Lele, C. and Jindal, M., 2022. *Data Analytics: Principles, Tools, and Practices: A Complete Guide for Advanced Data Analytics Using the Latest Trends, Tools, and Technologies* (English Edition). BPB Publications.

Batko, K. and Ślęzak, A., 2022. The use of big data analytics in healthcare. *Journal of Big Data*, 9(1), p. 3.

Berisha, B., Mëziu, E. and Shabani, I., 2022. Big data analytics in cloud computing: an overview. *Journal of Cloud Computing*, 11(1), p. 24.

Bhattacharya, P., Kumari, A., Budhiraja, I. and Tanwar, S., 2024. MetaEd: metaverse-assisted virtual classroom and content generation framework underlying 5G. In: *2024 IEEE International Conference on Communications Workshops (ICC)*, pp. 311–319. IEEE.

Bhattacharya, P., Kumari, A., Tanwar, S., Budhiraja, I. and Patel, S., 2024. Quant-Jack: Quantum Machine Learning to detect cryptojacking attacks in IIoT networks. In: *2024 IEEE International Conference on Communications Workshops (ICC)*, pp. 1–12. IEEE.

Eckroth, J., 2018. A course on big data analytics. *Journal of Parallel and Distributed Computing*, 118, pp. 166–176.

Jan, B., Farman, H., Khan, M., Imran, M., Islam, I.U., Ahmad, A., Ali, S. and Jeon, G., 2019. Deep learning in big data analytics: a comparative study. *Computers & Electrical Engineering*, 75, pp. 275–287.

Kaddoura, S. and Grati, R., 2021. Blockchain for healthcare and medical systems. In: *Enabling Blockchain Technology for Secure Networking and Communications*, pp. 249–270. IGI Global.

Khan, M., Jan, B. and Farman, H., 2019. *Deep Learning: Convergence to Big Data Analytics*. Singapore: Springer.

Kumari, A., Kakkar, R., Tanwar, S., Garg, D., Polkowski, Z., Alqahtani, F. and Tolba, A., 2024. Multi-agent-based decentralized residential energy management using Deep Reinforcement Learning. *Journal of Building Engineering*, 87, p. 109031.

Kumari, A., Nehra, A., Bhattacharya, P., Tanwar, S., Gupta, R. and Rodrigues, J.J.P.C., 2024. A secure Stackelberg game framework for profit maximization in Vehicle-to-Grid systems using 5G. In: *ICC 2024-IEEE International Conference on Communications*, pp. 4263–4268. IEEE.

Moreira, J., Carvalho, A. and Horvath, T., 2018. *A General Introduction to Data Analytics*. John Wiley & Sons.

Prokofieva, M. and Miah, S.J., 2019. Blockchain in healthcare [Online]. *Australasian Journal of Information Systems*, 23.

Vanani, I.R. and Majidian, S., 2019. Literature review on big data analytics methods. In: *Social Media and Machine Learning, pp.* 2–10. IntechOpen.

Vassakis, K., Petrakis, E. and Kopanakis, I., 2018. Big data analytics: applications, prospects and challenges. In: *Mobile Big Data: A Roadmap from Models to Technologies*, pp. 3–20. Springer.

2

Data Management Technologies and Tools

LEARNING OBJECTIVES

- Effective data management is discussed with firms to exploit big data and obtain a competitive advantage in today's business world.
- This chapter delves into analytics, visualization, integration, and real-time processing technologies that are critical for handling and interpreting large data.
- It describes technologies and solutions that use statistical techniques and machine learning algorithms to extract actionable insights from massive datasets.
- It explores technologies for converting complex datasets into intuitive visual forms, hence improving understanding and interpretation.
- It emphasizes real-time data analytics technologies that allow enterprises to rapidly process and analyze data streams, allowing for the agile detection of patterns, anomalies, and trends.

2.1 Introduction

In the contemporary landscape of business, the term "data" has transcended its conventional connotations to become a cornerstone of modern enterprise operations. We find ourselves engulfed in a deluge of data, stemming from an array of sources including social media interactions, transactional records, sensor data from Internet of Things (IoT) devices, and more. This data surge presents both opportunities and challenges for organizations across industries. On the one hand, it offers unprecedented potential for extracting valuable insights, driving innovation, and enhancing decision-making processes. On the other hand, managing and harnessing this vast volume of data poses formidable challenges in terms of scalability, security, and complexity. Amid this data deluge, the concept of big data has emerged as a paradigm-shifting force, reshaping the way businesses operate and compete in the digital age. Big data, characterized by the three Vs—volume, velocity, and variety, encompasses datasets that are voluminous, generated at high velocity, and exhibit diverse structures and formats. Traditional data management approaches and tools are often ill-equipped to handle the scale and complexity of big data, necessitating the adoption of innovative technologies and strategies.

At the heart of effective big data management lies the ability to extract actionable insights from raw data, thereby transforming information into strategic assets. This process of data analytics involves the application of statistical techniques, machine learning algorithms, and artificial intelligence (AI) to uncover patterns, trends, and correlations hidden within the data. By leveraging analytics, organizations can gain valuable insights into customer behavior, market trends, operational performance, and more, enabling them to make data-driven decisions with confidence. Figure 2.1 shows the management of data in big data analytics. However, the journey from raw data to actionable insights is fraught with challenges, chief among them being the sheer volume and variety of data sources. Traditional relational databases and spreadsheet-based tools are often inadequate for processing and analyzing big data, necessitating the adoption of specialized technologies and platforms designed for scalability and performance. Additionally, ensuring data quality, consistency, and integrity is paramount to

Figure 2.1 Management of data in big data analytics.

deriving accurate and reliable insights. Data integration and preparation tools and technologies play a crucial role in harmonizing data from disparate sources, resolving inconsistencies, and cleansing noisy or incomplete data.

Furthermore, the ability to visualize and communicate insights effectively is essential for driving organizational alignment and decision-making. Data visualization tools enable stakeholders to explore complex datasets through interactive charts, graphs, and dashboards, thereby facilitating better understanding and interpretation. By transforming raw data into compelling visual narratives, organizations can democratize access to insights and empower decision-makers at all levels of the organization. In the quest for real-time insights, organizations are increasingly turning to streaming analytics technologies that process and analyze data in motion. These platforms enable organizations to detect patterns, anomalies, and emerging trends in real time, empowering them to respond swiftly to changing market dynamics and customer needs. Whether it's detecting fraudulent transactions, optimizing supply chain operations, or personalizing customer experiences, real-time data analytics has become indispensable for driving agility and competitiveness in today's hyper-connected world.

In essence, effective data management is no longer a choice but a necessity for organizations seeking to thrive in the era of big data. By embracing advanced technologies and tools in analytics, visualization, integration, and real-time processing, businesses can unlock the full potential of their data assets and gain a competitive edge in today's data-driven landscape. However, achieving success in the realm of big data requires more than just technology; it demands a holistic approach encompassing organizational culture, talent management, and strategic alignment. As we embark on this journey of exploration and discovery, let us navigate the complexities of big data with curiosity, resilience, and a relentless pursuit of innovation.

2.1.1 Motivation

In an era where data drives decision-making, mastering data management technologies is essential for organizations striving to stay competitive. This chapter explores the fundamental tools and techniques that empower businesses to harness the full potential of big data. From analytics technologies that extract actionable insights to visualization tools that translate complex datasets into intuitive representations, each section delves into critical aspects of modern data management. Additionally, it highlights the importance of data integration and preparation in ensuring consistency and accuracy, while real-time analytics technologies enable organizations to detect trends and anomalies with agility. By understanding these key components, readers will gain a solid foundation to navigate the evolving data landscape and leverage cutting-edge tools for innovation and strategic growth.

2.1.2 Chapter Contributions

- Provides a comprehensive overview of key data management technologies and tools for handling big data effectively.
- Explores advanced analytics techniques for extracting meaningful insights from large datasets. Discusses data visualization tools that enhance interpretability and facilitate better decision-making.
- Examines data integration and preparation tools to ensure accuracy, consistency, and seamless data harmonization.
- Analyzes real-time analytics technologies that enable swift detection of patterns, trends, and anomalies.
- Bridges theoretical concepts with practical applications to support data-driven decision-making. Serves as a valuable resource for researchers, professionals, and organizations aiming to leverage data for innovation and strategic growth.

2.1.3 Organization of the Chapter

The remainder of the chapter is structured as follows: Section 2.2 presents analytics technologies and tools. Section 2.3 discusses the data visualization tools. Section 2.4 covers the data integration and preparation tools. Section 2.5 highlights real-time data analytics technologies along with big data analytics tools, and Section 2.6 comprises closing thoughts.

2.2 Analytics Technologies and Tools

Figure 2.2 illustrates the tools and technologies used in big data analytics. These technologies and tools encompass a wide array of methodologies and software platforms designed to extract meaningful insights from data. These tools enable organizations to analyze large volumes of structured and unstructured data to uncover patterns, trends, correlations, and actionable insights. Here's a detailed exploration of analytics technologies and tools, along with examples of their applications:

a. **Statistical Analysis:** Statistical analysis forms the foundation of analytics, involving the application of mathematical principles to quantify and analyze data. For example, a retail company may use statistical analysis to analyze sales data and identify trends in customer purchasing behavior. By conducting regression analysis, the company can determine the factors that influence sales and optimize its marketing strategies accordingly.

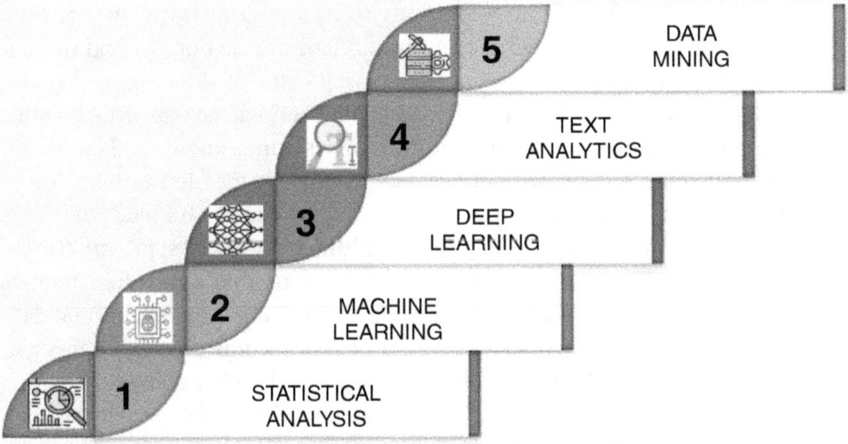

Figure 2.2 Tools and technologies used in big data analytics.

b. **Machine Learning:** Machine learning algorithms leverage computational methods to identify patterns and make predictions based on data. For instance, a health-care provider may use machine learning algorithms to analyze patient data and predict the likelihood of disease onset or progression. By training a classification model on historical patient records, the provider can identify patients at high risk of developing certain conditions and intervene with preventive measures.

c. **Deep Learning:** Deep learning represents a subset of machine learning techniques that involve neural networks with multiple layers of interconnected nodes. An example application of deep learning is in image recognition, where a technology company may use convolutional neural networks (CNNs) to develop a system that can automatically classify and tag images uploaded by users. This enables efficient content organization and retrieval in photo-sharing platforms.

d. **Text Analytics:** Text analytics tools analyze unstructured textual data to extract insights and derive meaning from documents, social media posts, emails, and other text-based sources. For example, a marketing agency may use sentiment analysis to analyze customer reviews and social media conversations about a product or service. By gauging the sentiment expressed in these texts, the agency can assess customer satisfaction levels and identify areas for improvement.

e. **Data Mining:** Data mining techniques involve the exploration and analysis of large datasets to discover hidden patterns, relationships, and anomalies. An example application of data mining is in fraud detection, where a financial institution may use association rule mining to identify suspicious patterns of transactions indicative of fraudulent activity. By analyzing transactional data, the institution can detect and prevent fraudulent transactions in real time. It is estimated that ETL processes account for 70–80% of the costs, risks, and time associated with data warehousing. This overhead makes even modest data analysis prototyping or exploratory analysis quite expensive. Traditional relational database management systems (RDBMSs) face limitations due to the growing variety of data types that need to be stored and analyzed. This data can be unstructured, like emails or multimedia files, or semi-structured, like clickstream data. The speed and diversity of this data often require schema adjustments in real time, which is challenging for conventional data warehouses to support. This is why Hadoop has become a game-changer in the fields of data warehousing and data mining. Hadoop's architecture, which separates storage from processing, allows organizations to keep their raw data in HDFS without needing ETL processes to standardize it into a single model. Additionally, YARN's flexible processing layer enables direct access and querying of raw data from various angles and using different methods, such as SQL or non-SQL, depending on the specific use case. As a result, Hadoop facilitates exploratory analysis and data mining prototyping and supports a broader range of data types and analytical approaches.

2.2.1 Evolution of Data Analytics

The historical evolution of data analytics traces back to ancient civilizations, where rudimentary methods were employed to collect and analyze data for various purposes, as shown in Figure 2.3.

However, the modern concept of data analytics as we understand it today has evolved significantly over the past few decades, driven by technological advancements and changing business needs. Here's a detailed exploration of the historical evolution of data analytics:

i. **Early Beginnings:** The roots of data analytics can be traced back to ancient civilizations such as Mesopotamia and Egypt, where records of agricultural yields, trade transactions, and census data were kept and analyzed to inform decision-making. Methods such as tallying, counting, and basic arithmetic were used to process and interpret data.
ii. **Statistical Analysis:** The emergence of statistics as a formal discipline in the seventeenth century laid the groundwork for modern data analytics. Pioneers like William Playfair, Francis Galton, and Florence Nightingale developed techniques for visualizing and analyzing data, paving the way for the systematic exploration of quantitative data.

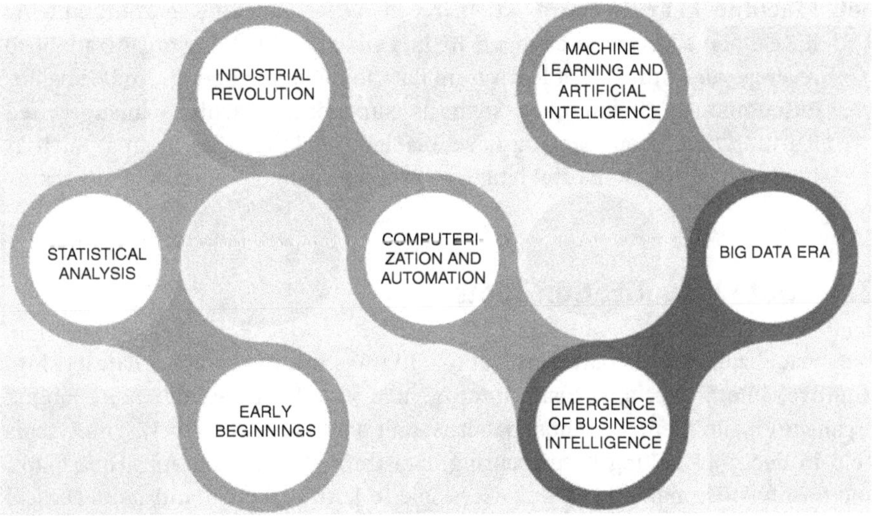

Figure 2.3 The historical development of data analytics.

iii. **Industrial Revolution:** The Industrial Revolution brought about significant advancements in data collection and analysis, particularly in the fields of economics, demography, and social sciences. Statistical methods such as regression analysis, hypothesis testing, and sampling gained prominence, enabling researchers to draw insights from large datasets.

iv. **Computerization and Automation:** The advent of computers in the mid-twentieth century revolutionized data analytics by enabling the processing and analysis of large volumes of data with unprecedented speed and accuracy. Early computer systems facilitated tasks such as data entry, storage, and retrieval, laying the foundation for more sophisticated analytics techniques.

v. **Emergence of Business Intelligence:** The late twentieth century saw the rise of business intelligence (BI) systems, which integrated data from multiple sources to provide insights for decision-making. Technologies such as data warehouses, online analytical processing (OLAP), and executive information systems (EISs) enabled organizations to gain a holistic view of their operations and performance.

vi. **Big Data Era:** The twenty-first century ushered in the era of big data, characterized by the exponential growth in data volume, velocity, and variety. This proliferation of data, coupled with advancements in computing power and storage, necessitated the development of new analytics techniques and tools to extract insights from large and complex datasets.

vii. **Machine Learning and AI:** In recent years, machine learning and AI have emerged as game-changers in data analytics, enabling organizations to leverage algorithms that learn from data to make predictions and decisions autonomously. Techniques such as supervised learning, unsupervised learning, and deep learning have enabled breakthroughs in areas such as image recognition, natural language processing, and predictive analytics.

2.3 Data Visualization Tools

Data visualization tools play a crucial role in transforming complex datasets into intuitive, interactive, and easily interpretable visual representations, enabling organizations to identify trends, patterns, and anomalies effectively. These tools help in decision-making by presenting data through charts, graphs, heatmaps, and dashboards, making insights accessible to both technical and nontechnical users. Popular data visualization tools include *Tableau*, which offers interactive dashboards and real-time data analysis; *Power BI*, a Microsoft tool known for its seamless integration with various data sources; *Google Data Studio*, which allows users to create customizable reports; and *D3.js*, a JavaScript library for creating dynamic, web-based visualizations. By leveraging these tools, businesses and researchers can enhance data storytelling, improve operational efficiency, and drive strategic decisions with clarity and confidence.

2.4 Data Integration and Preparation Tools

Data integration and preparation tools are essential components of the data management process, enabling organizations to consolidate, cleanse, and harmonize data from disparate sources for analysis and decision-making. Here's a step-by-step explanation of how these tools work, illustrated in Figure 2.4 with an example:

Step 1: Data Collection
The first step in the data integration and preparation process involves collecting data from various sources, which may include databases, spreadsheets, cloud applications, IoT devices, and external data sources. For example, a retail company collects sales data from point-of-sale systems, customer data from CRM systems, and inventory data from warehouse management systems.

Step 2: Data Extraction
Once the data sources are identified, data extraction tools are used to retrieve relevant data from each source. These tools extract data in its raw form, typically in

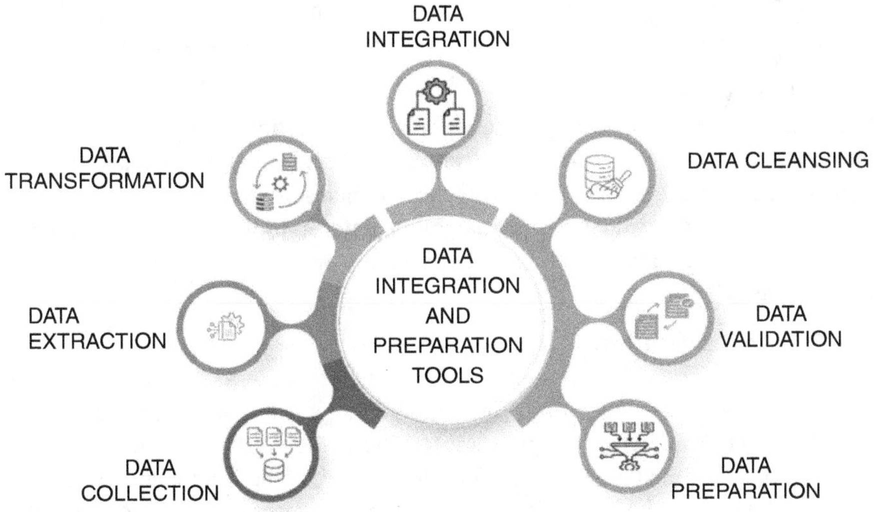

Figure 2.4 Data integration and the tools used for data preparation.

structured formats such as CSV, Excel, or databases. Continuing with the retail example, the company uses an ETL (Extract, Transform, Load) tool to extract sales data from its database, customer data from its CRM system, and inventory data from its warehouse management system.

Step 3: Data Transformation
After extraction, the raw data often requires transformation to ensure consistency, quality, and compatibility across different datasets. Transformation tools enable organizations to cleanse, normalize, and standardize data, as well as perform calculations, aggregations, and data enrichment. For instance, the retail company may use data transformation rules to standardize product names, convert currencies, and calculate total sales revenue.

Step 4: Data Integration
Once the data is transformed, it needs to be integrated into a unified dataset for analysis. Data integration tools facilitate the merging of data from multiple sources into a single, cohesive dataset. These tools may use techniques such as joins, unions, and merges to combine data based on common identifiers or attributes. In our example, the retail company integrates sales, customer, and inventory data into a single dataset for comprehensive analysis.

Step 5: Data Cleansing
Data cleansing tools identify and rectify errors, duplicates, inconsistencies, and missing values within the dataset. These tools employ techniques such as data profiling, deduplication, and outlier detection to ensure data quality and integrity.

For example, the retail company uses data cleansing tools to remove duplicate customer records, correct misspelled product names, and fill in missing sales data.

Step 6: Data Validation
After cleansing, the integrated dataset undergoes validation to ensure its accuracy and reliability. Data validation tools compare the integrated dataset against predefined rules or benchmarks to identify discrepancies or anomalies. For instance, the retail company validates the integrated dataset by comparing total sales revenue against financial records and verifying customer demographics against market research data.

Step 7: Data Preparation
Finally, the prepared dataset is ready for analysis and decision-making. Data preparation tools enable users to format, filter, aggregate, and summarize data to meet specific analytical requirements. These tools empower analysts and decision-makers to explore insights and derive actionable intelligence from the prepared dataset. In our example, the retail company uses data preparation tools to create reports, dashboards, and visualizations that provide insights into sales performance, customer behavior, and inventory management. Table 2.1 highlights key analytics technologies and tools across various categories, including big data processing, storage, visualization, machine learning, integration, and statistical analysis. These tools empower organizations to efficiently manage, analyze, and visualize data for actionable insights. Statistical analysis offers descriptive insights, machine learning provides predictive capabilities, and data mining helps discover hidden patterns, together forming a comprehensive approach to BI. Combining these techniques allows organizations to not only understand past performance but also predict future outcomes.

In summary, data integration and preparation tools play a crucial role in the data management process, facilitating the consolidation, cleansing, and harmonization of data from disparate sources for analysis and decision-making. By following these steps and leveraging the capabilities of integration and preparation tools, organizations can unlock the full potential of their data assets and drive business success.

2.5 Real-time Data Analytics Technologies

Real-time data analytics technologies enable organizations to process and analyze data as it is generated, providing insights and actionable intelligence in near real time. This capability is particularly valuable in scenarios where immediate decisions or responses are required, such as in financial trading, fraud detection, predictive maintenance, and personalized marketing. Figure 2.5 shows

Table 2.1 Popular analytics technologies and tools.

Category	Technology/tool	Description
Big data processing	Hadoop	An open-source framework for processing large datasets across distributed computing environments, which uses the MapReduce programming model, where the "Map" function processes and filters data, and the "Reduce" function aggregates and consolidates the results
	Apache Spark	A fast, in-memory data processing engine for big data analytics
	Google BigQuery	A fully managed, serverless data warehouse for large-scale data analysis
Data storage	Amazon S3	Scalable cloud storage for storing and retrieving large volumes of data
	MongoDB	A NoSQL database designed for flexible and scalable data storage
	Apache Cassandra	A distributed database system for handling large amounts of structured data
Data visualization	Tableau	A tool for creating interactive dashboards and data visualizations
	Power BI	A business analytics tool by Microsoft for data visualization and reporting
	D3.js	A JavaScript library for creating data-driven, dynamic visualizations on the web
Machine learning	TensorFlow	An open-source platform for building and deploying machine learning models
	Scikit-learn	A Python library for machine learning and data mining
	PyTorch	A flexible deep learning framework widely used in research and production

Note: Big Data Processing using MapReduce is available as a free supplementary material over: www.wiley.com\go\kumaribigdatatechnologies1

technologies used for real-time data analytics. Here's a step-by-step explanation of how real-time data analytics technologies work, along with an example:

- **Data Ingestion:** The process begins with the ingestion of data from various sources, such as sensors, social media feeds, transactional systems, and IoT devices. Data is continuously streamed into the analytics platform, ensuring that the most up-to-date information is available for analysis. One of Hadoop's

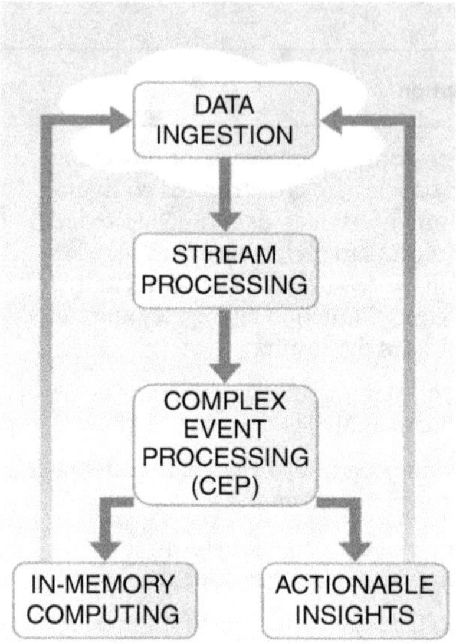

Figure 2.5 Types of real-time data analytics.

key advantages is its ability to operate without a fixed schema, accommodating any type or format of data, whether structured or unstructured, from various sources. As long as you use Hadoop's Writable or DBWritable interfaces and write your MapReduce code to interpret the data correctly, Hadoop can handle it. However, when dealing with data that is already structured in a relational database, it would be more efficient to utilize this existing schema to import the data into Hadoop rather than manually uploading and parsing CSV files. Sqoop (SQL-to-Hadoop) is specifically designed to facilitate the transfer of data between RDBMS and Hadoop. It automates much of the data transformation by using the RDBMS schema to streamline the import process. While Sqoop is effective for bulk-loading data from relational databases into Hadoop, modern applications often generate high-speed data streams, such as application logs, GPS data, social media updates, and sensor information. To manage and process this high-throughput, event-based data directly in HDFS, we need a system that supports continuous data ingestion from various sources. Apache Flume addresses this need by efficiently collecting, aggregating, and transferring large volumes of log data from multiple sources to a centralized data store. Although Flume is commonly used to stream log data into Hadoop (typically HDFS or HBase), it is versatile and can be customized to handle a wide range of event data, including network traffic, social media content, and sensor data, routing it to any Flume-compatible destination.

Table 2.2 Real-time data analytics technologies.

Technology/tool	Description
Apache Kafka	A distributed event streaming platform for real-time data processing
Apache Flink	A stream-processing framework for high-throughput, low-latency analytics
Amazon Kinesis	A cloud-based service for collecting, processing, and analyzing real-time data
Google Dataflow	A fully managed stream and batch data processing service
Spark Streaming	A real-time extension of Apache Spark for streaming analytics

Example: A smart city initiative utilizes sensors deployed across the city to collect real-time data on traffic flow, air quality, and energy consumption. This data is continuously ingested into a real-time analytics platform to monitor environmental conditions and optimize city services in response to changing needs.

- **Stream Processing:** Once data is ingested, it undergoes stream processing, where it is analyzed and transformed in real time. Stream-processing engines such as Apache Kafka, Apache Flink, and Spark Streaming enable the processing of high-velocity data streams with low latency. Table 2.2 shows more real-time data analytics technologies.
  Example: A financial services firm uses stream processing to analyze market data feeds from stock exchanges. By applying algorithms for trend analysis and anomaly detection in real time, the firm can identify trading opportunities and execute buy/sell orders swiftly to capitalize on market fluctuations.
- **Complex Event Processing (CEP):** Real-time analytics platforms often incorporate complex event processing capabilities to detect patterns, correlations, and events of interest in the data streams. CEP engines analyze incoming data streams against predefined rules and patterns to identify significant events or anomalies.
  Example: An e-commerce retailer employs CEP to monitor website traffic and customer behavior in real time. By defining rules for detecting unusual spikes in website traffic or sudden changes in shopping cart abandonment rates, the retailer can proactively investigate and address potential issues to improve the online shopping experience.
- **In-Memory Computing:** Real-time analytics platforms leverage in-memory computing technologies to store and process data in memory, enabling faster access and analysis compared to traditional disk-based systems. This enables

low-latency processing of high-volume data streams, ensuring timely insights and responses.

Example: An online gaming company utilizes in-memory computing to analyze player interactions and gaming sessions in real time. By storing game telemetry data in memory, the company can detect cheating behaviors or performance issues instantly, allowing for immediate intervention to maintain a fair and enjoyable gaming experience.

- **Actionable Insights:** Finally, the insights derived from real-time data analytics are translated into actionable intelligence that informs decision-making and drives operational improvements. Dashboards, alerts, and automated actions enable stakeholders to respond promptly to emerging trends, threats, or opportunities.

  Example: A telecommunications provider uses real-time analytics to monitor network performance and customer usage patterns. By analyzing streaming data from network devices and customer interactions, the provider can identify network congestion issues in real time and dynamically allocate resources to optimize service delivery and enhance customer satisfaction.

Effective big data management relies on a diverse ecosystem of tools designed for various stages of the data life cycle. **Data storage and management** tools like Hadoop, Apache HBase, and Amazon S3 provide scalable and reliable solutions for handling massive datasets. **Data processing and analysis** platforms such as Apache Spark, Apache Flink, and Google BigQuery enable efficient computation and real-time analytics. For better insights, **data visualization** tools like Tableau, Power BI, and D3.js transform complex datasets into intuitive visual formats. **Data integration and ETL** tools, including Talend, Apache NiFi, and Informatica, streamline data aggregation from multiple sources, ensuring accuracy and consistency. In the realm of **machine learning and AI**, frameworks like TensorFlow, H2O.ai, and RapidMiner facilitate predictive analytics and model development. **Data streaming** solutions such as Apache Kafka, Amazon Kinesis, and Apache Pulsar support real-time data ingestion and event-driven architectures. Lastly, **big data querying** tools like Hive, Presto, and Drill enable efficient querying and retrieval of large-scale structured and semi-structured data, empowering organizations to make data-driven decisions with speed and accuracy. Figure 2.6 shows big data analytics tools across different categories. These categories include:

1. **Data Storage and Management**: Tools like Hadoop, Apache HBase, and Amazon S3.
2. **Data Processing and Analysis**: Tools like Apache Spark, Apache Flink, and Google BigQuery.
3. **Data Visualization**: Tools like Tableau, Power BI, and D3.js.

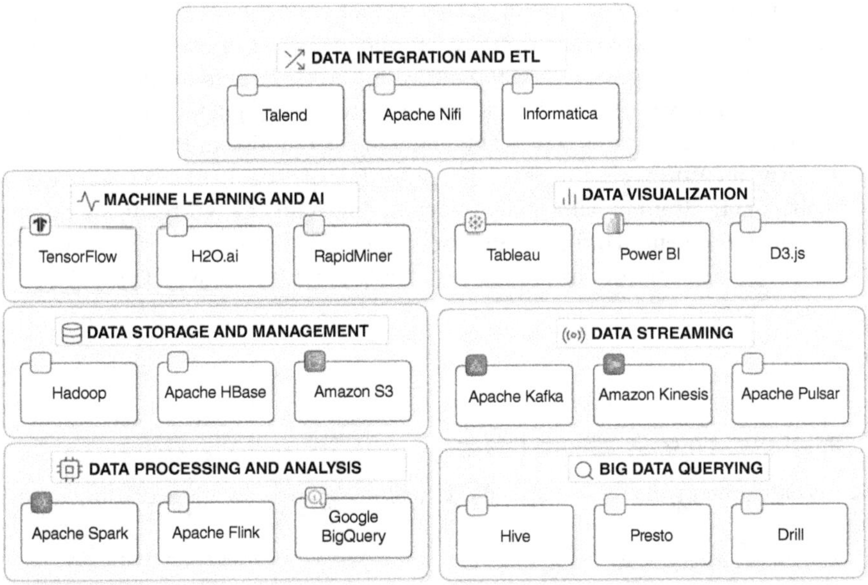

Figure 2.6 Big data analytics tools.

4. **Data Integration and ETL**: Tools like Talend, Apache NiFi, and Informatica.
5. **Machine Learning and AI**: Tools like TensorFlow, H2O.ai, and RapidMiner.
6. **Data Streaming**: Tools like Apache Kafka, Amazon Kinesis, and Apache Pulsar.
7. **Big Data Querying**: Tools like Hive, Presto, and Drill.

2.6 Conclusion

In the ever-evolving landscape of data management, the exploration of analytics technologies and tools unveils a transformative potential for organizations across industries. As evidenced by the diverse range of methodologies and software platforms discussed in this chapter, analytics serves as a cornerstone for extracting actionable insights from vast and complex datasets. From statistical analysis to machine learning, deep learning, text analytics, and data mining, organizations have at their disposal a myriad of tools to navigate the intricacies of big data. These tools empower businesses to uncover hidden patterns, trends, and correlations, enabling informed decision-making, predictive analytics, and innovation. Moreover, the examples provided illustrate the real-world applications of analytics technologies, spanning diverse domains such as retail, health care, technology, marketing, and finance. Whether it's optimizing marketing strategies, predicting disease outcomes, automating content classification, or detecting fraudulent activity, analytics tools play a pivotal role in driving operational efficiency, enhancing customer experiences, and mitigating risks. As organizations continue to harness the power of analytics, it is imperative to recognize that success lies not only in the adoption of advanced technologies but also in the cultivation of a data-driven culture and the development of talent capable of leveraging these tools effectively. By embracing analytics technologies and tools, organizations can unlock the full potential of their data assets, gaining a competitive edge in today's data-driven landscape and paving the way for future innovation and growth.

Practice Set

A Multiple Choice Questions (MCQ)

1 What is the primary role of analytics technologies and tools according to the chapter?
- **a** Data storage
- **b** Extracting actionable insights from datasets
- **c** Enhancing hardware performance
- **d** Managing software licenses

2 Which analytics tool is NOT mentioned in the chapter?
- **a** Statistical analysis
- **b** Deep learning
- **c** Text analytics
- **d** Virtual Reality

3 What does predictive analytics help organizations with?
- **a** Optimizing marketing strategies
- **b** Automating content classification
- **c** Forecasting future outcomes
- **d** Detecting fraudulent activity

4 In which domain is analytics technology NOT explicitly mentioned as having applications?
- **a** Retail
- **b** Health care
- **c** Manufacturing
- **d** Finance

5 What is necessary for organizations to successfully leverage analytics tools?
   a High-speed Internet
   b Advanced hardware
   c A data-driven culture and skilled talent
   d Large budgets

6 How do analytics tools contribute to customer experiences according to the chapter?
   a By reducing data storage costs
   b By automating customer service
   c By enhancing decision-making and innovation
   d By improving software interfaces

7 Which of the following is a key component of big data analytics mentioned in the chapter?
   a Data warehousing
   b Data mining
   c Data visualization
   d Data encryption

8 What is the role of deep learning in big data analytics?
   a Data organization
   b Data security
   c Extracting complex patterns from data
   d Data storage

9 What can organizations uncover using analytics tools?
   a Market trends
   b Hidden patterns and correlations
   c Network security breaches
   d Data entry errors

10 Which factor is crucial for unlocking the full potential of data assets?
   a Expanding hardware resources
   b Implementing data-driven strategies
   c Increasing data volume
   d Reducing data collection frequency

B Fill-in-the-Blanks

11 Analytics technologies help businesses navigate the complexities of big data through tools like __________, deep learning, and data mining.

12 To drive operational efficiency and enhance customer experiences, organizations utilize analytics tools for tasks such as __________ and predicting disease outcomes.

13 A data-driven __________ and the development of skilled talent are crucial for organizations to leverage analytics tools effectively.

14 The chapter highlights the use of analytics technologies in diverse domains such as retail, health care, and __________.

15 Success in utilizing analytics technologies involves not only advanced tools but also __________ and effective talent development.

C Short Answer Questions

16 What are some of the tools available for big data analytics as discussed in the chapter?

17 How do analytics tools contribute to innovation within organizations?

18 Explain the role of machine learning in big data analytics.

19 Describe the impact of analytics technologies on decision-making processes.

20 What are the benefits of adopting a data-driven culture in organizations?

D Long Answer Questions

21 Discuss the transformative potential of big data analytics technologies across different industries and provide examples.

22 Analyze how organizations can benefit from combining statistical analysis, machine learning, and data mining.

23 Evaluate the challenges organizations might face in cultivating a data-driven culture and how they can be addressed.

24 Examine the role of advanced analytics tools in optimizing marketing strategies and improving customer experiences.

25 Explore the implications of analytics technologies for future innovation and growth in organizations.

Further Readings

Acharya, S., 2019. *Big Data and Analytics*. Wiley.

Andronie, M., Lăzăroiu, G., Iatagan, M., Hurloiu, I., Ştefănescu, R., Dijmărescu, A. and Dijmărescu, I., 2023. Big data management algorithms, deep learning-based object detection technologies, and geospatial simulation and sensor fusion tools in the internet of robotic things. *ISPRS International Journal of Geo-Information*, 12(2), p. 35.

Andronie, M., Lăzăroiu, G., Karapalevski, O.L., Ştefănescu, R., Hurloiu, I., Dijmărescu, A. and Dijmărescu, I., 2022. Remote big data management tools, sensing and computing technologies, and visual perception and environment mapping algorithms in the Internet of Robotic Things. *Electronics*, 12(1), p. 22.

Arfat, Y., Usman, S., Mehmood, R. and Katib, I., 2020. Big data tools, technologies, and applications: a survey. In: *Smart Infrastructure and Applications: Foundations for Smarter Cities and Societies*, pp. 453–490. Springer.

Gajbe, S.B., Tiwari, A. and Singh, R.K., 2021. Evaluation and analysis of data management plan tools: a parametric approach. *Information Processing & Management*, 58(3), p. 102480.

Gupta, I., Purohit, G., Kumari, A., Ray, S., Kumar, P. and Kumar, S., 2024. Brace: a pairing algorithm for mentorship using compatibility score. In: *2024 IEEE International Conference on Electronics, Computing and Communications*, pp. 1–6. IEEE.

Hussain, T., Sanga, A. and Mongia, S., 2019. Big data Hadoop tools and technologies: a review. In: *Proceedings of International Conference on Advancements in Computing & Management (ICACM)*, pp. 574–578. Social Science Research Network.

Kaddoura, S. and Grati, R., 2021. Blockchain for healthcare and medical systems. In: *Enabling Blockchain Technology for Secure Networking and Communications*, pp. 249–270. IGI Global.

Kondam, A. and Yella, A., 2022. *Navigating the Complexities of Big Data*. Springer Nature.

Kumari, A., Kumar, P. and Golyan, A., 2024. Introduction of blockchain for biomedical and healthcare system. In: *Blockchain for Biomedical Research and Healthcare: Concept, Trends, and Technologies*, pp. 1–16. Singapore: Springer.

Kumari, A., Obaidat, M., Panchal, S., Raval, N., Kumar, P. and Yadav, D.K., 2024. M-VMT-PC: Metaverse-enabled Virtual Medical Training and Patient Care framework underlying 5G. In: *2024 International Conference on Communications, Computing, Cybersecurity*, pp. 1–7. IEEE.

Miah, S.J., Miah, M. and Shen, J., 2020. Editorial note: learning management systems and big data technologies for higher education. *Education and Information Technologies*, 25, pp. 725–730.

Po, L., Bikakis, N., Desimoni, F. and Papastefanatos, G., 2022. *Linked Data Visualization: Techniques, Tools, and Big Data*. Springer Nature.

Prokofieva, M. and Miah, S.J., 2019. Blockchain in healthcare [Online]. *Australasian Journal of Information Systems*, 23.

Rao, T.R., Mitra, P., Bhatt, R. and Goswami, A., 2019. The big data system, components, tools, and technologies: a survey. *Knowledge and Information Systems*, 60, pp. 1165–1245.

Shihab, L.A., 2020. Technological tools for data security in the treatment of data reliability in big data environments. *International Transaction Journal of Engineering, Management, & Applied Sciences & Technologies*, 11(9), pp. 1–13.

Subbiah, A., Mahfoud, A. and Kumari, A., 2024. Smart Urban Traffic Management: leveraging automatic control and intelligent systems for improved safety in commercial vehicle road banning operations. In: *2024 IEEE 6th Symposium on Computers & Informatics (ISCI)*, pp. 78–83. IEEE.

Tandel, V., Kumari, A., Tanwar, S., Singh, A., Sharma, R. and Yamsani, N., 2024. Intelligent wearable-assisted digital healthcare industry 5.0. *Artificial Intelligence in Medicine*, 157, p. 103000.

3

AI-based Big Data Analytics Techniques

LEARNING OBJECTIVES

- This chapter investigates how AI technologies are transforming big data analytics by introducing new approaches for extracting insights from massive and heterogeneous datasets.
- It covers sophisticated statistical methodologies, machine learning models, deep learning architectures, and natural language processing (NLP).
- It discusses how AI may improve data quality and processing efficiency in big data analytics.
- This chapter looks at AI approaches that can unlock actionable insights and improve organizational decision-making processes.
- It provides an in-depth look at real-world applications of AI-based methodologies, highlighting their impact on driving innovation and competition. Next, provides readers with the knowledge and tools to successfully navigate AI-based big data analytics, allowing them to exploit AI.

3.1 Introduction

In the digital age, the proliferation of data has ushered in a new era of possibilities and challenges for organizations across industries. As the volume, velocity, and variety of data continue to grow exponentially, the need for advanced analytics techniques becomes increasingly imperative to extract meaningful insights and drive informed decision-making processes. At the forefront of this evolution lies the convergence of artificial intelligence (AI) with big data analytics, where AI-based techniques offer unprecedented capabilities to unlock the latent value hidden within vast and complex datasets.

This chapter explores the transformative potential of AI-based big data analytics techniques, providing a comprehensive examination of methodologies that leverage AI to derive actionable insights from data. From ensuring data quality and processing efficiency to employing advanced statistical approaches, machine learning models, deep learning architectures, and natural language processing (NLP) techniques, this chapter illuminates the diverse array of AI-driven techniques shaping the future of big data analytics.

As organizations navigate the complexities of the digital landscape, the integration of AI technologies presents a pathway to innovation, optimization, and competitive advantage. By harnessing the power of AI-based big data analytics, organizations can gain deeper insights into their data assets, anticipate market trends, mitigate risks, and capitalize on emerging opportunities. Through a combination of theoretical insights and practical applications, this chapter aims to equip readers with the knowledge and tools needed to harness the transformative potential of AI in driving value and unlocking new frontiers in big data analytics.

3.1.1 Motivation

The rapid growth of data in various domains has led to an urgent need for advanced analytical techniques capable of extracting meaningful insights from vast and complex datasets. AI-based big data analytics techniques offer powerful solutions by leveraging machine learning, deep learning, and NLP to analyze structured and unstructured data efficiently. These techniques enable automated pattern recognition, predictive modeling, and real-time decision-making, making them invaluable in fields such as health care, finance, cybersecurity, and smart cities. The integration of AI with big data analytics enhances scalability, accuracy, and processing speed, allowing organizations to uncover hidden trends, optimize resource allocation, and improve overall operational efficiency. This chapter aims to explore the latest advancements in AI-driven big data analytics, discussing state-of-the-art methodologies, frameworks, and applications that drive innovation in data-driven decision-making. By understanding these techniques, researchers and practitioners can develop intelligent systems that not only process massive datasets but also generate actionable insights, ultimately leading to smarter and more efficient technological solutions.

3.1.2 Chapter Contributions

- Offers a comprehensive analysis of AI-driven big data analytics techniques, emphasizing their role in managing large-scale datasets.
- Investigates various machine learning and deep learning methodologies for data processing, pattern detection, and predictive modeling.
- Explores the fusion of AI with big data frameworks, focusing on scalability, efficiency, and real-time analytical capabilities.
- Identifies key challenges and constraints in AI-powered big data analytics, including concerns related to data privacy, computational demands, and model transparency.

- Showcases real-world implementations and case studies to illustrate the effectiveness of AI-based big data solutions. Highlights emerging innovations and future research opportunities in AI-enhanced data analytics to advance decision-making and automation.

3.1.3 Organization of the Chapter

The remainder of the chapter is structured as follows: Section 3.2 highlights data quality and preprocessing techniques. Next, Section 3.3 focuses on statistical methodologies such as data distributions, hypothesis testing, regression models, and correlation analysis, which are essential for understanding patterns within large datasets. Section 3.4 comprises various machine learning techniques, including decision trees, support vector machines (SVMs), and clustering algorithms, which are discussed for their role in trend identification, classification, and prediction. Section 3.5 explores deep learning methods such as convolutional neural networks (CNNs), recurrent neural networks (RNNs), and transformers, showcasing how these architectures process unstructured data like images, audio, and text with high accuracy. Finally, Section 3.6 covers NLP techniques such as sentiment analysis, entity recognition, and text summarization, demonstrating how they can be applied to analyze unstructured textual data from sources like social media and clinical records to derive valuable insights for various applications.

3.2 Data Quality and Processing Technologies

In the realm of big data analytics, ensuring data quality is paramount for deriving accurate and reliable insights from vast and diverse datasets. Data quality refers to the fitness for use of data in a specific context, encompassing aspects such as accuracy, completeness, consistency, timeliness, and relevance. Data processing technologies play a crucial role in enhancing data quality by facilitating the transformation, cleansing, and enrichment of data to meet the desired standards. Figure 3.1 illustrates data quality and processing technologies, which are further explained in detail below:

- **Data Integration:** Data integration technologies enable organizations to consolidate data from disparate sources, such as databases, files, cloud services, and IoT devices, into a unified and coherent dataset. Extract, transform, load (ETL) tools automate the process of extracting data from source systems, transforming it into a consistent format, and loading it into a target database or data warehouse. Data integration ensures that data from various sources can be harmonized and analyzed together, enhancing the completeness and comprehensiveness of the dataset.

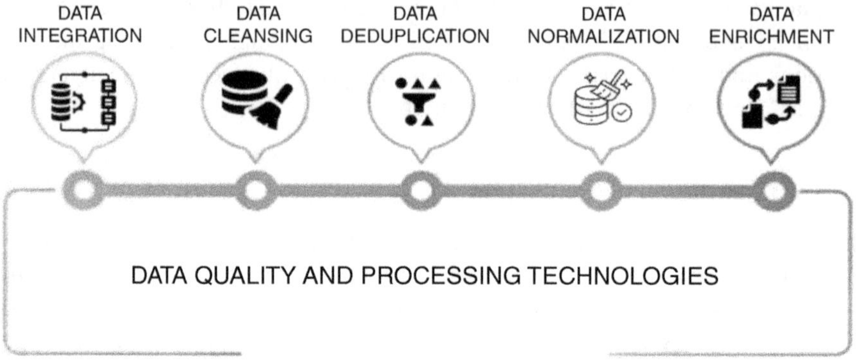

Figure 3.1 Data quality and processing technology.

- **Data Cleansing:** Data cleansing, also known as data scrubbing or data cleansing, involves identifying and correcting errors, inconsistencies, and anomalies in the dataset. Data cleansing technologies employ algorithms and rules-based processes to detect and rectify issues such as missing values, duplicate records, formatting errors, and outliers. By cleaning the data, organizations can improve their accuracy, reliability, and usability for analysis and decision-making.
- **Data Deduplication:** Data deduplication technologies identify and remove duplicate records or entries within the dataset. Duplicate data can arise from multiple sources, data entry errors, or system migrations, leading to inaccuracies and inefficiencies in analysis. Deduplication algorithms compare records based on key attributes and criteria, such as name, address, or unique identifiers, and eliminate redundant entries while preserving essential information. Data deduplication enhances data accuracy and reduces the risk of errors in analysis and reporting.
- **Data Normalization:** Data normalization involves organizing and structuring data to eliminate redundancy and reduce data anomalies. Normalization techniques standardize data formats, units of measurement, and naming conventions to ensure consistency and comparability across the dataset. By normalizing the data, organizations can improve data consistency, facilitate data aggregation and analysis, and enhance the effectiveness of data processing and modeling techniques.
- **Data Enrichment:** Data enrichment technologies augment the existing dataset with additional information or attributes to enhance its value and utility for analysis. Enrichment techniques may involve appending external data sources, such as demographic data, geographic information, or market intelligence, to the dataset. By enriching the data, organizations can gain deeper insights into customer behavior, market trends, and business performance, enabling more informed decision-making.

3.3 Statistical Approaches for Big Data Analytics

Statistical approaches are fundamental in big data analytics, providing tools and techniques to extract insights, identify patterns, and make informed decisions from vast and complex datasets. These approaches encompass a wide range of statistical methods tailored to address the unique challenges posed by big data, including high dimensionality, heterogeneity, and variability. Let's explore statistical approaches for big data analytics with a real-world example: *Predictive Maintenance in Manufacturing*.

In the manufacturing industry, unplanned equipment downtime can result in significant losses in productivity, revenue, and customer satisfaction. Predictive maintenance aims to address this challenge by leveraging statistical approaches to anticipate equipment failures before they occur, thereby enabling proactive maintenance actions to be taken.

- **Data Collection and Preparation:** The first step in predictive maintenance is to collect and preprocess data from sensors installed on machinery. These sensors continuously monitor various parameters such as temperature, vibration, and pressure, generating large volumes of time-series data. Statistical techniques are employed to clean, normalize, and aggregate the raw sensor data to prepare it for analysis.
- **Statistical Analysis:** Statistical methods such as time-series analysis, survival analysis, and reliability analysis are applied to the preprocessed data to identify patterns indicative of impending equipment failures. For example, time-series analysis techniques like autoregressive integrated moving average (ARIMA) models can be used to forecast equipment performance degradation based on historical sensor data (Figure 3.2).
- **Failure Prediction Models:** Using historical data on equipment failures and maintenance activities, statistical models such as logistic regression, decision trees, and random forests are trained to predict the likelihood of future failures. These models incorporate features extracted from sensor data, maintenance logs, and environmental factors to identify early warning signs of potential equipment breakdowns.
- **Anomaly Detection:** Statistical approaches for anomaly detection, such as z-score analysis, kernel density estimation, and clustering algorithms, are utilized to detect deviations from normal equipment behavior. Anomalies in sensor readings may indicate underlying issues or impending failures, prompting maintenance personnel to investigate and take corrective actions.
- **Decision Support Systems:** Statistical analysis results are integrated into decision support systems that provide actionable insights to maintenance technicians and asset managers. Real-time dashboards and alerts highlight equipment health status, maintenance priorities, and recommended actions based on statistical models and predictive analytics.

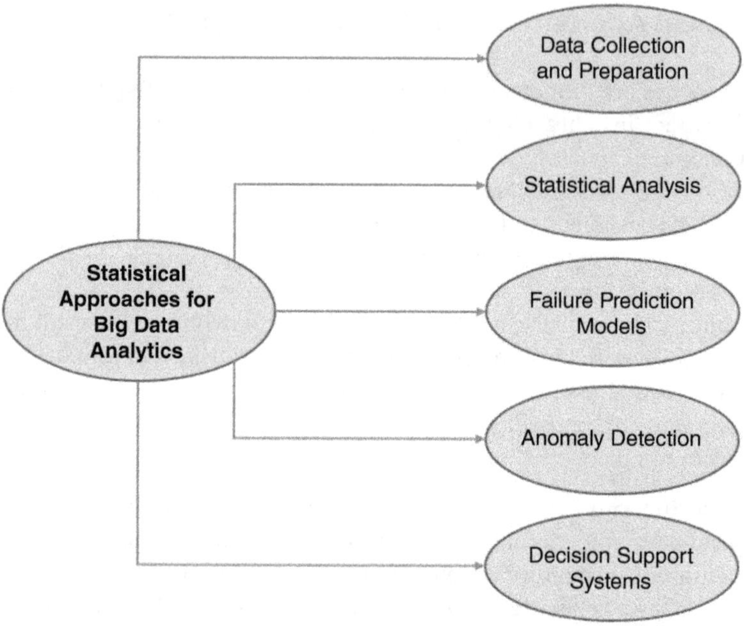

Figure 3.2 Statistical approaches for big data analytics.

Statistical approaches play a crucial role in big data analytics, enabling organizations to extract actionable insights and drive value from their data assets. By applying statistical techniques to real-world challenges such as predictive maintenance in manufacturing, organizations can optimize operations, reduce costs, and enhance customer satisfaction. As big data continues to proliferate across industries, the application of statistical approaches will remain indispensable in unlocking the full potential of data-driven decision-making.

3.3.1 Benefits

By leveraging statistical approaches for predictive maintenance, manufacturing companies can achieve several benefits shown in Table 3.1.

3.4 Machine Learning Models for Big Data Analysis

Machine learning (ML) models are at the forefront of big data analysis, offering powerful tools to extract insights, predict outcomes, and uncover patterns from vast and complex datasets. In this section, we'll delve into the details of machine

Table 3.1 Benefits of leveraging statistical approaches for predictive maintenance.

Key benefit	Explanation
Cost reduction	Proactive maintenance reduces downtime and minimizes repair costs by addressing issues before they escalate.
Improved efficiency	Predictive maintenance optimizes equipment utilization and prolongs asset lifespan through timely interventions.
Enhanced safety	Early detection of equipment failures enhances workplace safety by preventing accidents and ensuring compliance with regulatory standards.
Customer satisfaction	Reliability and uptime improvements result in better product quality and delivery performance, enhancing customer satisfaction and loyalty.

learning models and explore real-world examples of their applications in big data analysis (Figure 3.3).

1. **Supervised Learning:** Supervised learning algorithms learn from labeled data to make predictions or decisions. Examples include:
   - **Classification:** Identifying which category or class new data belongs to. For instance, a bank can use a classification model to predict whether a loan applicant is likely to default or not based on historical data.
   - **Regression:** Predicting a continuous value. For example, an e-commerce company can use regression to forecast sales based on factors like advertising spend, seasonality, and economic indicators.
2. **Unsupervised Learning:** Unsupervised learning algorithms uncover patterns and structures in unlabeled data. Examples include:
   - **Clustering:** Grouping similar data points together. An online retailer can use clustering to segment customers based on purchasing behavior, allowing for targeted marketing campaigns.
   - **Dimensionality Reduction:** Reducing the number of features in a dataset while preserving its essential information. This can help visualize high-dimensional data and improve model performance.
3. **Ensemble Learning:** Ensemble learning combines multiple models to improve prediction accuracy and robustness. Examples include:
   - **Random Forest:** A collection of decision trees trained on different subsets of the data. This method is used in applications like fraud detection, where multiple weak classifiers combine to make a strong prediction.
   - **Gradient Boosting:** Sequentially adding models that correct errors made by the previous ones. Gradient boosting is widely used in applications such as recommendation systems and search engine ranking.

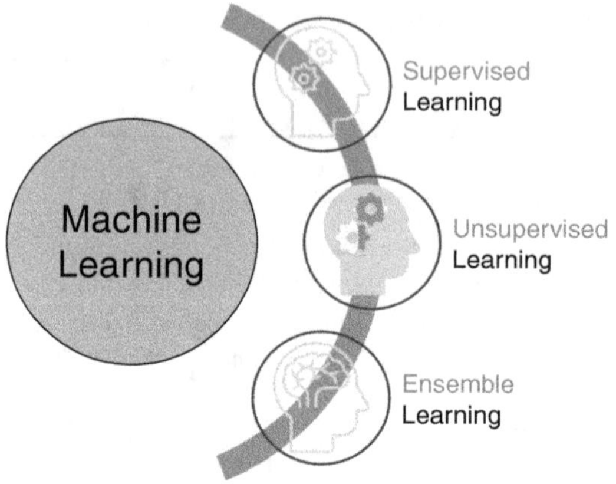

Figure 3.3 Machine learning model.

Table 3.2 Popular models in big data analysis.

Model	Use case
Linear regression	Predicting continuous values
Decision trees	Classification and regression
Random forest	Ensemble learning for accuracy
K-means	Clustering large datasets
SVM	Classification tasks
Neural networks	Complex tasks (e.g., image recognition, and speech analysis)
Gradient boosting	Ensemble technique for accuracy

Various machine learning models are used for analyzing big data, each suited to different types of tasks. These models range from simple algorithms like linear regression to more complex techniques such as deep learning and neural networks, allowing for effective handling of large datasets and complex patterns. Table 3.2 shows some popular models and their common use cases in big data analysis.

3.4.1 Real-world Example

3.4.1.1 Health Care: Predictive Modeling for Disease Diagnosis

In health care, machine learning models play a crucial role in disease diagnosis and prognosis. For example, researchers at the Mayo Clinic developed a machine learning model to predict the risk of heart failure in patients with diabetes. The model analyzes electronic health records, genetic data, and lifestyle factors to identify patients at high risk of developing heart failure. By leveraging supervised learning techniques such as logistic regression and random forest, the model can accurately predict the likelihood of heart failure onset within a certain time frame. Additionally, unsupervised learning algorithms like clustering can help identify subgroups of patients with similar risk profiles, enabling personalized treatment plans and interventions. Ensemble learning techniques further enhance prediction accuracy by combining multiple models trained on different data sources and features.

By deploying machine learning models for big data analysis in health-care settings, organizations can improve patient outcomes, reduce health-care costs, and optimize resource allocation. These models empower clinicians with valuable insights and decision support tools, enabling proactive interventions and personalized care pathways for patients at risk of chronic diseases like heart failure. Algorithm 3.4.2 presents all the steps for a machine learning model for big data analytics in any application area.

3.4.2 Algorithm for Machine Learning Models for Big Data Analysis

Step 1: Data Collection

1. Collect datasets from sensors, logs, and databases.
2. Store in distributed systems like Hadoop or cloud storage.

Step 2: Data Preprocessing

1. Clean data (handle missing values, remove duplicates).
2. Normalize features (e.g., Min-Max scaling).
3. Extract features (e.g., time series, categorization).

Step 3: Model Selection

1. Supervised Learning:
   - Classification: decision trees, random forest.
   - Regression: linear regression, SVM, and so on.
2. Unsupervised Learning:
   - Clustering: K-means, DBSCAN, and so on.
   - Dimensionality Reduction: PCA, t-SNE, and so on.
3. Ensemble Learning:
   - Combine models like random forest or gradient boosting.

Step 4: Model Training

1. Split data into training and testing sets.
2. Train the selected model on the training set.

Step 5: Model Evaluation

1. Use metrics (accuracy, precision, recall, and RMSE).
2. Validate the model with cross-validation.

Step 6: Hyperparameter Tuning

1. Optimize parameters using grid search or random search.

Step 7: Model Deployment

1. Deploy the model to production.
2. Use it for real-time predictions.

Step 8: Continuous Monitoring and Updates

1. Monitor performance with real-time data.
2. Update the model with new data when needed.
3. Integrate the outputs of machine learning models executed on different nodes of the Hadoop cluster into application dashboards.

3.5 Deep Learning Architectures in Big Data Analytics

Deep learning architectures represent a subset of machine learning techniques that leverage neural networks with multiple layers of interconnected nodes to extract features and patterns from data. In the context of big data analytics, deep learning offers unparalleled capabilities to analyze vast and complex datasets, ranging from images and videos to text and sensor data. Let's explore this topic in detail with a real-world example.

3.5.1 Example: Image Recognition in Health Care Using Deep Learning Architectures

Consider a scenario in the health-care industry where deep learning architectures are employed for image recognition tasks, such as diagnosing medical conditions from diagnostic images like X-rays, MRIs, or CT scans. Deep learning models, particularly CNNs, have revolutionized medical imaging by enabling automated interpretation of images with accuracy comparable to human experts. Next, detailed steps are shown in Algorithm 3.5.2. Figure 3.4 shows the deep learning architectures in big data analytics, which comprises various steps that is as follows:

- **Data Collection and Preprocessing:** In this example, the health-care organization collects a large volume of medical images from various sources, including hospitals, clinics, and research institutions. These images are typically stored in digital formats and may vary in terms of quality, resolution, and format. Before feeding the images into the deep learning model, preprocessing steps such as resizing, normalization, and augmentation may be applied to enhance data quality and consistency.

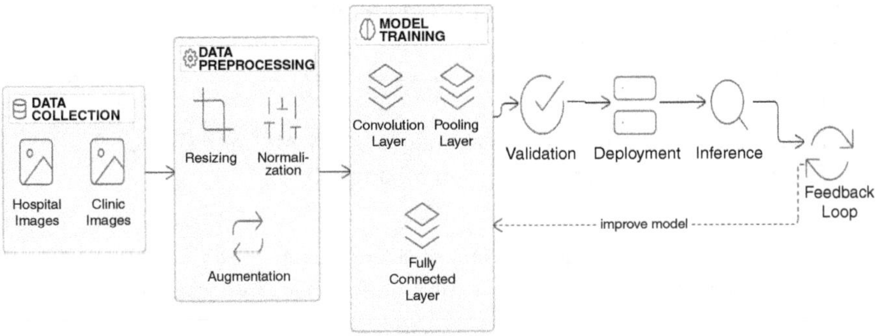

Figure 3.4 Deep learning architectures in big data analytics.

- **Model Training:** The organization leverages a deep learning framework such as TensorFlow or PyTorch to train a CNN model on the collected image dataset. The CNN architecture consists of multiple layers, including convolutional layers, pooling layers, and fully connected layers, designed to extract hierarchical features from the input images. During training, the model learns to recognize patterns and features indicative of different medical conditions, such as tumors, fractures, or abnormalities.
- **Validation and Fine-tuning:** The trained model is validated using a separate dataset to evaluate its performance and generalization capabilities. Techniques such as cross-validation and hyperparameter tuning may be employed to optimize the model's performance and prevent overfitting. The model's accuracy, sensitivity, specificity, and other performance metrics are carefully evaluated to ensure its reliability and effectiveness in real-world applications.
- **Deployment and Inference:** Once validated, the trained deep learning model is deployed into production environments, where it performs inference on new incoming images in real time. When a medical image is input into the system, the model analyzes the image and generates predictions regarding the presence or absence of specific medical conditions. These predictions are then reviewed by health-care professionals for further diagnosis and treatment planning.
- **Continuous Learning and Improvement:** The deployed model continues to learn and improve over time as it receives feedback from health-care professionals and encounters new cases. Techniques such as transfer learning and online learning enable the model to adapt to evolving datasets and emerging medical trends, ensuring its efficacy and relevance in dynamic health-care settings.

3.5.2 Algorithm for Deep Learning-driven Medical Image Recognition in Big Data Analytics

Input:
- Large dataset of labeled medical images (X-ray, MRI, and CT scans)
- Patient metadata and clinical history (optional)

Output:
- Classified medical images with disease prediction
- Continuous model improvement through feedback integration

Steps:
1. **Data Collection and Preprocessing:**
   - Acquire large-scale medical image datasets from hospitals and healthcare repositories.
   - Normalize images (e.g., resizing, grayscale conversion, and noise removal).
   - Apply data augmentation (rotation, flipping, and contrast adjustment) to enhance robustness.
   - Convert images into tensors for deep learning model processing.
2. **Model Selection and Training:**
   - Choose a deep learning architecture (CNN, ResNet, EfficientNet, or Vision Transformers).
   - Train the model using labeled images (healthy vs. diseased) with supervised learning.
   - Optimize model parameters using loss functions (e.g., cross-entropy, Dice loss).
   - Validate model performance using metrics like accuracy, precision, recall, and F1-score.
3. **Disease Classification and Prediction:**
   - Feed new patient images into the trained model.
   - Extract deep feature representations and classify them into predefined disease categories.
   - Generate heatmaps (Grad-CAM) for explainability in diagnosis.
4. **Feedback Loop for Continuous Learning:**
   - Integrate expert radiologist feedback to correct misclassified images.
   - Retrain the model with corrected labels and new datasets to improve accuracy.
   - Implement active learning, where uncertain predictions are flagged for manual review.
   - Update the model periodically to adapt to new medical findings and variations in imaging.

5. **Big Data Integration and Deployment:**
   - Store patient imaging data in distributed storage (e.g., Hadoop, cloud-based solutions).
   - Deploy the model on cloud/edge devices for real-time disease detection in hospitals using master-slave architecture of cluster environment.
   - Ensure compliance with health-care regulations (HIPAA, GDPR).
6. **Evaluation and Continuous Improvement:**
   - Regularly assess model performance with new test datasets.
   - Fine-tune hyperparameters using reinforcement learning techniques.
   - Implement federated learning to enhance security while using global medical datasets.

3.6 NLP for Textual Big Data

NLP is a branch of AI that focuses on the interaction between computers and human language. In the context of textual big data, NLP techniques enable the analysis, understanding, and generation of natural language text, facilitating tasks such as sentiment analysis, entity recognition, topic modeling, and text summarization. Let's explore NLP in detail with a real-world example:

3.6.1 Example: Sentiment Analysis in Social Media Monitoring

Consider a scenario where a company wants to monitor social media conversations about its products to gauge customer sentiment and identify potential issues or opportunities. By leveraging NLP techniques, the company can analyze large volumes of textual data from social media platforms such as Twitter, Facebook, and Instagram to extract insights and trends. Algorithm 3.6.2 presents all the steps for NLP for big data analytics for sentiment analysis for any application area. NLP could be useful for various application areas as discussed below:

1. **Data Collection:** The first step involves collecting textual data from social media platforms using APIs or web scraping techniques. The data may include tweets, posts, comments, and reviews related to the company's products or brand.
2. **Preprocessing:** Textual data often contains noise, such as punctuation, stopwords, and special characters, which can impact analysis. Preprocessing techniques such as tokenization, lowercasing, and removing stopwords are applied to clean the data and prepare it for analysis.

3. **Sentiment Analysis:** Sentiment analysis is a common NLP task that involves determining the sentiment expressed in a piece of text, such as positive, negative, or neutral. ML algorithms, such as SVMs, logistic regression, or deep learning models like RNNs or transformer-based architectures, are trained on labeled data to classify text sentiment.
   Example: A tweet that reads "I love the new iPhone, it's amazing!" would be classified as positive sentiment, while "The customer service experience was terrible" would be classified as negative sentiment.
4. **Named Entity Recognition:** Entity recognition involves identifying named entities such as people, organizations, locations, and products mentioned in the text. Named entity recognition (NER) models, trained on annotated data, are used to extract entities from textual data.
   Example: In the sentence "I bought a MacBook Pro from Apple Store," the NER model would identify "MacBook Pro" as a product and "Apple Store" as an organization.
5. **Topic Modeling:** Topic modeling is a technique used to discover latent topics or themes present in a collection of documents. Algorithms such as Latent Dirichlet Allocation or Non-Negative Matrix Factorization are applied to identify topics and their associated keywords from textual data.
   Example: Topic modeling analysis of customer reviews may reveal topics such as product features, customer service, pricing, and user experience.
6. **Text Summarization:** Text summarization techniques condense large volumes of text into concise summaries while preserving key information and meaning. Extractive summarization methods select important sentences or phrases from the original text, while abstractive summarization techniques generate new sentences to convey the essence of the text.
   Example: A news article about a recent product launch can be summarized into a few sentences highlighting key announcements, features, and reactions.

3.6.2 Algorithm for Natural Language Processing with Big Data for Sentiment Analysis

Step 1: Data Collection

- Gather textual big data from various sources such as social media, news articles, or online reviews.
- Store the collected data in a structured format (CSV, database, or cloud storage) in a distributed system like Hadoop or others.

Step 2: Data Preprocessing

- Convert text to lowercase for uniformity.
- Remove special characters, punctuation, and stopwords.

- Perform tokenization to split sentences into words.
- Apply stemming or lemmatization to normalize words.

Step 3: Feature Extraction

- Convert text into numerical representations using techniques like:
- Bag of Words (BoW).
- Term Frequency-Inverse Document Frequency (TF-IDF).
- Word Embeddings (Word2Vec, GloVe, BERT, etc.).

Step 4: Model Selection and Training

- Choose a machine learning or deep learning model:
- Traditional ML models: Naïve Bayes, support vector machines (SVMs), and random forest.
- Deep learning models: recurrent neural networks (RNNs), long short-term memory (LSTM), transformer-based models (BERTs).
- Train the model using labeled sentiment datasets.

Step 5: Sentiment Classification

- Input the processed text into the trained model.
- Classify the sentiment as positive, negative, or neutral based on model predictions.

Step 6: Performance Evaluation

- Use performance metrics such as accuracy, precision, recall, and F1-score to assess the model.
- Optimize hyperparameters if necessary to improve results.

Step 7: Real-Time Processing and Deployment

- Deploy the trained model for real-time sentiment analysis on new data streams.
- Integrate all results from different nodes of the Hadoop cluster into applications, dashboards, or business intelligence systems.

3.6.3 Real-world Impact

By applying NLP techniques such as sentiment analysis, entity recognition, topic modeling, and text summarization to textual big data, organizations can gain valuable insights into customer preferences, market trends, brand perception, and competitive landscape. These insights enable organizations to make data-driven decisions, enhance customer experiences, optimize marketing strategies, and identify areas for improvement or innovation. For example, a company can use sentiment analysis to assess customer feedback on a new product launch and adjust its marketing or product development strategy accordingly. Similarly, entity recognition can help businesses identify influencers or brand ambassadors on social media platforms and engage with them to amplify their brand message. Overall, NLP for textual big data has a profound impact on various industries, including marketing, customer service, health care, finance, and e-commerce, driving innovation and competitiveness in the digital age. Furthermore, NLP techniques play a crucial role in enhancing decision-making processes, improving customer experiences, and driving innovation. By understanding customer preferences, market trends, and competitive landscape through textual analysis, organizations can make informed decisions, optimize resource allocation, and identify new opportunities for growth and differentiation.

As organizations continue to harness the power of NLP for textual big data analytics, the potential for innovation and value creation remains boundless. By embracing advanced NLP techniques and integrating them into their analytics workflows, organizations can gain a competitive edge in today's data-driven landscape, driving efficiency, agility, and strategic advantage. In conclusion, NLP for textual big data analytics represents a cornerstone of modern data-driven decision-making, empowering organizations to extract actionable insights, drive innovation, and unlock new opportunities for growth and success in the digital age.

3.7 Conclusion

In conclusion, this chapter explores how AI technologies are revolutionizing big data analytics by introducing advanced methods for extracting insights from vast and diverse datasets. It covers key AI-driven approaches, including statistical methodologies, machine learning models, deep learning architectures, and NLP, demonstrating their role in enhancing data quality and processing efficiency. By unlocking actionable insights, AI empowers organizations to make informed decisions, optimize strategies, and drive innovation. Real-world applications highlight its transformative impact on various industries, fostering competitiveness and efficiency. Ultimately, this chapter equips readers with the knowledge and tools needed to effectively leverage AI for big data analytics, enabling them to harness its full potential. This chapter has provided a comprehensive exploration of NLP techniques and methodologies, showcasing their diverse applications in analyzing, understanding, and generating natural language text within the context of big data analytics. NLP is a powerful tool in big data analytics, enabling organizations to derive valuable insights from vast amounts of textual data. This chapter explored key NLP techniques, including sentiment analysis, entity recognition, topic modeling, and text summarization, which help analyze data from sources like social media, customer reviews, and news articles. By leveraging machine learning and deep learning models, organizations can automate sentiment classification, entity extraction, and topic identification for faster, more accurate analysis. Real-world applications span multiple domains, such as marketing, health care, finance, and e-commerce, enhancing decision-making, customer experience, and innovation. As businesses continue integrating NLP into their analytics workflows, its potential to drive efficiency, agility, and competitive advantage remains immense, making it a cornerstone of data-driven decision-making in the digital era.

Practice Set

A Multiple Choice Questions (MCQ)

1 What is the main role of natural language processing (NLP) in big data analytics?
- **a** Automating hardware functions
- **b** Extracting actionable insights from textual data
- **c** Managing data storage
- **d** Improving data encryption

2 Which NLP technique is used to understand the sentiment of text data?
- **a** Entity recognition
- **b** Sentiment analysis
- **c** Topic modeling
- **d** Text summarization

3 Which application area does NLP NOT directly impact, as mentioned in the chapter?
- **a** Marketing
- **b** Health care
- **c** Manufacturing
- **d** Finance

4 What is the purpose of entity recognition in NLP?
- **a** Summarizing text
- **b** Identifying key entities and relationships
- **c** Analyzing sentiment
- **d** Topic modeling

5 Which method is NOT mentioned as a part of NLP techniques?
   a Sentiment classification
   b Deep learning architectures
   c Data encryption
   d Statistical models

6 How does sentiment analysis benefit businesses?
   a By improving hardware efficiency
   b By gauging customer sentiment and adjusting strategies
   c By increasing data storage
   d By automating data entry

7 What role does text summarization play in NLP?
   a Identifying topics
   b Creating brief versions of texts
   c Classifying sentiments
   d Extracting entities

8 Which domain benefits from NLP through personalized recommendations and targeted marketing?
   a Health care
   b E-commerce
   c Manufacturing
   d Telecommunications

9 What does topic modeling help organizations understand?
   a Customer sentiment
   b Key entities
   c Main themes and topics in textual data
   d Text summaries

10 What advantage does integrating advanced NLP techniques into analytics workflows provide?
   a Increased hardware requirements
   b Competitive edge and strategic advantage
   c Reduced data collection
   d Simplified data entry

B Fill-in-the-Blanks

11 NLP techniques such as sentiment analysis and __________ are used to analyze and generate natural language text.

12 Entity recognition helps identify key __________ and relationships within textual data.

13 Text summarization creates __________ versions of longer texts to make them more manageable.

14 Sentiment analysis helps businesses gauge __________ sentiment on social media platforms.

15 Advanced NLP techniques can drive __________ and unlock new opportunities for growth.

C Short Answer Questions

16 What are some common applications of NLP in big data analytics?

17 Explain how machine learning algorithms are used in NLP.

18 Describe the benefits of sentiment analysis for businesses.

19 How does entity recognition contribute to personalized recommendations in e-commerce?

20 What is the impact of NLP on decision-making processes within organizations?

D Long Answer Questions

21 Discuss the role of NLP in transforming textual big data into actionable insights and provide examples from different domains.

22 Analyze how sentiment analysis and topic modeling can be combined to enhance marketing strategies.

23 Evaluate the potential challenges organizations might face when implementing NLP techniques and propose solutions.

24 Examine how NLP can drive innovation and efficiency in customer service and health care.

25 Explore the future potential of NLP technologies in big data analytics and their implications for organizational growth.

Further Readings

Alkurd, R., Abualhaol, I. and Yanikomeroglu, H., 2020. Big-data-driven and AI-based framework to enable personalization in wireless networks. *IEEE Communications Magazine*, 58(3), pp. 18–24.

Bhat, S.A. and Huang, N.F., 2021. Big data and AI revolution in precision agriculture: survey and challenges. *IEEE Access*, 9, pp. 110209–110222.

Fong, S., Fortino, G., Ghista, D. and Piccialli, F., 2023. Special issue on deep learning and big data analytics for medical e-diagnosis/AI-based e-diagnosis. *Neural Computing and Applications*, 35(22), pp. 15961–15965.

Himeur, Y., Elnour, M., Fadli, F., Meskin, N., Petri, I., Rezgui, Y., Bensaali, F. and Amira, A., 2023. AI-big data analytics for building automation and management systems: a survey, actual challenges and future perspectives. *Artificial Intelligence Review*, 56(6), pp. 4929–5021.

Kamrowska-Załuska, D., 2021. Impact of AI-based tools and urban big data analytics on the design and planning of cities. *Land*, 10(11), p. 1209.

Khan, Z.F. and Alotaibi, S.R., 2020. Applications of artificial intelligence and big data analytics in m-health: a healthcare system perspective. *Journal of Healthcare Engineering*, 2020(1), p. 8894694.

Kumari, A., Obaidat, M., Panchal, S., Raval, N., Kumar, P. and Yadav, D.K., 2024. M-VMT-PC: Metaverse-enabled Virtual Medical Training and Patient Care framework underlying 5G. In: *2024 International Conference on Communications, Computing, Cybersecurity*, pp. 1–7. IEEE.

Kumari, A. and Tanwar, S., 2020. Secure data analytics for smart grid systems in a sustainable smart city: challenges, solutions, and future directions. *Sustainable Computing: Informatics and Systems*, 28, p. 100427.

Kumari, A. and Tanwar, S., 2021. ρReveal: an AI-based big data analytics scheme for energy price prediction and load reduction. In: *2021 11th International Conference on Cloud Computing, Data Science & Engineering (Confluence)*, pp. 321–326. IEEE.

Kumari, A. and Tanwar, S., 2022. GrAb: a deep learning-based data-driven analytics scheme for energy theft detection. *Sensors*, 22(11), p. 4048.

Kusal, S., Patil, S., Kotecha, K., Aluvalu, R. and Varadarajan, V., 2021. AI-based emotion detection for textual big data: techniques and contribution. *Big Data and Cognitive Computing*, 5(3), p. 43.

Li, J., Ye, Z. and Zhang, C., 2022. Study on the interaction between big data and artificial intelligence. *Systems Research and Behavioral Science*, 39(3), pp. 641–648.

Lokesh, S., Chakraborty, S., Pulugu, R., Mittal, S., Pulugu, D. and Muruganantham, R., 2022. AI-based big data analytics model for medical applications. *Measurement: Sensors*, 24, p. 100534.

Punia, S.K., Kumar, M., Stephan, T., Deverajan, G.G. and Patan, R., 2021. Performance analysis of machine learning algorithms for big data classification: ML and AI-based algorithms for big data analysis. *International Journal of E-Health and Medical Communications (IJEHMC)*, 12(4), pp. 60–75.

Rahmani, A.M., Azhir, E., Ali, S., Mohammadi, M., Ahmed, O.H., Ghafour, M.Y., Ahmed, S.H. and Hosseinzadeh, M., 2021. Artificial intelligence approaches and mechanisms for big data analytics: a systematic study. *PeerJ Computer Science*, 7, p. e488.

Ren, S., Patrick Hui, C.L. and Jason Choi, T.M., 2018. AI-based fashion sales forecasting methods in big data era. In: *Artificial Intelligence for Fashion Industry in the Big Data Era*, pp. 9–26. Springer.

Samuel, P., Reshmy, A.K., Rajesh, S., Kanipriya, M. and Karthika, R.A., 2023. AI-based big data algorithms and machine learning techniques for managing data in E-governance. In: *AI, IoT, and Blockchain Breakthroughs in E-governance*, pp. 19–35. IGI Global.

Tandel, V., Kumari, A., Tanwar, S., Singh, A., Sharma, R. and Yamsani, N., 2024. Intelligent wearable-assisted digital healthcare industry 5.0. *Artificial Intelligence in Medicine*, 157, p. 103000.

Vekaria, D., Kumari, A., Tanwar, S. and Kumar, N., 2020. ξboost: an AI-based data analytics scheme for COVID-19 prediction and economy boosting. *IEEE Internet of Things Journal*, 8(21), pp. 15977–15989.

4

Real-world Applications of Big Data

LEARNING OBJECTIVES

- Big data can predict equipment failures to minimize downtime and optimize maintenance schedules in manufacturing industries.
- Understand how big data enables personalized recommendations and enhances customer experiences in the e-commerce industry.
- Explore how big data analytics helps in risk assessment, fraud detection, and decision-making in the financial services sector.
- Learn how big data improves patient care by enabling predictive analytics, personalized treatments, and efficient health-care management.
- Discover how big data supports the development of smart cities through data-driven urban planning and optimization of resources.
- Understand how big data analytics enhances the safety, navigation, and efficiency of autonomous vehicles and transportation systems.

4.1 Introduction

Big data has become an indispensable force in revolutionizing industries, enabling businesses and governments to derive actionable insights, optimize processes, and drive innovation. This chapter explores the real-world applications of big data across diverse sectors, emphasizing its transformative role when combined with technologies like artificial intelligence (AI), the Internet of Things (IoT), and blockchain. From enhancing operational efficiency to enabling smarter decision-making, big data analytics is the backbone of many cutting-edge solutions shaping modern society. In this chapter, we delve into key applications such as AI-driven predictive maintenance in manufacturing, which reduces downtime by predicting and preventing failures, and data-driven personalization in e-commerce, enhancing customer satisfaction and profitability. Big data's impact on financial services is profound, offering advanced tools for risk analysis and fraud detection. Similarly, health-care analytics utilizes big data to improve patient care and optimize resource allocation. The chapter also highlights how big data empowers smart cities with efficient urban planning and contributes to the development of autonomous vehicles and intelligent transportation systems, revolutionizing mobility and safety. Through these examples, the chapter demonstrates the immense potential of big data in solving real-world challenges and shaping the future.

4.1.1 Motivation

The motivation behind exploring real-world applications of big data is rooted in its transformative potential to revolutionize industries and improve everyday life. As technology continues to advance, the ability to harness vast amounts of data from diverse sources presents unparalleled opportunities for innovation, efficiency, and personalized experiences. From manufacturing and e-commerce to health care and smart cities, big data is enabling organizations to make more informed, data-driven decisions that drive growth, optimize resources, and enhance customer satisfaction. Understanding how big data can be applied across various sectors not only highlights its current impact but also opens the door to new possibilities for tackling complex challenges and shaping a smarter, more connected future.

4.1.2 Chapter Contributions

- Demonstrates how AI-driven predictive maintenance optimizes manufacturing operations by reducing downtime and preempting equipment failures. Explores data-driven decision-making in e-commerce, highlighting personalized customer experiences and enhanced sales through targeted recommendations.
- Analyzes the application of big data in financial services, emphasizing improved risk analysis, fraud detection, and informed investment strategies. Showcases the transformative impact of health-care analytics on patient care, including predictive modeling, real-time monitoring, and personalized treatment plans.
- Investigates how big data contributes to the development of smart cities by enhancing urban planning, traffic management, and resource optimization.
- Examines the integration of big data in autonomous vehicles and intelligent transportation systems, underlining advancements in navigation, safety, and traffic flow management.

4.1.3 Organization of the Chapter

Chapter 4 explores diverse real-world applications of big data across various industries. It begins with AI-driven predictive maintenance in manufacturing, showcasing how big data optimizes operations and reduces downtime in Section 4.2. This chapter then discusses data-driven decision-making in e-commerce personalization, highlighting tailored customer experiences in Section 4.3. It further delves into financial services and risk analysis, demonstrating big data's role in enhancing decision-making and reducing risks in Section 4.4. In Section 4.5, the application of big data in health-care analytics is examined, focusing on improved patient care outcomes. Next, the impact of big data on smart cities, urban planning, and intelligent transportation systems in Sections 4.6 and 4.7. Finally, the chapter concludes in Section 4.8.

4.2 AI-driven Predictive Maintenance in Manufacturing

In the manufacturing industry, predictive maintenance has emerged as a game-changer, leveraging the power of AI and big data. By continuously monitoring equipment performance through IoT sensors, manufacturers can collect vast amounts of data, such as machine temperature, vibration, and operational parameters. This data is then analyzed using advanced algorithms to identify patterns and anomalies, enabling proactive identification of potential issues before they lead to equipment failure. This approach not only minimizes unplanned downtime but also reduces maintenance costs and improves overall production efficiency, making it an indispensable tool for modern manufacturing. In manufacturing, predictive maintenance powered by big data analytics has emerged as a game-changer, enabling companies like General Electric (GE) and Siemens to minimize downtime, enhance equipment performance, and reduce maintenance costs through proactive fault detection and maintenance scheduling.

4.2.1 Case Study

A global automotive manufacturer faced frequent disruptions in its production line due to unexpected machine breakdowns in the Gujarat, India region. These unexpected halts were not only slowing down production but also increasing maintenance costs. To address this issue, the company installed IoT sensors across its machinery to collect real-time data on key performance metrics such as vibration, temperature, and operational cycles. This data was then fed into an AI-powered analytics system designed to detect early signs of wear and tear.

However, the data used in this example is generated synthetically to simulate the scenario to reflect real-world possibilities. By feeding this sensor data into an AI-powered analytics platform, the company built a predictive maintenance system that could anticipate equipment failures with up to 95% accuracy, and production uptime improved dramatically, reaching nearly 98%. It clearly shows the powerful potential of combining IoT and AI for smarter, more efficient manufacturing operations and it sets a promising benchmark for the future of the industry.

In another scenario, GE Aviation employs predictive maintenance to keep a close watch on the health of its jet engines. Equipped with sensors, the engines gather data on crucial metrics like temperature, pressure, vibrations, and more. This information is sent to GE's Predix platform for analysis. The Predix platform utilizes machine learning algorithms to process the data, uncover patterns, and forecast potential failures in the engines. As a result of this approach, GE has notably decreased instances of unscheduled maintenance, enhanced engine performance, and reduced operational costs (GE Aviation, 2023).

Furthermore, Siemens leverages AI-powered predictive maintenance to optimize the performance of its industrial gas turbines. By implementing this system, Siemens has significantly enhanced the reliability and efficiency of its turbine operations, reducing both downtime and maintenance expenses (Siemens, 2023). Toyota employs predictive maintenance in its manufacturing plants to ensure continuous production. Toyota has enhanced its production efficiency, reduced maintenance costs, and minimized unexpected breakdowns (Toyota, 2023).

4.2.2 Architecture Diagram

Figure 4.1 shows a simplified architecture diagram for an AI-driven predictive maintenance system in manufacturing. Here, the architecture of AI-driven predictive maintenance consists of several key components that work together to monitor, analyze, and predict equipment performance. At its core, the system begins with IoT sensors installed on machinery, which continuously collect real-time data such as temperature, vibration, pressure, and operational cycles. This raw data is transmitted to a data processing layer, often hosted on cloud-based platforms, where it is cleansed, aggregated, and stored in scalable databases. The next step involves the use of machine learning models for predictive/root cause analytics, which are trained on historical and real-time data to identify patterns, trends, and anomalies that could indicate potential failures. These models employ techniques such as regression analysis, neural networks, and time-series forecasting.

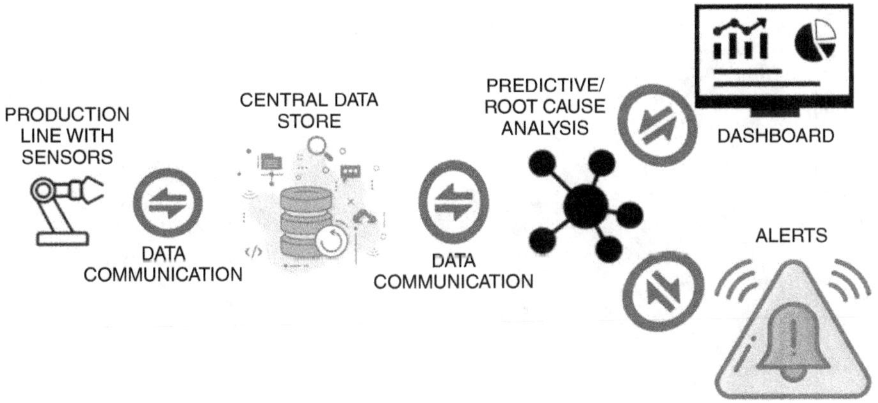

Figure 4.1 Architecture of AI-driven predictive maintenance.

The processed insights are fed into a decision-making layer, where predictive algorithms generate actionable insights, such as predicting the remaining useful life of equipment or identifying the likelihood of specific failures. These insights are then visualized using dashboard interfaces or communicated directly to maintenance teams through automated alerts, enabling them to take proactive action. A feedback loop is also integrated into the architecture, allowing the system to refine its predictions by incorporating outcomes from past maintenance actions. Additionally, the architecture often includes edge computing to process data locally for real-time decision-making in environments with low latency requirements. This cohesive structure ensures efficiency, reduces costs, and maximizes equipment uptime.

By integrating this automotive sensor data with AI-powered analytics, the company developed a predictive maintenance system capable of forecasting equipment uptime with 98% accuracy. This system allowed maintenance teams to address issues proactively, resulting in a 35% reduction in maintenance costs and a significant increase in production uptime, as shown in Figure 4.2. The bar graph illustrates the impact of implementing a predictive maintenance system on maintenance costs and production uptime. Before implementation, maintenance costs are at their peak (close to 95%), while production uptime was relatively low (around 65%). After the AI-driven system was introduced, maintenance costs dropped significantly to approximately 60%, indicating a 35% cost reduction. Conversely, production uptime improved dramatically, reaching nearly 98%, highlighting the effectiveness of predictive maintenance in enhancing operational efficiency and minimizing unplanned downtime. The success of this implementation not only enhanced operational efficiency but also set a new benchmark for the industry.

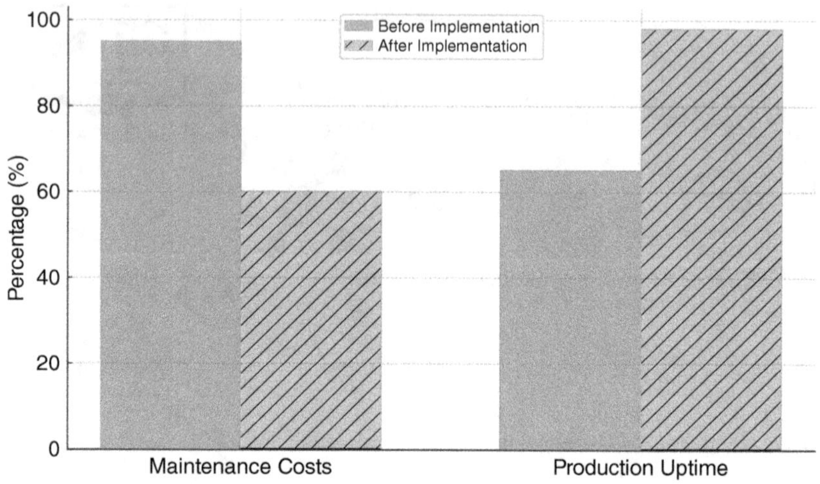

Figure 4.2 Impact of predictive maintenance system.

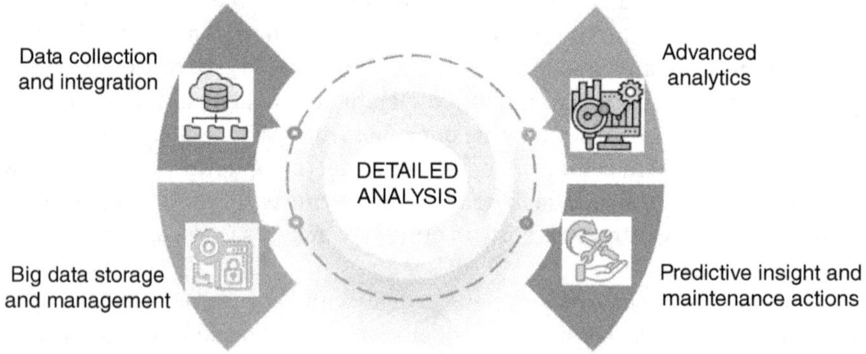

Figure 4.3 Detailed analysis of AI-driven predictive maintenance in manufacturing.

4.2.3 Detailed Analysis

1. **Data Collection and Integration**
   - **Sources**: Data is sourced from various sensors installed on manufacturing equipment. These sensors monitor operational metrics such as temperature, vibration, sound, and pressure, shown in Figure 4.3.
   - **Transmission**: Data is transmitted in real time to edge devices, which perform initial processing to filter out noise and reduce data volume before sending it to the central system.

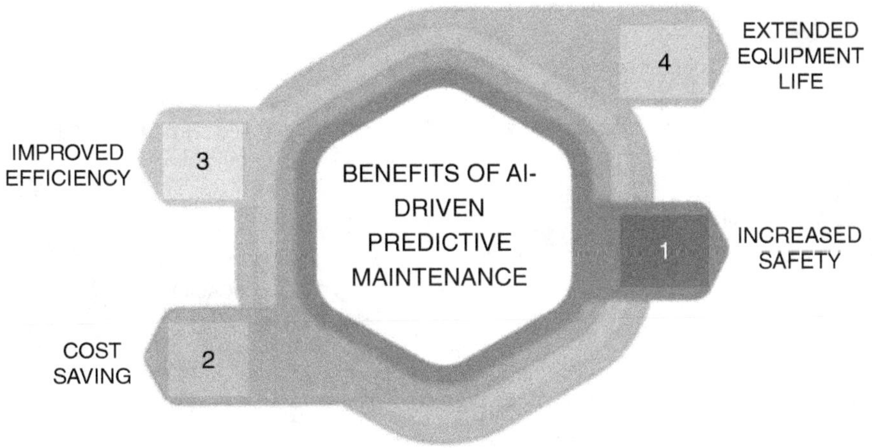

Figure 4.4 Benefits of AI-driven predictive maintenance.

2. **Big Data Storage and Management**
   - **Data Lake**: A data lake stores raw data in its native format until it is needed. This provides flexibility in data management and supports various data types.
   - **NoSQL Databases**: For more structured data storage, NoSQL databases like Apache Cassandra or MongoDB are used, enabling fast read/write operations.
3. **Advanced Analytics**
   - **Machine Learning Models**: Models are trained on historical data to learn the normal operational patterns of machinery. Techniques such as regression analysis, neural networks, and anomaly detection are used.
   - **Real-time Processing**: Using frameworks like Apache Kafka and Spark Streaming, real-time data is continuously analyzed to provide immediate insights.

4.2.4 Benefits of AI-driven Predictive Maintenance in Manufacturing

Figure 4.4 illustrates the comprehensive benefits of AI-driven predictive maintenance, including enhanced safety, significant cost savings, and improved operational efficiency. These advantages further contribute to extended equipment lifespan, showcasing the value of this advanced maintenance approach.

4.2.5 Challenges and Solutions

AI-driven predictive maintenance offers significant advantages, but it also comes with several challenges that require thoughtful solutions, as depicted in

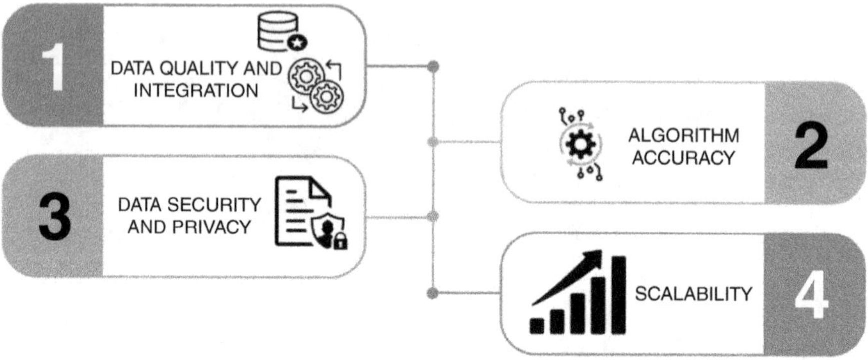

Figure 4.5 The challenges of AI-driven predictive maintenance.

Figure 4.5. A primary concern is *data quality and integration*, where ensuring consistent, high-quality input from diverse sensors is essential. This issue can be addressed by deploying edge-level data preprocessing to clean and normalize data before transmission. *Algorithm accuracy* is also critical for generating reliable maintenance predictions; this can be improved by continual model refinement, using updated data, real-world outcomes, and feedback loops. *Data security and privacy* present further concerns, especially with the handling of sensitive operational data. These are countered with robust encryption, secure transmission protocols, and strong access control mechanisms. *Scalability* is another challenge, given the exponential increase in data from multiple sources. This is mitigated through scalable cloud storage and distributed processing frameworks capable of efficiently managing large datasets. Lastly, maintaining the scalability of predictive models is vital to ensuring their long-term reliability and adaptability across evolving industrial environments.

4.3 Data-driven Decision-making for E-commerce Personalization

In the highly competitive e-commerce industry, personalization is key to attracting and retaining customers. Big data enables e-commerce platforms to analyze vast amounts of customer data, including browsing behavior, purchase history, and demographic information. By leveraging this data, companies can create tailored shopping experiences that resonate with individual preferences. Personalized product recommendations, targeted marketing campaigns, and dynamic pricing strategies are just a few examples of how data-driven decision-making can significantly boost customer satisfaction and drive sales. In e-commerce, data-driven decision-making has transformed the way businesses interact with customers, with industry giants like Amazon, Netflix, and Alibaba leveraging customer data to personalize recommendations, boost engagement, and drive sales.

4.3.1 Case Study

A leading online retailer struggled to convert website traffic into sales despite having a large customer base. To tackle this challenge, the retailer adopted a big data analytics platform to analyze customer behavior, including browsing patterns, clickstreams, and purchase histories. Using machine learning algorithms, the platform generated personalized product recommendations for each user and displayed them in real time on the website. Here, website traffic data is used, and some parts of the data are generated synthetically for better analysis. The retailer also used predictive analytics to send targeted marketing emails and optimize pricing strategies based on demand patterns. These efforts led to a 20% increase in sales and a 15% boost in customer retention rates, transforming the retailer into a leader in personalized e-commerce, as shown in Figure 4.6.

Amazon uses advanced machine learning algorithms to power its recommendation engine. By analyzing customer purchase history, browsing behavior, and product ratings, Amazon's system generates personalized product recommendations. Personalized recommendations contribute significantly to Amazon's sales, accounting for a large portion of overall revenue (Amazon, 2023).

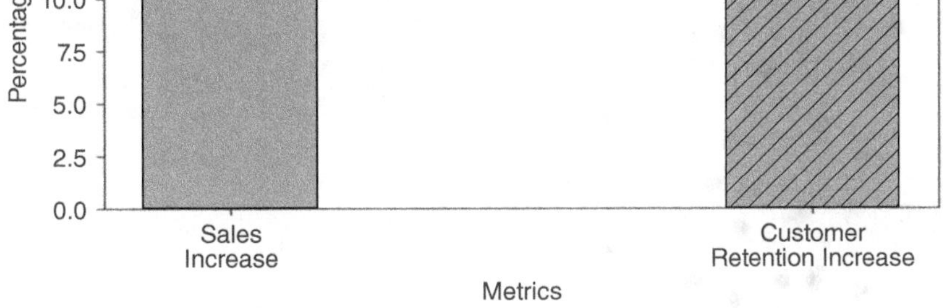

Figure 4.6 Impact of big data analytics on E-commerce performance.

4.3.2 Architecture Diagram

Figure 4.7 presents a conceptual architecture diagram for a data-driven decision-making system for e-commerce personalization. In this figure, data-driven decision-making in e-commerce personalization illustrates the integration of various components required to deliver personalized experiences to users. At the core, it leverages user data, including browsing behavior, purchase history, and demographic information, which is collected through various touchpoints such as websites, mobile apps, and customer interactions. This data is then processed through data storage and analytics platforms, where machine learning algorithms and AI models are applied to segment users and predict their preferences. These insights are fed into personalization engines, which dynamically recommend products or content tailored to individual users. The architecture also incorporates feedback loops, where continuous data collection and model refinement ensure that recommendations evolve over time, improving customer engagement and conversion rates. This seamless flow of data from collection to personalization enables a more customized and engaging e-commerce experience through the user interface.

4.3.3 Benefits of Data-driven Personalization

- **Increased Customer Engagement**: Personalized experiences make users feel valued and understood, leading to higher engagement.

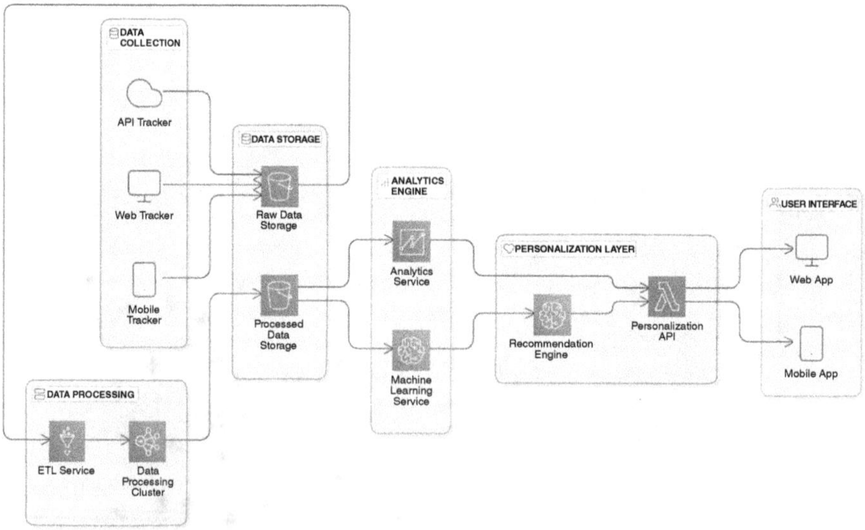

Figure 4.7 E-commerce personalization architecture.

- **Higher Conversion Rates**: Tailored recommendations and offers are more likely to convert browsers into buyers.
- **Customer Retention**: Personalization fosters customer loyalty by continuously meeting individual needs and preferences.
- **Improved Customer Insights**: Data analytics provide deep insights into customer behavior and preferences, informing business strategies.
- **Operational Efficiency**: Automation of personalized recommendations and marketing reduces the manual effort required.

4.3.4 Challenges and Solutions

In the realm of e-commerce, managing customer data effectively is crucial for personalized experiences. However, this also presents various challenges. Table 4.1 outlines some of the common issues faced and the solutions that can be implemented to overcome them.

4.4 Financial Services and Risk Analysis

The financial services sector relies heavily on big data for risk analysis, fraud detection, and investment decision-making. By analyzing transaction data, market trends, and customer profiles, financial institutions can identify potential

Table 4.1 Challenges and solutions.

Aspect	Challenge	Solution
Data privacy and security	Protecting sensitive customer data and complying with regulations like GDPR	Implement robust encryption, access controls, and privacy policies to ensure data security and compliance
Data integration	Integrating data from diverse sources and formats	Use advanced ETL tools and data integration platforms to consolidate and harmonize data
Scalability	Managing and processing large volumes of data in real time	Leverage scalable cloud infrastructure and distributed processing frameworks
Algorithm bias	Ensuring fairness and avoiding biases in recommendation algorithms	Regularly audit and update algorithms to detect and mitigate biases
Customer trust	Gaining and maintaining customer trust in data usage	Be transparent about data usage policies and provide options for customers to control their data

risks and opportunities with greater precision. Big data also enhances fraud detection systems by spotting unusual patterns in real time, thereby protecting customers and reducing financial losses. Furthermore, it empowers organizations to offer more personalized financial products, improving customer satisfaction and loyalty. Financial services have also benefited significantly from big data analytics, with institutions like JPMorgan Chase, HSBC, and Mastercard employing advanced analytics to mitigate risks, enhance compliance, and improve financial performance.

4.4.1 Case Study

A multinational bank experienced increasing instances of fraudulent transactions, leading to financial losses and reduced customer trust. To address this issue, the bank implemented a big data platform to analyze transaction data in real time, along with some part of the data being generated synthetically. By using AI algorithms, the platform identified anomalies in transaction patterns, such as unusually high spending or transactions from multiple locations within a short time frame. This allowed the bank to flag and investigate suspicious activities immediately, reducing fraudulent transactions by 40% and improving the credit risk by 25%. Additionally, the platform improved credit risk assessments by analyzing historical data and market trends, enabling the bank to make more informed lending decisions and enhance overall financial stability show in Figure 4.8.

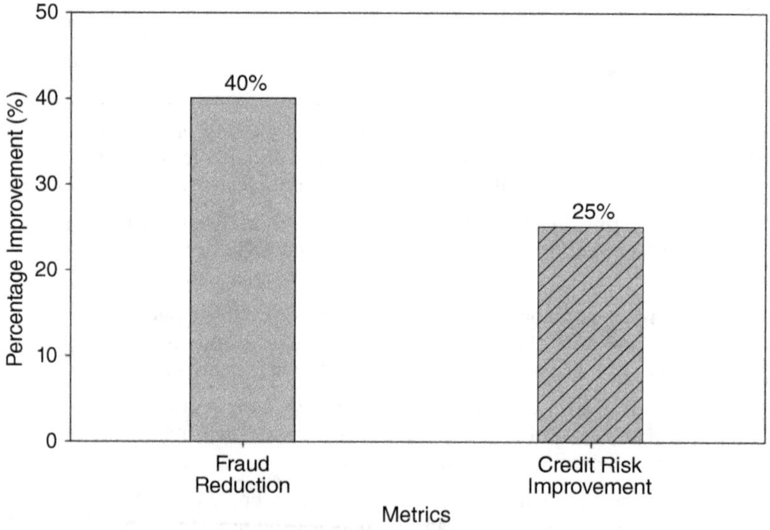

Figure 4.8 Impact of big data platform on fraud and credit risk.

JP Morgan Chase uses machine learning models to detect and prevent fraudulent transactions by analyzing real-time transaction data. These models identify fraud patterns by examining transaction history, geolocation data, and user behavior, leading to enhanced fraud detection rates, reduced false positives, and improved customer trust. Credit Suisse employs AI-driven risk management tools to assess credit risk by analyzing a wide range of data points, including financial statements, market conditions, and macroeconomic indicators. This approach results in more accurate credit risk assessments and informed lending decisions, leading to a lower default rate.

4.4.2 Architecture Diagram

Figure 4.9 is a proposed architecture diagram for a risk analysis system in financial services.

The architecture diagram for financial services and risk analysis typically involves several key components designed to manage data flow, analysis, and decision-making processes. At the core, there is a centralized data repository where structured and unstructured financial data is collected and stored in big data storage. This data is then processed through various modules, including IoT data integration platforms that clean and standardize the information. On top of this, advanced analytics engines, powered by AI algorithms, perform risk assessment and predictive modeling. These models evaluate financial risks such as credit risk, market risk, and fraud detection and are passed to the financial API and risk API. To handle the data security and privacy issue, blockchain services can be integrated with a financial API, and the smart contract could be designed.

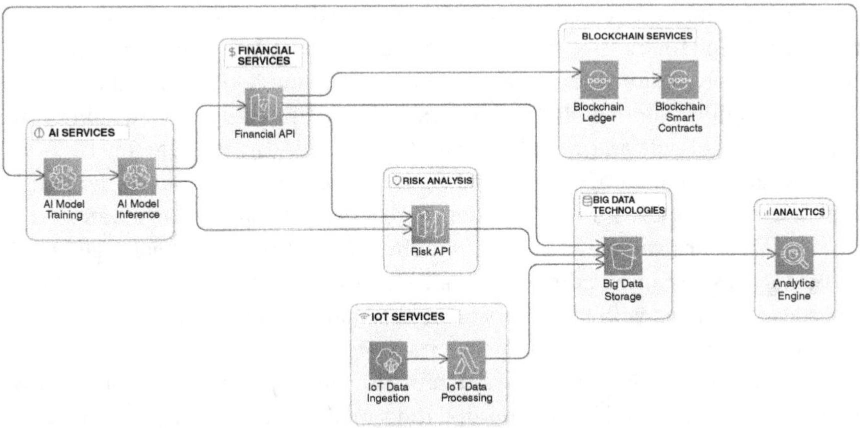

Figure 4.9 Financial services risk analysis architecture for big data analytics.

The system is supported by a scalable cloud infrastructure, which ensures seamless handling of large data volumes and computational power. Furthermore, compliance and security layers are integrated throughout the architecture, including real-time monitoring tools, encryption protocols, and access controls to ensure regulatory adherence and protect sensitive financial information. The output of the system is used to generate actionable insights and reports, which are then visualized via analytics dashboards for decision-makers.

4.4.3 Benefits of Data-driven Risk Analysis

1. **Enhanced Risk Detection**: Advanced analytics and machine learning improve the ability to detect and respond to potential risks, such as fraud and credit defaults.
2. **Informed Decision-Making**: Data-driven insights enable financial institutions to make more informed and strategic decisions regarding investments, lending, and risk management.
3. **Regulatory Compliance**: Automated risk analysis helps ensure compliance with regulatory requirements by providing accurate and timely reporting.
4. **Operational Efficiency**: Reduces manual effort and errors in risk assessment processes, increasing overall efficiency.
5. **Customer Trust**: Improved risk management enhances customer trust and satisfaction by safeguarding their assets and providing reliable financial services.

4.4.4 Challenges and Solutions

Ensuring the quality and consistency of data from diverse sources is a significant challenge in the financial sector. To address this, robust data governance policies and integration platforms are essential for maintaining high-quality data across the organization. Another challenge is scalability, particularly when dealing with large volumes of data and complex computations. This can be overcome by leveraging scalable cloud infrastructure and distributed computing frameworks, which can efficiently handle growing data and processing demands. Regulatory compliance is also critical, with the need to adhere to stringent financial regulations and standards. By integrating compliance checks into risk analysis workflows and staying updated with regulatory changes, organizations can ensure they meet these requirements.

Furthermore, model accuracy and fairness are key concerns in predictive analytics. Regularly validating and updating models, along with implementing techniques to mitigate biases, ensures both accuracy and fairness in predictions.

Lastly, protecting sensitive financial data from cyber threats remains a top priority. Employing advanced cybersecurity measures such as encryption, access controls, and continuous monitoring can safeguard data against potential risks and breaches.

4.5 Health-care Analytics for Patient Care

In the health-care industry, big data has paved the way for transformative advancements in patient care. By analyzing electronic health records, diagnostic imaging, and genomic data, health-care providers can gain deeper insights into patient conditions and treatment effectiveness. Big data enables early disease detection, personalized treatment plans, and better resource allocation, ultimately improving patient outcomes. Additionally, it supports health-care research by uncovering patterns and correlations that were previously impossible to identify, driving innovation in medical science. In health care, organizations such as Mayo Clinic, IBM Watson Health, and Kaiser Permanente are leveraging big data to deliver personalized care, improve treatment outcomes, and drive preventive measures.

4.5.1 Case Study

A large hospital network sought to improve patient outcomes by leveraging big data analytics. The network implemented a platform that integrated data from electronic health records (EHRs), lab results, diagnostic imaging, and wearable devices. By analyzing this data, the system identified early warning signs of sepsis, a life-threatening condition, in patients admitted to the intensive care unit. The predictive model enabled health-care professionals to intervene earlier, reducing mortality rates by 20%, as shown in Figure 4.10. Furthermore, the system optimized resource allocation by predicting patient recovery times, resulting in a 15% reduction in hospital stay durations as well. This data-driven approach not only saved lives but also enhanced the overall efficiency of the health-care system.

Mayo Clinic employs big data analytics to enhance patient care and outcomes. By analyzing data from EHRs, lab results, and patient surveys using machine learning algorithms, Mayo Clinic identifies disease patterns, predicts patient deterioration, and recommends personalized treatment plans. This approach has resulted in better patient outcomes, reduced hospital readmissions, and improved care delivery efficiency. Next, IBM Watson Health utilizes big data analytics to support clinical decision-making and research. Watson Health collects and processes extensive datasets from clinical trials, medical literature, and patient records. AI-driven models analyze this data to provide evidence-based

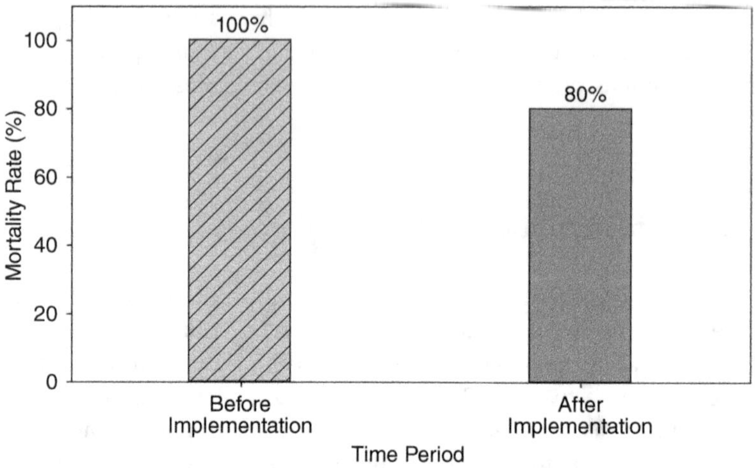

Figure 4.10 Reduction in mortality rates due to early sepsis detection.

treatment recommendations and identify potential drug interactions, enhancing diagnostic accuracy, accelerating medical research, and personalizing patient care.

4.5.2 Architecture Diagram

The architecture diagram for health-care analytics for patient care integrates various systems and technologies that support the efficient collection, processing, and analysis of patient data, as shown in Figure 4.11. At the core, the diagram includes a centralized EHR system where patient data is stored. The proposed architecture is divided into three layers: (i) data collection layer, (ii) analytics layer, and (iii) decision support system layer. In the data collection layer, data is collected from various sources, such as wearables, diagnostic devices, and hospital information systems. Data integration platforms ensure seamless aggregation and standardization of data across multiple health-care providers.

Once integrated, advanced analytics tools and machine learning algorithms are employed to assess patient health risks, predict future health events, and provide insights for personalized care in the analytics layer. These analytics are delivered via dashboards and decision support tools for health-care professionals, aiding them in making informed decisions in the decision support system layer. In addition, cloud infrastructure is leveraged to provide scalability and ensure access to resources as the volume of data grows. Security and compliance layers are built into the architecture to ensure patient data privacy and adhere to health-care regulations like HIPAA. Furthermore, real-time monitoring and alerting systems provide continuous insights and allow for timely intervention in critical cases.

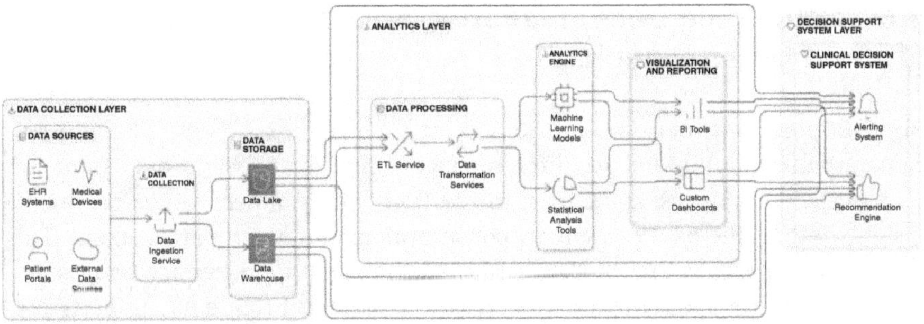

Figure 4.11 Architecture diagram of health-care analytics system for patient care.

Table 4.2 Benefits of health-care analytics for patient care.

Benefit	Description
Improved patient outcomes	Analytics help in early diagnosis and personalized treatment, leading to better health outcomes.
Cost reduction	Predictive analytics help optimize resource allocation and reduce unnecessary procedures or hospital readmissions.
Enhanced decision-making	Health-care professionals can make informed decisions by analyzing real-time data and predictive models.
Personalized treatment plans	Analytics enable tailored treatment recommendations based on individual patient data and health history.
Operational efficiency	Automation and predictive modeling improve workflow and resource management within health-care facilities.
Real-time monitoring and alerts	Continuous monitoring of patient data allows for real-time alerts, enabling timely interventions and reducing risks.
Regulatory compliance	The architecture ensures data privacy and adherence to health-care regulations, such as HIPAA, protecting patient information.

4.5.3 Benefits of Health-care Analytics for Patient Care

The integration of health-care analytics into patient care provides numerous advantages by leveraging data to enhance decision-making, optimize resource usage, and improve patient outcomes. Table 4.2 outlines the key benefits of using analytics in health care, showcasing how it helps health-care providers deliver more efficient, personalized, and cost-effective care while ensuring regulatory compliance.

4.6 Role of Big Data in Creating Smart Cities and Efficient Urban Planning

Big data plays a pivotal role in the development of smart cities, enabling efficient urban planning and resource management. By analyzing data from IoT sensors, public services, and citizen interactions, city planners can gain valuable insights into traffic patterns, energy consumption, and waste management. This data-driven approach helps optimize public transportation, reduce congestion, and enhance the quality of life for residents. Moreover, big data supports predictive modeling for disaster management and urban development, ensuring sustainable growth and resilience.

4.6.1 Case Study

A rapidly growing metropolitan city like Ahmedabad, Gujarat, faced challenges with traffic congestion and inefficient public transportation systems. To address these issues, the city deployed IoT-enabled traffic sensors and collected data on vehicle movement, road usage, and public transit schedules. This data was analyzed using big data analytics to identify bottlenecks and optimize transportation routes. The city also introduced a real-time traffic monitoring system that provided commuters with live updates and alternative routes. As a result, traffic congestion decreased by 25%, and public transportation efficiency improved significantly, leading to higher commuter satisfaction and reduced environmental impact, as shown in Figure 4.12.

New York City leverages big data for efficient urban planning and infrastructure management. Big data from public transportation, social services, and emergency response systems is collected and analyzed. Big data analytics helps in understanding urban dynamics, predicting infrastructure needs, and planning for future growth. New York City has enhanced its public transportation system, improved emergency response times, and effectively planned for urban expansion.

4.6.2 Architecture Diagram

Figure 4.13 shows a simplified architecture diagram for a big data analytics system used in smart cities and urban planning.

The architecture diagram for big data in smart cities and urban planning integrates various data sources and technologies to support the development of efficient, sustainable, and liveable urban environments. Here, it is divided into three major parts: (i) data ingestion, (ii) data management, and (iii) data analysis. In data ingestion, data from numerous IoT sensors deployed throughout the city is collected, ranging from traffic management systems to air quality monitors and energy

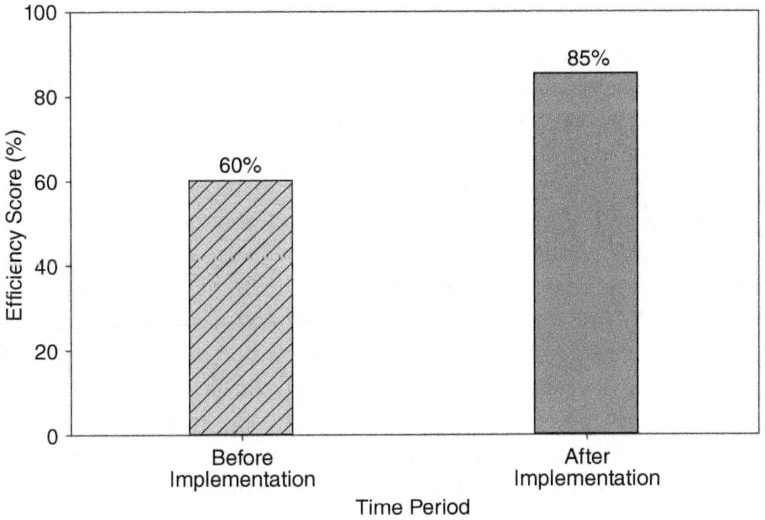

Figure 4.12 Improvement in public transportation efficiency.

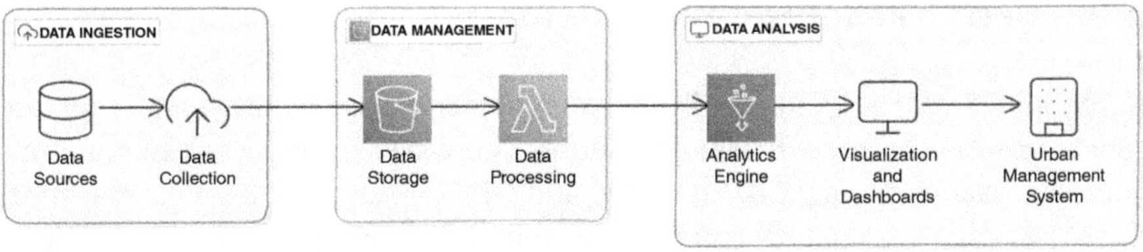

Figure 4.13 Architecture diagram for smart cities and urban planning using big data analytics.

meters. This data is transmitted to centralized data lakes or cloud-based storage platforms, where it is stored and processed in data management systems.

In data analysis, advanced analytics platforms and machine learning algorithms are then employed to analyze this vast amount of data in real time, providing actionable insights for urban planning and management. These insights are used to optimize traffic flow, reduce energy consumption, improve waste management, and enhance public safety. Furthermore, geospatial data and geographic information systems (GISs) are integrated to assist with spatial planning and infrastructure development. The system also includes dashboards and decision support tools for city planners, enabling them to make informed decisions based on real-time and historical data. Security layers are implemented throughout the architecture to ensure the privacy and safety of citizens' data, and compliance frameworks are maintained to align with local regulations.

4.6.3 Benefits of Big Data in Smart Cities and Urban Planning

Big data in smart cities and urban planning offers numerous benefits that enhance the overall efficiency, sustainability, and safety of urban environments. Real-time analysis of traffic patterns enables improved traffic management, reducing congestion and enhancing mobility. Additionally, big data facilitates more efficient resource allocation, optimizing energy usage, waste management, and water supply. By analyzing patterns in crime, accidents, and emergencies, cities can proactively improve public safety. Data-driven insights also support sustainable urban development, helping to plan and construct infrastructure that minimizes environmental impact while improving quality of life. In terms of energy, big data aids in smart energy management, optimizing consumption and promoting the use of renewable energy sources. Furthermore, real-time data fosters better citizen engagement, improving communication and transparency in urban planning. Finally, by optimizing resource usage and infrastructure development, cities can achieve significant cost savings, benefiting both city governments and residents.

4.7 Big Data Analytics for Autonomous Vehicles and Intelligent Transportation Systems

Autonomous vehicles and intelligent transportation systems heavily rely on big data to ensure safe and efficient operations. These systems process vast amounts of sensor data, including LiDAR, radar, and GPS information, to make real-time decisions. Big data enables autonomous vehicles to navigate complex environments, avoid obstacles, and optimize routes. Additionally, intelligent transportation systems use analytics to enhance traffic flow, reduce accidents, and improve overall road safety, paving the way for a smarter and more connected future. The role of big data in creating smart cities and enabling intelligent transportation systems cannot be overstated. Cities like Barcelona, Singapore, and New York City are leveraging data analytics to optimize urban infrastructure, enhance public services, and improve the quality of life for residents. Similarly, companies like Waymo, Tesla, and Uber ATG are harnessing big data to develop autonomous vehicles and intelligent transportation systems that promise safer, more efficient, and more sustainable mobility solutions.

4.7.1 Case Study

An autonomous vehicle company faced challenges in processing the massive volumes of data generated by its fleet during pilot tests. To overcome this, the company implemented a big data framework capable of handling terabytes of

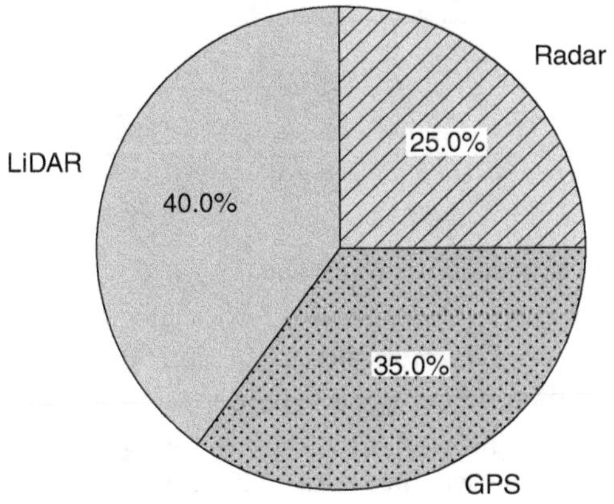

Figure 4.14 Types of data processed by the big data framework.

sensor data. We simulate the scenarios for the testing of autonomous vehicles in intelligent transportation systems (ITSs). This included information from LiDAR sensors for mapping surroundings, GPS data for navigation, and radar inputs for detecting nearby objects. The analytics platform enabled the vehicles to make split-second decisions, such as avoiding collisions and selecting optimal routes. The pie chart shown in Figure 4.14 highlights the relative contribution of each data source, emphasizing their roles in enabling real-time decision-making for autonomous vehicles. This breakdown underscores the importance of integrating diverse data streams to ensure the safety and reliability of autonomous transportation systems. During pilot tests, the implementation resulted in a 35% reduction in accidents, showcasing the potential of big data in ensuring the safety and reliability of autonomous transportation.

Tesla leverages big data for its autopilot and full self-driving (FSD) features. Data is gathered from vehicle sensors, including cameras, ultrasonic sensors, and radar. Deep learning models process this big data to enable features like automatic lane-keeping, adaptive cruise control, and self-parking. Tesla has enhanced the autonomous driving capabilities of its vehicles, providing a safer and more efficient driving experience.

4.7.2 Architecture Diagram

In Figure 4.15, the architecture diagram for big data analytics in autonomous vehicles and ITS integrates multiple layers of technology to support real-time decision-making, optimize traffic flow, and ensure the safe operation of autonomous vehicles. These layers are (i) data ingestion, (ii) data management,

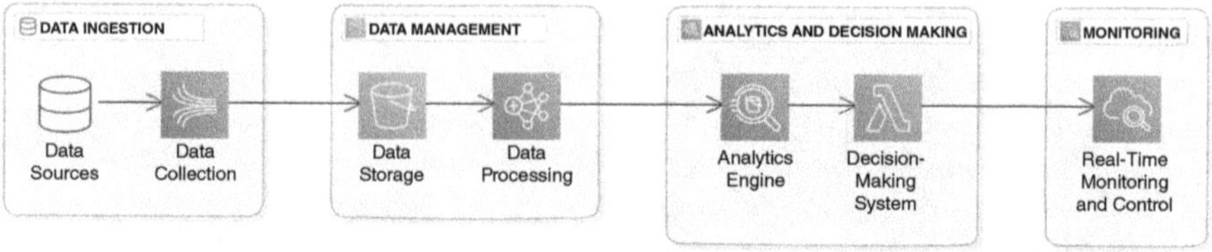

Figure 4.15 Big data analytics system for autonomous vehicles and ITS.

(iii) analytics and decision-making, and (iv) monitoring. In data ingestion layer, data are collected from various data sources, such as in-vehicle sensors (LIDAR, radar, cameras, GPS), traffic management systems, and infrastructure data (e.g., road conditions, traffic lights, and weather data). These data sources provide continuous streams of information about the environment, traffic patterns, and vehicle status.

In the data management layer, data collected from these sources is sent to a centralized cloud-based platform or data lake, where it is stored and processed. Next, advanced analytics platforms and machine learning models are employed to process this data and generate actionable insights, such as predicting traffic patterns, identifying hazards, or optimizing routes in the analytics and decision-making layer. Real-time data processing is critical, as autonomous vehicles must react quickly to dynamic road conditions and make instant decisions to ensure safety. Furthermore, data from autonomous vehicles is also shared with ITS to enhance overall traffic flow and safety in cities. The communication between vehicles and infrastructure is facilitated by vehicle-to-everything (V2X) technology, enabling vehicles to exchange information with each other and traffic infrastructure in real time.

In the monitoring layer, the system also includes geospatial data and GIS for precise location tracking and route optimization. Dashboards and visualization tools are employed for operators and decision-makers to monitor and manage traffic flows, vehicle health, and other relevant metrics. Security and privacy of data are integrated throughout the architecture to safeguard data transmission and protect against cyber threats, especially as autonomous vehicles are highly dependent on secure communication and sensor data integrity.

4.7.3 Big Data Analytics for Autonomous Vehicles and Intelligent Transportation Systems—Challenges and Solutions

Autonomous vehicles and intelligent transportation systems face several challenges related to big data analytics. Securing the large amounts of sensitive data generated by these vehicles is a key concern, requiring strong encryption and secure transmission protocols. Integrating data from multiple sources in real time, such as sensors and traffic management systems, is complex but can be addressed with unified data platforms and cloud-based solutions. Real-time data processing is crucial for quick decision-making, and technologies like edge computing help reduce delays. Sensor reliability is another issue, with redundancy and advanced algorithms improving accuracy. Regulatory compliance also presents challenges, with evolving laws requiring collaboration with policymakers and adaptive systems. Outdated infrastructure may hinder these systems, but upgrades to smart traffic signals and communication technologies are necessary. Lastly, ethical and liability concerns must be addressed through clear legal frameworks and transparent decision-making. By solving these challenges, big data analytics will enhance the safety and efficiency of autonomous vehicles and transportation systems, contributing to smarter cities.

4.8 Conclusion

In conclusion, the advent of big data technologies and analytics has revolutionized various aspects of our modern world, particularly in the realms of manufacturing, e-commerce, finance, health care, urban planning, and transportation. Throughout this chapter, we have explored a myriad of real-world applications where big data has been harnessed to drive innovation, efficiency, and optimization. In this chapter, we explored the transformative potential of big data across a diverse range of sectors, illustrating how data-driven insights are reshaping the way organizations operate and innovate. From AI-driven predictive maintenance in manufacturing to personalized customer experiences in e-commerce, big data has proven to be a powerful catalyst for operational efficiency and enhanced decision-making. In financial services, advanced analytics are enabling better risk management and fraud detection, while in health care, real-time data integration is supporting proactive patient care and resource optimization. The chapter also highlighted the vital role of big data in developing smart cities for optimizing infrastructure, energy, and public services for sustainable urban growth. Lastly, the use of big data in autonomous vehicles and intelligent transportation systems showcased how real-time analytics can improve safety, mobility, and environmental impact. Collectively, these applications underscore the critical importance of big data as a foundational element of innovation and progress in today's digital age.

Practice Set

A Multiple Choice Questions (MCQ)

1 Which sector has been transformed by predictive maintenance powered by big data analytics?

a E-commerce
b Health care
c Manufacturing
d Urban Planning

2 Which company is mentioned as using big data for predictive maintenance?

a Amazon
b JPMorgan Chase
c General Electric
d Waymo

3 How has big data analytics impacted e-commerce?

a By reducing hardware costs
b By personalizing recommendations and boosting engagement
c By enhancing customer service infrastructure
d By automating supply chain logistics

4 Which financial institution is listed as employing advanced analytics to enhance compliance?

a IBM Watson Health
b Alibaba
c JPMorgan Chase
d Siemens

5 Which organization is NOT mentioned in the health-care sector's use of big data?

a Mayo Clinic
b IBM Watson Health
c Kaiser Permanente
d Mastercard

6 What role does big data play in creating smart cities?

a Optimizing urban infrastructure
b Reducing data storage costs
c Enhancing software development
d Improving hardware performance

7 Which company is associated with developing autonomous vehicles using big data?

- **a** Netflix
- **b** Tesla
- **c** HSBC
- **d** Waymo

8 What is a major benefit of big data analytics in transportation?

- **a** Enhancing vehicle design
- **b** Developing intelligent transportation systems
- **c** Reducing fuel consumption
- **d** Improving vehicle aesthetics

9 Which city is mentioned as leveraging data analytics for urban planning?

- **a** Los Angeles
- **b** Barcelona
- **c** Tokyo
- **d** London

10 What is a key focus of big data analytics in health care?

- **a** Reducing administrative costs
- **b** Delivering personalized care and improving treatment outcomes
- **c** Enhancing medical device performance
- **d** Streamlining hospital management

B Fill-in-the-Blanks

11 In manufacturing, predictive maintenance powered by big data analytics helps companies like General Electric and Siemens minimize __________.

12 Big data analytics has transformed e-commerce by allowing companies to personalize __________ and boost engagement.

13 Financial institutions use big data to mitigate risks and enhance __________.

14 Smart cities use data analytics to optimize urban __________ and enhance public services.

15 Companies like Waymo and Tesla are using big data to develop __________ vehicles and intelligent transportation systems.

C Short Answer Questions

16 How has big data analytics improved manufacturing processes?

17 What benefits have e-commerce businesses gained from big data analytics?

18 In what ways does big data enhance financial services?

19 Describe how big data is used in health care.

20 How do intelligent transportation systems benefit from big data?

D Long Answer Questions

21 Discuss the impact of big data technologies on the manufacturing sector with examples.

22 Analyze the role of big data in enhancing e-commerce strategies and customer interactions.

23 Evaluate the significance of big data in the financial services industry and its impact on risk management.

24 Examine the contributions of big data to the development of smart cities and urban planning.

25 Explore the future potential of big data technologies and their implications for various industries.

Bibliography

Abu-Salih, B., Wongthongtham, P., Zhu, D., Chan, K.Y. and Rudra, A., 2021. *Social Big Data Analytics*. Singapore: Springer.

Acharya, S. and Chellappan, S., 2022. *Big Data and Analytics* (2nd ed.). Wiley.

Alwan, H.B. and Ku-Mahamud, K.R., 2020. Big data: definition, characteristics, life cycle, applications, and challenges. In: *IOP Conference Series: Materials Science and Engineering*, Vol. 769, No. 1, p. 012007. IOP Publishing.

Amazon, 2023. Powering personalized recommendations through machine learning. *https://www.aboutamazon.com/recommendation-engine*.

Barcelona City Council, 2023. Transforming into a smart city with Big Data. *https://smartcity.barcelona.cat/big-data*.

Credit Suisse, 2023. AI-driven credit risk assessment: enhancing decision-making in lending. *https://www.credit-suisse.com/ai-credit-risk.*

Djerdjouri, M., 2020. Data and Business Intelligence Systems for Competitive Advantage: prospects, challenges, and real-world applications. *Mercados y Negocios*, 41, pp. 5–18.

GE Aviation, 2023. Predictive maintenance with Predix: enhancing jet engine performance. https://www.geaviation.com/predictive-maintenance.

Gunjal, B.L., 2022. Real-world applications of data science. In: *Data Science*, pp. 33–56. Chapman and Hall/CRC.

IBM Watson Health, 2023. Enhancing clinical decision-making with Big Data analytics. *https://www.ibm.com/watson-health/big-data.*

Iqbal, R., Doctor, F., More, B., Mahmud, S. and Yousuf, U., 2020. Big data analytics: computational intelligence techniques and application areas. *Technological Forecasting and Social Change*, 153, p. 119253.

JP Morgan Chase, 2023. Leveraging machine learning for fraud detection and prevention. *https://www.jpmorganchase.com/machine-learning-fraud-detection.*

Kaiser Permanente, 2023. Advancing preventive care and chronic disease management with Big Data. *https://www.kaiserpermanente.org/big-data-healthcare.*

Khan, M.A., Karim, M.R. and Kim, Y., 2018. A two-stage big data analytics framework with real world applications using Spark machine learning and long short-term memory network. *Symmetry*, 10(10), p. 485.

Kumari, A., Kakkar, R., Tanwar, S., Garg, D., Polkowski, Z., Alqahtani, F. and Tolba, A., 2024. Multi-agent-based decentralized residential energy management using Deep Reinforcement Learning. *Journal of Building Engineering*, 87, p. 109031.

Lim, C., Kim, K.J. and Maglio, P.P., 2018. Smart cities with big data: reference models, challenges, and considerations. *Cities*, 82, pp. 86–99.

Liu, F. and Panagiotakos, D., 2022. Real-world data: a brief review of the methods, applications, challenges and opportunities. *BMC Medical Research Methodology*, 22(1), p. 287.

Mayo Clinic, 2023. Improving patient care with Big Data analytics. *https://www.mayoclinic.org/big-data-analytics.*

Netflix, 2023. Personalizing content recommendations with data-driven algorithms. *https://www.netflixtechblog.com/personalized-recommendations.*

NYC Mayor's Office of Data Analytics, 2023. Using Big Data for urban planning and infrastructure management. *https://www1.nyc.gov/nyc-resources/big-data-urban-planning.*

Ramkumar, P.N., Haeberle, H.S., Bloomfield, M.R., Schaffer, J.L., Kamath, A.F., Patterson, B.M. and Krebs, V.E., 2019. Artificial intelligence and arthroplasty at a single institution: real-world applications of machine learning to big data, value-based care, mobile health, and remote patient monitoring. *The Journal of Arthroplasty*, 34(10), pp. 2204–2209.

Sarker, I.H., 2021. Machine learning: algorithms, real-world applications and research directions. *SN Computer Science*, 2(3), p. 160.

Siemens, 2023. AI-driven predictive maintenance for industrial gas turbines. *Siemens.* https://www.siemens.com/predictive-maintenance.

Spotify, 2023. Enhancing user experience through personalized music recommendations. *https://newsroom.spotify.com/personalized-playlists.*

Tesla, 2023. Leveraging Big Data for Autopilot and Full Self-Driving features. *https://www.tesla.com/autopilot-big-data*.

Toyota, 2023. Predictive maintenance in the Toyota Production System. *Toyota Global.* https://www.toyota-global.com/tps/predictive-maintenance.

Yousefi, S., Derakhshan, F. and Karimipour, H., 2020. Applications of big data analytics and machine learning in the Internet of Things. In: *Handbook of Big Data Privacy*, pp. 77–108. Springer.

5

Cybersecurity Issues with Big Data and Handling Using Blockchain

LEARNING OBJECTIVES

- Recognizes different cyber threats that have an impact on large data systems.
- Explain how blockchain technology can enhance cybersecurity.
- Analyze how decentralized architectures improve data security and integrity.
- Demonstrate the use of smart contracts for managing and processing large datasets.
- Evaluate the role of blockchain in improving transparency within supply chains by presenting a case study.
- Identify and assess the challenges in implementing blockchain-based solutions for big data systems.

5.1 Introduction

The exponential growth of data generation from various sources like social media, Internet of Things (IoT) devices, and online transactions has led to the need for efficient big data management solutions. However, this massive data collection and storage also bring significant cybersecurity challenges. Traditional security measures are often inadequate to protect the vast volumes of sensitive information stored in big data repositories. We're living in the era of big data, where every click, swipe, and transaction adds to a massive digital footprint. While this data drives innovation and smarter decision-making, it also attracts cyber threats like moths to a flame. The sheer scale, speed, and diversity of big data make it a prime target for sophisticated attacks, leaving organizations scrambling to keep their digital assets safe. In this chapter, we dive into the core cybersecurity issues haunting big data systems. From stealthy malware and deceptive phishing tactics to crippling ransomware, insider threats, and denial-of-service (DoS) attacks, the landscape of vulnerabilities is vast and constantly evolving. To fight back, we explore a rising star in the cybersecurity realm, that is, blockchain technology. With its decentralized structure and tamper-proof records, blockchain is changing the game for data protection. You'll discover how it secures data, strengthens trust, and brings new levels of transparency and accountability to digital ecosystems.

In this chapter, we'll also unpack the power of smart contracts for managing large-scale data securely and automatically and look at how blockchain is redefining supply chain visibility. To balance the hype with reality, we wrap up by addressing the key challenges and scalability concerns that come with implementing blockchain in big data environments.

5.1.1 Motivation

The increasing reliance on data-driven processes across sector from health care and finance to transportation and governance has amplified the need for advanced cybersecurity frameworks. Traditional security models often fall short when confronted with the complexity and scale of big data. This gap motivates the exploration of innovative, future-ready solutions like blockchain, which promise not only enhanced security but also trust, automation, and data integrity.

5.1.2 Chapter Contributions

This chapter makes the following key contributions:

- Identifies and categorizes prevalent cyber threats impacting big data systems. Explores blockchain's role in enhancing cybersecurity through decentralization and immutability.
- Highlights blockchain's application in improving supply chain transparency. Investigates the use of smart contracts for secure and automated big data management.
- Discusses the technical and scalability challenges in deploying blockchain-based big data solutions.
- Provides a comprehensive foundation for researchers and practitioners aiming to secure big data environments using emerging technologies.

5.1.3 Organization of the Chapter

The remainder of the chapter is structured as follows: Sections 5.2 and 5.3 outline major types of cyber threats and vulnerabilities that commonly affect these systems, including malware attacks, phishing and social engineering, ransomware incidents, insider threats, and DoS attacks in a big data environment. Section 5.4 presents the fundamentals of blockchain technology, focusing on its relevance in strengthening cybersecurity frameworks. Section 5.5 delves into how blockchain's decentralized structure enhances data security and integrity. Section 5.6 highlights the application of smart contracts for secure, automated management of big data processes. Section 5.7 illustrates the role of blockchain in ensuring supply chain transparency, particularly in data-intensive industries such as health care. Section 5.8 discusses the challenges and scalability considerations that must be addressed for the successful integration of blockchain into big data environments. Lastly, Section 5.9 provides the concluding remarks on the chapter.

5.2 Cybersecurity Issues with Big Data

The centralized storage and processing of big data make it a lucrative target for cyberattackers. Here are some of the major cybersecurity issues, shown in Figure 5.1, associated with big data in more detail:

1. **Data Breaches:** The concentration of vast amounts of sensitive data, such as personal information, financial records, and intellectual property, in a single location or centralized repository increases the risk of data breaches. A successful cyberattack on these big data systems can lead to unauthorized access, theft, or exposure of this sensitive information. The consequences of such data breaches can be severe, including identity theft, financial losses, regulatory fines, and reputational damage for the affected organizations and individuals.

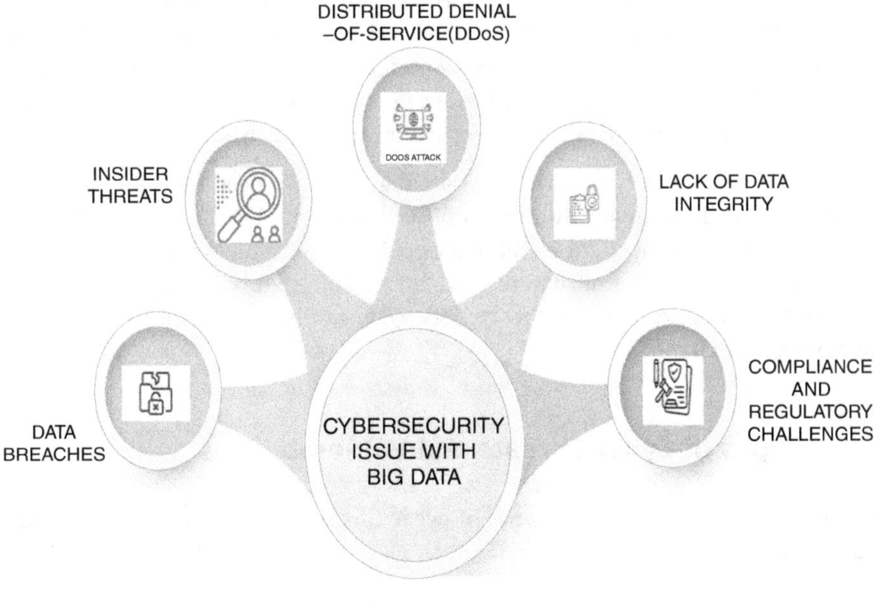

Figure 5.1 Cybersecurity challenges faced in big data.

2. **Insider Threats:** While big data systems are designed to protect against external threats, they can be vulnerable to insider threats posed by malicious or disgruntled employees, contractors, or third-party service providers with legitimate access to the system. These insiders can misuse their privileged access to steal sensitive data, sabotage systems, or carry out other malicious activities. Insider threats are particularly challenging to detect and mitigate as they often involve trusted individuals with authorized access.
3. **Distributed Denial-of-Service (DDoS) Attacks:** Big data systems rely on high-performance computing resources and network infrastructure to process and analyze massive volumes of data. These systems can be overwhelmed by DDoS attacks, where an attacker floods the system with a large number of requests or traffic, leading to service disruptions, data loss, and potential system crashes. DDoS attacks can be challenging to defend against, especially when launched from a distributed network of compromised devices or botnets.
4. **Lack of Data Integrity:** In centralized big data systems, data integrity is a critical concern. With a single point of control and storage, it becomes challenging to ensure the authenticity and integrity of data throughout its life cycle. Data can be intentionally or unintentionally altered, tampered with, or corrupted, leading to inaccurate or unreliable analyses and decision-making based on compromised data.
5. **Compliance and Regulatory Challenges:** Big data often involves processing and storing sensitive personal data, which is subject to various data protection regulations and privacy laws, such as the General Data Protection Regulation (GDPR) in the European Union or the California Consumer Privacy Act in the United States. Ensuring compliance with these regulations and protecting individuals' privacy rights can be a significant challenge in the context of big data, where vast amounts of personal information are collected, processed, and stored.

These cybersecurity issues with big data highlight the need for robust security measures and innovative solutions to protect the confidentiality, integrity, and availability of sensitive data in big data environments. Blockchain technology, with its decentralized, transparent, and immutable nature, offers a promising approach to address many of these challenges, as discussed in the subsequent sections of the chapter.

5.3 Types of Cyber Threats and Vulnerabilities

Figure 5.2 shows the different types of cyber threats and vulnerabilities in a big data environment.

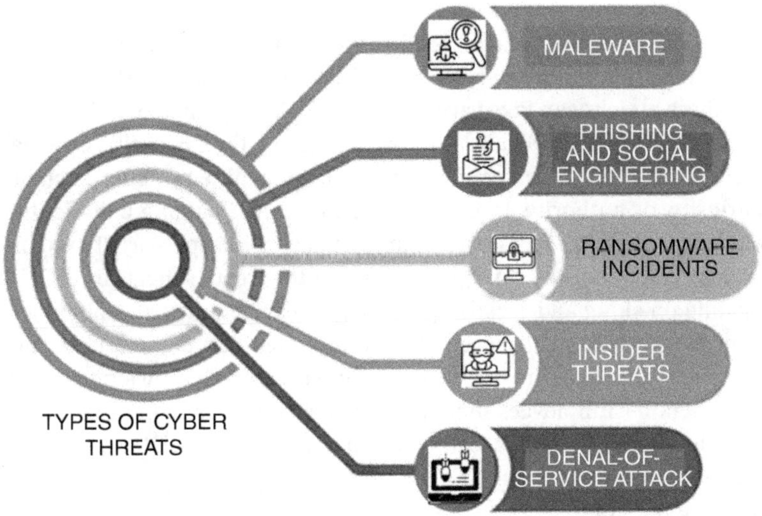

Figure 5.2 Various types of cyber threats.

i. Malware Attacks

Malware attacks can take various forms, including viruses, worms, Trojans, spyware, and advanced persistent threats (APTs). These attacks can be particularly devastating for big data systems due to the vast amounts of sensitive information they store and process. Viruses are self-replicating malicious code that can spread across systems, corrupting or deleting data, and causing system failures. Worms are similar to viruses but can replicate and propagate independently without requiring a host program or user intervention.

Trojans are disguised as legitimate software but contain malicious code that can grant unauthorized access, steal data, or disrupt systems. Spyware is a type of malware that covertly monitors user activities, collects sensitive information, and transmits it to external parties. APTs are sophisticated, targeted attacks carried out by well-resourced adversaries, such as nation-states or cybercriminal organizations. APTs often involve a combination of social engineering, malware, and exploitation of vulnerabilities to gain a persistent foothold within an organization's systems, including big data environments.

Mitigating malware threats in big data systems requires a multilayered approach, including regularly updating and patching systems, implementing robust antivirus and anti-malware solutions, conducting regular vulnerability assessments, and providing employee training on cybersecurity best practices.

ii. Phishing and Social Engineering
Phishing attacks often leverage social engineering techniques to manipulate individuals into revealing sensitive information or executing malicious actions. These attacks can take various forms, such as spoofed emails, fraudulent websites, or phone calls impersonating legitimate entities. Social engineering attacks exploit human psychology and emotions, such as fear, curiosity, or authority, to trick individuals into divulging confidential information or granting access to systems. Attackers may pose as IT support staff, executives, or trusted third parties to gain the trust of their targets.

Mitigating phishing and social engineering threats requires a combination of technical controls, such as email filtering, web content filtering, and multi-factor authentication, as well as regular employee awareness and training programs. Employees should be educated on recognizing and reporting suspicious emails, phone calls, or other forms of social engineering attempts.

iii. Ransomware Incidents
Ransomware attacks have become increasingly prevalent and sophisticated, posing a significant threat to big data systems and the valuable information they store. These attacks can encrypt or lock down data, rendering it inaccessible until a ransom is paid, often in the form of cryptocurrencies like Bitcoin. Ransomware can spread through various vectors, including phishing emails, malicious websites, or exploiting software vulnerabilities. Once inside a system, ransomware can propagate rapidly, encrypting data on local drives, network shares, and even cloud storage repositories.

Mitigating ransomware threats requires a multilayered approach, including regular data backups, software updates, and patching, restricting administrative privileges, implementing robust access controls, and providing employee awareness training. Additionally, organizations should have an incident response plan in place to manage and contain ransomware incidents effectively.

iv. Insider Threats
Insider threats can be particularly challenging to detect and mitigate, as they involve individuals with legitimate access to systems and data. These threats can arise from disgruntled employees, contractors, or third-party service providers who may intentionally or unintentionally cause data breaches, sabotage systems, or expose sensitive information. Insider threats can manifest in various ways, such as unauthorized data access, theft of intellectual property, sabotage of systems or data, or inadvertent data exposure due to negligence or lack of awareness.

Mitigating insider threats requires a comprehensive approach that includes robust access controls, data encryption, continuous monitoring and logging, background checks for personnel with privileged access, and implementing strict data handling policies and procedures. Additionally, fostering a positive workplace culture and providing employee awareness training can help reduce the risk of insider threats.

v. DoS Attacks

DoS attacks aim to overwhelm systems or networks with a high volume of traffic or requests, rendering them unavailable or unresponsive to legitimate users or services. These attacks can be particularly disruptive for big data systems, which often rely on high-performance computing resources and networks to process and analyze massive volumes of data. DoS attacks can be launched from a single source (single-source DoS) or from a distributed network of compromised devices or botnets (DDoS). DDoS attacks can generate overwhelming traffic from multiple sources, making them more difficult to mitigate.

Mitigating DoS and DDoS attacks requires a multipronged approach, including implementing load balancing and traffic filtering mechanisms, deploying web application firewalls, and utilizing cloud-based DDoS mitigation services. Additionally, regular monitoring and incident response planning are crucial to detect and respond to these attacks promptly. By understanding the various types of cyber threats and vulnerabilities in detail, organizations can better prepare and implement effective security measures to protect their big data systems and the valuable information they store and process.

5.4 Understanding Blockchain in Cybersecurity

Figure 5.3 shows the explanation of blockchain in cybersecurity, which is explained below.

- **Decentralization**: Blockchain technology is built on a decentralized architecture, where data and processing power are distributed across a network of nodes, rather than relying on a centralized authority or single point of failure. This decentralized nature makes blockchain systems inherently more resilient to cyberattacks targeting centralized systems.

  Case Study: The Equifax data breach in 2017 highlighted the vulnerabilities of centralized data storage systems. Hackers exploited a vulnerability in

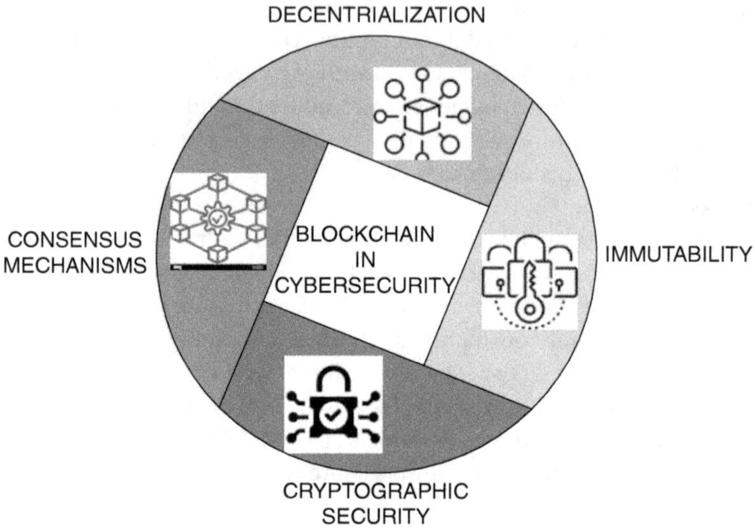

Figure 5.3 Blockchain in cybersecurity.

Equifax's systems, gaining access to sensitive personal information of nearly 145 million consumers. If Equifax had leveraged a decentralized system such as a blockchain-based system for storing and managing consumer data, the impact of the breach could have been significantly reduced. With data distributed across multiple nodes, it becomes much harder for attackers to compromise the entire system, as they would need to breach a majority of nodes simultaneously.

- **Immutability:** Once data is recorded on the blockchain, it becomes immutable, meaning it cannot be altered or tampered with without being detected. This immutability is achieved through the use of cryptographic hash functions and consensus mechanisms. Each block in the blockchain contains a cryptographic hash, which is a unique digital fingerprint of the data contained within that block. Any modification to the data would result in a different hash value, making the tampering immediately detectable. Additionally, each block is linked to the previous block through its hash, forming an immutable chain of data.

  In the financial sector, immutability is crucial for maintaining the integrity of transaction records. By leveraging blockchain technology, financial institutions can ensure that their transaction data cannot be altered or tampered with, reducing the risk of fraud, double-spending, or data manipulation.
- **Cryptographic Security**: Blockchain technology relies on advanced cryptographic techniques, such as digital signatures and hash functions, to secure transactions and data. Digital signatures ensure data authenticity and

non-repudiation, while hash functions ensure data integrity and tamper-resistance. Digital signatures are created using public-key cryptography, where each participant in the blockchain network has a unique private key and a corresponding public key. Transactions or data are digitally signed using the private key, and the signature can be verified using the public key, ensuring the authenticity of the data and the identity of the sender.

In the supply chain industry, cryptographic security can be leveraged to ensure the authenticity and provenance of goods. Each participant in the supply chain, such as manufacturers, logistics providers, and retailers, can digitally sign transactions or data related to the movement and handling of goods. This digital signature ensures that the data cannot be repudiated and that any tampering or modification can be immediately detected.

- **Consensus Mechanisms:** Blockchain networks use consensus algorithms to validate transactions and maintain data consistency across the distributed network. The most widely used consensus mechanisms are proof-of-work (PoW) and proof-of-stake (PoS). In a PoW consensus mechanism, nodes in the network compete to solve complex cryptographic puzzles, and the first node to solve the puzzle gets to add a new block to the blockchain and receive a reward. This process ensures that all nodes agree on the state of the blockchain and prevents unauthorized modifications.

  Case Study: Bitcoin, the world's first and most well-known cryptocurrency, uses a PoW consensus mechanism called mining. Miners compete to solve complex mathematical problems, and the winner gets to add a new block of transactions to the Bitcoin blockchain, receiving a reward in the form of newly minted Bitcoin.

  In a PoS consensus mechanism, instead of computational power, the likelihood of a node being chosen to validate and add a new block to the blockchain is based on the number of cryptocurrency tokens (or "stake") held by that node. This mechanism is generally considered more energy-efficient and environmentally friendly than PoW.

  Case Study: Ethereum, one of the largest blockchain platforms, has been transitioning from a PoW consensus mechanism to a more energy-efficient PoS consensus mechanism called Casper. This transition aims to address the high energy consumption and environmental impact associated with PoW mining while maintaining the security and decentralization of the Ethereum blockchain. By understanding the underlying principles and features of blockchain technology, organizations can better leverage its capabilities to enhance cybersecurity in big data environments. However, it's important to note that the successful implementation of blockchain solutions requires careful consideration of factors such as scalability, interoperability, regulatory compliance, and the development of skilled professionals in this emerging field.

5.5 Decentralized Data Security and Integrity Using Blockchain

By leveraging blockchain technology, big data can be stored and managed in a decentralized and secure manner, addressing many of the cybersecurity challenges faced by traditional centralized systems. Here's how blockchain can enhance data security and integrity. Figure 5.4 illustrates the decentralized data security and integrity using blockchain in big data environments.

1. **Distributed Data Storage:** Instead of storing big data in a centralized repository, blockchain enables the distribution and replication of data across multiple nodes in the network. This distributed storage approach reduces the risk of single-point failures or data breaches, as an attacker would need to compromise a majority of nodes to gain control over the data.
   Case Study: In the health-care industry, blockchain-based solutions like MediLedger and Patientory allow for the secure and decentralized storage of electronic medical records (EMRs). Patient data is encrypted and distributed across multiple nodes, ensuring data privacy and reducing the risk of large-scale data breaches that can occur with centralized storage systems.
2. **Data Provenance and Integrity:** The immutable nature of the blockchain ensures that data stored on the network cannot be altered or tampered with without being detected. This characteristic maintains data integrity and enables the tracking of data provenance, providing a transparent audit trail of data access, modifications, and transactions.

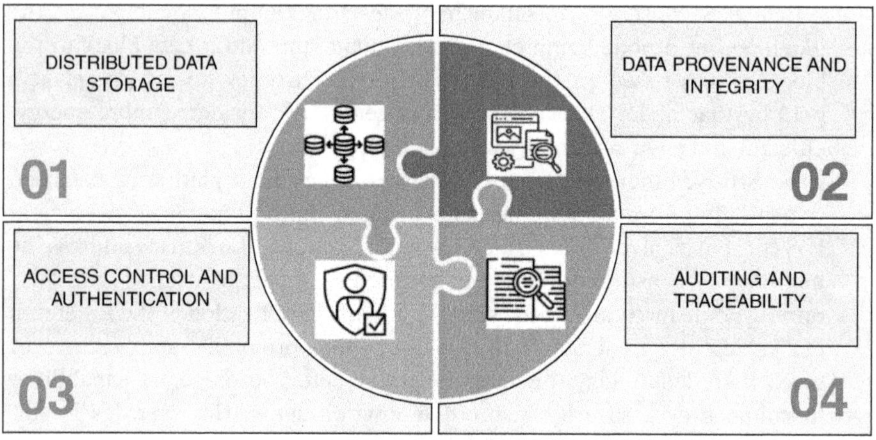

Figure 5.4 Ensuring data security and integrity.

Example: In the supply chain industry, blockchain can be used to track the provenance and movement of goods from the point of origin to the final destination. Each step in the supply chain process, such as manufacturing, shipping, and distribution, can be recorded on the blockchain, ensuring data integrity and enabling the verification of product authenticity and origin.

3. **Access Control and Authentication:** Blockchain-based access control mechanisms, such as digital identities and cryptographic keys, can ensure secure and authenticated access to big data resources. Only authorized parties with the correct credentials can access, modify, or add data to the blockchain network.
   Case Study: In the financial sector, blockchain-based identity management solutions like Civic and SelfKey enable secure and decentralized storage of personal and financial data. Users can control access to their data through digital identities and cryptographic keys, reducing the risk of unauthorized access or data breaches.
4. **Auditing and Traceability:** The transparent and immutable ledger provided by the blockchain enables comprehensive auditing and traceability of data access, modifications, and transactions. This feature is particularly valuable in regulated industries, where data integrity and audit trails are critical for compliance purposes.
   Example: In the pharmaceutical industry, blockchain can be used to track the movement of drugs and medications from manufacturers to distributors, pharmacies, and, ultimately, patients. This end-to-end traceability can help prevent counterfeiting, ensure drug safety, and facilitate product recalls if necessary.

By leveraging these features of blockchain technology, organizations can enhance the security and integrity of their big data systems, ensuring data confidentiality, integrity, and availability. However, it's important to note that the successful implementation of blockchain solutions requires careful consideration of factors such as scalability, interoperability, and regulatory compliance, as well as the development of skilled professionals in this emerging field.

5.6 Smart Contracts in Big Data Management

Definition: Smart contracts are self-executing programs or code deployed on the blockchain network. Smart contracts automatically execute predefined conditions or actions when certain criteria are met, without the need for intermediaries or manual intervention.

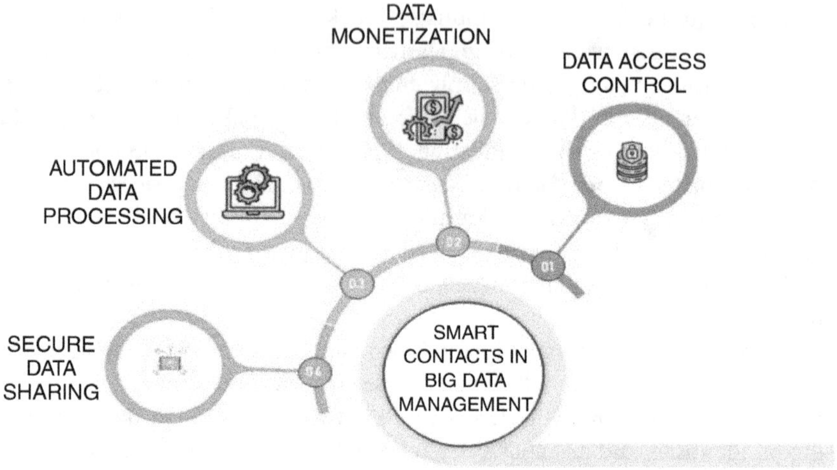

Figure 5.5 Use of smart contracts in big data management.

Figure 5.5 illustrates the use of smart contracts in big data management. Next, smart contracts can play a pivotal role in enhancing security, transparency, and efficiency in big data management.

1. **Data Access Control**: Smart contracts can be used to enforce predefined rules and policies for accessing and sharing big data, ensuring that only authorized parties can access sensitive information. These contracts can automatically grant or revoke access based on predetermined conditions, such as user roles, permissions, or specific data attributes.
   Real-world Example: Opu Labs, a health-care technology company, has developed a blockchain-based platform called Opu Rizr that uses smart contracts to manage access to EMRs. The platform allows patients to grant or revoke access to their medical data through smart contracts, ensuring that only authorized health-care providers and entities can access sensitive information. This approach enhances data privacy and security while enabling efficient data sharing among health-care stakeholders.
2. **Data Monetization:** Smart contracts can facilitate secure and transparent data monetization by enabling controlled access and micropayments for accessing valuable big data resources. This feature can help organizations monetize their data assets while maintaining control over data access and usage.
   Real-world Example: Ocean Protocol is a decentralized data exchange platform that leverages blockchain and smart contracts to enable secure and transparent data monetization. Data providers can publish their datasets on the Ocean Protocol network and utilize smart contracts to define access conditions, pricing models, and usage rights. Interested parties can then access and acquire

these datasets by executing the corresponding smart contracts and making micropayments in the platform's native cryptocurrency.

3. **Automated Data Processing:** Smart contracts can trigger and execute predefined data processing tasks or analytics workflows based on specific conditions or events. This automation can reduce manual interventions and associated security risks, while ensuring data processing is carried out consistently and transparently.
   Real-world Example: Chainvine, a blockchain-based data management platform, utilizes smart contracts to automate data processing and analytics workflows. For instance, in the financial sector, Chainvine's platform can automatically trigger fraud detection algorithms or generate compliance reports based on predefined rules and thresholds encoded in smart contracts. This automation ensures the timely detection of suspicious activities and reduces the risk of human error or manual interventions.
4. **Secure Data Sharing:** Smart contracts can facilitate secure data sharing among multiple parties by enforcing predetermined conditions and rules. This feature can be particularly valuable in collaborative environments or industries where data needs to be shared among various stakeholders while maintaining data integrity and confidentiality.
   Real-world Example: The Energy Web Foundation has developed a blockchain-based platform for the energy sector, leveraging smart contracts to enable secure data sharing among utility companies, grid operators, and renewable energy providers. Each party can contribute relevant data, such as energy consumption patterns, grid performance metrics, or renewable energy production data, to the blockchain network. Smart contracts govern access and usage of this data based on predefined rules, allowing for efficient collaboration while protecting sensitive information.

While smart contracts offer numerous benefits for big data management, it's important to note that their successful implementation requires careful planning, robust security measures, and adherence to regulatory and compliance requirements. Additionally, the development and deployment of smart contracts should be carried out by skilled professionals with expertise in blockchain technology and secure coding practices

5.7 Supply Chain Transparency

Blockchain technology can enhance transparency and security in supply chain management, which often involves the exchange and analysis of large volumes of data. By leveraging the inherent features of blockchain, organizations can address various challenges in supply chain operations, such as product traceability, provenance tracking, and secure data sharing.

1. **Product Traceability:** By recording product data on the blockchain, businesses can ensure end-to-end traceability of goods, enabling better quality control, counterfeit prevention, and regulatory compliance. The immutable and decentralized nature of the blockchain provides a transparent and tamper-proof record of a product's journey from the point of origin to the final destination.
   Real-world Example: IBM Food Trust is a blockchain-based platform that enables food traceability and supply chain transparency. It allows participants, including farmers, processors, distributors, and retailers, to record and share data related to the origin, processing, and transportation of food products on the blockchain. This transparency helps to identify and prevent food fraud, ensure food safety, and facilitate targeted recalls in case of contamination or quality issues. Major companies like Walmart, Dole, and Nestlé have adopted IBM Food Trust to improve supply chain visibility and food traceability.
2. **Provenance Tracking:** Blockchain can track the provenance of raw materials, components, and finished products, ensuring the authenticity and integrity of supply chain data. This feature is particularly valuable in industries where product authenticity and origin are critical, such as luxury goods, pharmaceuticals, and precious metals.
   Real-world Example: Everledger is a blockchain-based platform that provides provenance tracking and authentication for diamonds and other valuable assets. Each diamond is assigned a unique digital fingerprint based on its physical characteristics, and its journey from mining to cutting, polishing, and sale is recorded on the blockchain. This immutable record of provenance helps to prevent fraud, identify synthetic diamonds, and ensure the ethical sourcing of gemstones.
3. **Secure Data Sharing:** Blockchain-based platforms can securely share supply chain data among multiple stakeholders, such as manufacturers, suppliers, logistics providers, and retailers, while maintaining data integrity and confidentiality. Smart contracts can govern data access and usage based on predefined rules, ensuring that only authorized parties can access sensitive information.
   Real-world Example: TradeLens is a blockchain-based supply chain platform developed by IBM and Maersk, the world's largest container shipping company. It enables secure and transparent sharing of shipping data among various stakeholders, including port operators, customs authorities, and logistics providers. By recording shipping events and documents on the blockchain, TradeLens provides a single source of truth for supply chain data, reducing errors, improving efficiency, and enhancing trust among participants.

4. **Supply Chain Financing:** Blockchain technology can streamline supply chain financing by providing a secure and transparent platform for recording and executing financial transactions. Smart contracts can automate processes such as invoice verification, payment processing, and letter of credit issuance, reducing the need for manual intervention and increasing efficiency.
 Real-world Example: The Hong Kong Monetary Authority (HKMA) and the Bank of Thailand have implemented a blockchain-based platform called the HKMA-BOT Corridor for conducting cross-border payments and supply chain financing. The platform utilizes smart contracts to automate processes like purchase order matching, invoice verification, and payment execution. This blockchain-based solution aims to enhance transparency, reduce fraud, and improve the efficiency of cross-border trade finance operations.

By leveraging the transparency, immutability, and decentralized nature of blockchain technology, organizations can address various challenges in supply chain management, such as product traceability, provenance tracking, secure data sharing, and efficient supply chain financing. However, successful implementation requires collaboration among supply chain participants, adherence to industry-specific regulations, and the development of robust blockchain solutions tailored to the unique requirements of each industry.

5.7.1 Case Study

In the health-care environment, the hospital network faced persistent issues in its medicine supply chain, including delivery delays, counterfeit drug infiltration, and high administrative workloads. To overcome these challenges, the system adopted blockchain-powered smart contracts to streamline and secure the entire pharmaceutical logistics process. Every step, from production and distribution to final delivery, was transparently recorded on a tamper-proof digital ledger. Smart contracts automatically executed tasks such as verifying drug quality, confirming regulatory compliance, and initiating payments once specific conditions were met. This reduced human intervention, minimized errors, and fostered trust among all parties involved. The hospital saw a 40% drop in inventory-related issues, achieved near real-time drug tracking, and significantly improved patient safety by ensuring medicine authenticity. This case illustrates the transformative potential of smart contracts in enhancing efficiency, traceability, and reliability within the health-care supply chain.

Figure 5.6 shows the proposed architecture of the smart contract-based medicine supply chain management system. This diagram presents a blockchain-enabled architecture for managing the medicine supply chain in health care. It connects major stakeholders such as regulators, manufacturers, hospitals, pharmacies,

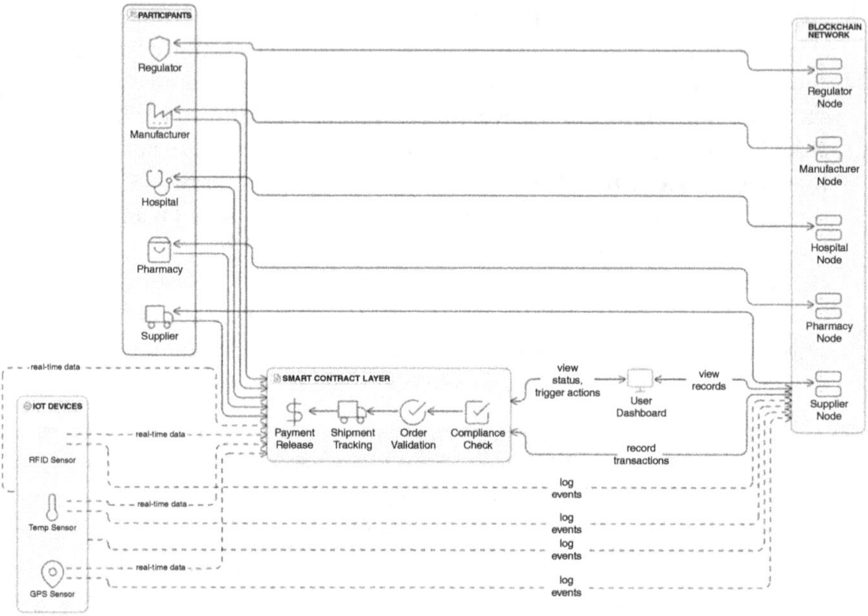

Figure 5.6 Smart contract-based medicine supply chain management.

and suppliers using a permissioned blockchain network, where each participant functions as a node. At the core is the smart contract layer, which automates essential processes like validating orders, monitoring shipments, ensuring regulatory compliance, and handling payments.

IoT devices such as RFID tags, GPS trackers, and temperature sensors gather live data during the transport of medicines, which is logged onto the blockchain using a smart contract layer (comprises compliance check, order validation, shipping tracking, and payment release) to guarantee transparency and drug integrity. A centralized dashboard enables all users to access real-time insights, improving supply chain efficiency, minimizing inventory-related challenges, and strengthening patient safety by verifying the authenticity of pharmaceuticals.

Here, Figure 5.7 shows the impact of smart contract-based medicine supply chain management in health care using the proposed architecture. hatched bar shows the issues before implementation of the architecture, and solid bar shows the results after the implementation of the proposed architecture. Here, the graph highlights:

- A 40% reduction in inventory-related issues
- A significant increase in drug tracking speed
- Enhanced patient safety through medicine authenticity

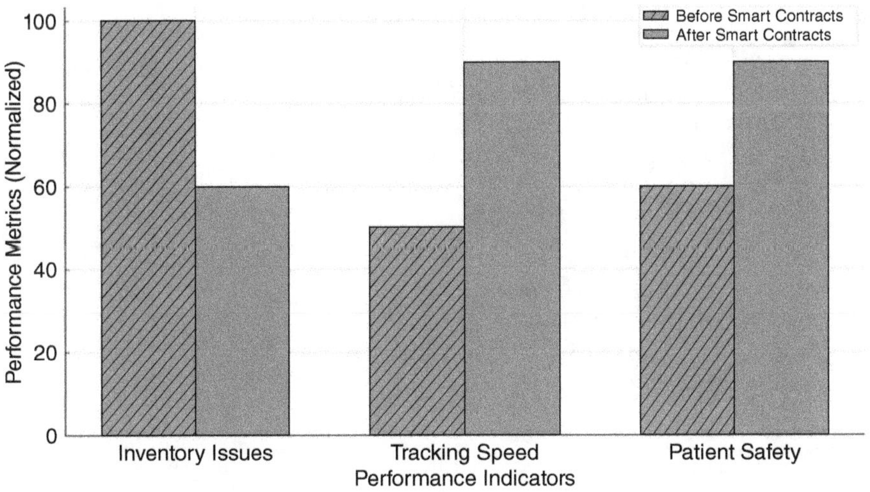

Figure 5.7 Performance metrics.

5.8 Challenges and Scalability Considerations

Figure 5.8 illustrates the challenges and scalability factors to consider when applying blockchain technology, which provides promising solutions for enhancing cybersecurity in big data environments. While blockchain technology offers promising solutions for cybersecurity in big data environments, several challenges and scalability considerations need to be addressed for successful implementation and widespread adoption.

1. **Performance and Scalability:** Traditional blockchain networks may struggle with the high throughput and low latency requirements of big data systems. The consensus mechanisms used in many blockchain platforms, such as PoW, can be computationally intensive and slow, potentially limiting the scalability of blockchain solutions for handling large volumes of data.
   Example: Bitcoin, the first and most well-known blockchain network, can process only a limited number of transactions per second due to its PoW consensus mechanism and block size limitations. This limited throughput makes it challenging to use Bitcoin's blockchain for handling high-velocity data streams or real-time data processing tasks associated with big data applications. To address these performance and scalability issues, various solutions are being explored, including:
   a. Sharding: Splitting the blockchain network into smaller partitions or "shards" that can process transactions in parallel, thereby increasing overall throughput.

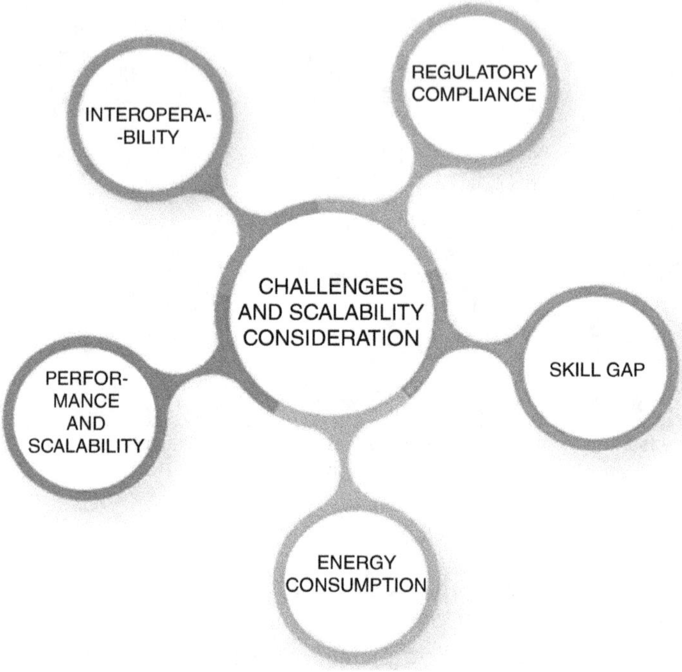

Figure 5.8 Challenges and scalability considerations.

   b. Off-chain Computations: Performing computationally intensive tasks or data processing off-chain and recording only the final results on the blockchain, reducing the on-chain load.
   c. Layer-2 Scaling Solutions: Building additional layers or protocols on top of the main blockchain to handle high-throughput transactions and data processing, while maintaining security through the underlying blockchain.

2. **Interoperability:** Integrating blockchain solutions with existing big data infrastructure and ensuring interoperability across different blockchain platforms can be challenging. Different blockchain networks may use different consensus mechanisms, data formats, and communication protocols, making it difficult to seamlessly integrate and share data across multiple systems.
   Example: The lack of interoperability between blockchain platforms like Ethereum, Hyperledger Fabric, and R3 Corda can hinder the seamless exchange of data and assets across different industries or organizations using different blockchain solutions. Initiatives like the Blockchain Interoperability Alliance and projects like *Polkadot and Cosmos* aim to address these interoperability challenges by developing standards and protocols for cross-chain communication and data exchange.

3. **Regulatory Compliance:** Navigating the evolving regulatory landscape surrounding blockchain technology and data privacy laws is crucial for widespread adoption in big data environments. Different industries and jurisdictions may have varying regulations and compliance requirements that need to be addressed when implementing blockchain-based solutions.

   Example: The European Union's GDPR has strict requirements for data privacy and user consent, which may pose challenges for certain blockchain implementations where personal data is recorded on an immutable ledger. Organizations need to carefully assess and comply with relevant regulations, such as data privacy laws, industry-specific regulations, and financial regulations (e.g., anti-money laundering and know-your-customer rules), when implementing blockchain solutions for big data management.
4. **Skill Gap:** There is a shortage of skilled professionals with expertise in both blockchain technology and big data management, hindering the widespread implementation of blockchain-based solutions. As an emerging field, there is a need for specialized education and training programs to develop a skilled workforce capable of designing, developing, and maintaining blockchain solutions for big data environments.

   Example: According to a report by Gartner, the lack of blockchain-skilled professionals is one of the top challenges facing organizations attempting to adopt blockchain technology. This skill gap can lead to poorly implemented solutions, security vulnerabilities, and suboptimal performance. Addressing this challenge requires collaboration between academia, industry, and professional organizations to develop comprehensive educational programs, certifications, and training initiatives focused on blockchain technology and its applications in big data management.
5. **Energy Consumption:** PoW consensus mechanisms used by some blockchain networks can be energy-intensive, raising sustainability concerns for large-scale big data applications. The computational resources required for mining and validating transactions in PoW blockchains can result in significant energy consumption and environmental impact.

   Example: Bitcoin's PoW consensus mechanism, which relies on energy-intensive mining operations, has been estimated to consume as much electricity as some small countries. This high energy consumption has raised concerns about the sustainability and environmental impact of PoW blockchains, especially in the context of big data applications with large-scale data processing requirements.

   To address this challenge, alternative consensus mechanisms, such as PoS and delegated proof-of-stake, are being explored and adopted by some blockchain platforms. These mechanisms are generally considered more energy-efficient and environmentally friendly than PoW.

By understanding and addressing these challenges and scalability considerations, organizations can better prepare for the successful implementation of blockchain solutions in big data environments. Collaboration among stakeholders, ongoing research and development, and the adoption of industry best practices will be crucial for overcoming these hurdles and unlocking the full potential of blockchain technology in enhancing cybersecurity and data integrity for big data applications.

5.9 Conclusion

The integration of blockchain technology with big data management offers a promising solution to address the cybersecurity challenges posed by the massive volumes of data generated and stored. In this chapter, we discussed the various aspects of blockchain in a big data environment. By leveraging the decentralized, immutable, and transparent nature of blockchain, organizations can enhance data security, integrity, and access control while enabling secure data sharing and supply chain transparency. This chapter also presented a case study of the smart contract-based medicine drug supply chain management system in permissioned blockchain-based health care. Apart from various benefits of blockchain in terms of cyber security issues in big data environment, scalability, performance, and regulatory compliance issues need to be carefully addressed to realize the full potential of this innovative technology in the realm of big data analytics and cybersecurity.

Practice Set

A Multiple Choice Questions (MCQ)

1 Which of the following is NOT a type of cyber threat discussed in the chapter?
   - **a** Malware attacks
   - **b** Phishing and social engineering
   - **c** Quantum computing attacks
   - **d** Ransomware incidents

2 What type of cyber threat involves deceiving individuals into revealing sensitive information?
   - **a** Insider threats
   - **b** Phishing and social engineering
   - **c** Denial-of-service (DoS) attacks
   - **d** Malware attacks

3 Which cyber threat is characterized by unauthorized access to data from within an organization?
  a Ransomware incidents
  b Insider threats
  c Phishing and social engineering
  d Denial-of-service (DoS) attacks

4 How does blockchain technology enhance data security in big data management?
  a By centralizing data storage
  b By enabling decentralized data security and integrity
  c By increasing data redundancy
  d By simplifying data access controls

5 What is the main benefit of using smart contracts in big data management?
  a Increasing data processing speed
  b Automating and securing data transactions
  c Reducing data storage costs
  d Enhancing user interface design

6 Which attack type involves overwhelming a system with excessive traffic?
  a Ransomware incidents
  b Denial-of-service (DoS) attacks
  c Insider threats
  d Malware attacks

7 What challenge is associated with implementing blockchain technology in big data management?
  a Increased data redundancy
  b Scalability and performance issues
  c Simplified data sharing
  d Enhanced data centralization

8 What is a key feature of blockchain that supports supply chain transparency?
  a Immutable ledger
  b High data redundancy
  c Centralized data control
  d Enhanced encryption methods

9 Which type of cyber threat involves encrypting data and demanding payment for decryption?
   a Ransomware incidents
   b Malware attacks
   c Phishing and social engineering
   d Denial-of-service (DoS) attacks

10 What aspect of blockchain technology helps in ensuring data integrity?
   a Data compression
   b Decentralized and immutable ledger
   c Centralized data storage
   d Enhanced encryption

B Fill-in-the-Blanks

11 Blockchain technology helps in managing cybersecurity by providing a __________ and immutable ledger.

12 Phishing and social engineering are types of cyber threats that involve deceiving individuals into revealing __________ information.

13 A __________ attack involves overwhelming a system with excessive requests, rendering it unavailable.

14 Smart contracts are used in blockchain to __________ and secure data transactions.

15 One of the challenges of integrating blockchain technology with big data is __________ and performance considerations.

C Short Answer Questions

16 What are some common types of cyber threats mentioned in the chapter?

17 Explain how insider threats can impact an organization's cybersecurity.

18 How does blockchain technology address issues related to data integrity?

19 Describe the role of smart contracts in enhancing big data management.

20 What are some of the scalability challenges associated with using blockchain in big data management?

D Long Answer Questions

21 Discuss the impact of malware attacks, phishing, and social engineering on cybersecurity and propose strategies to mitigate these threats.

22 Analyze how blockchain technology can be leveraged to improve supply chain transparency and security in big data management.

23 Evaluate the benefits and limitations of using blockchain technology to address cybersecurity challenges in big data environments.

24 Examine the role of smart contracts in automating data transactions and ensuring security in big data management.

25 Explore the scalability and performance issues associated with implementing blockchain technology and suggest potential solutions to these challenges.

Further Readings

Alotaibi, B., 2019. Utilizing blockchain to overcome cyber security concerns in the Internet of Things: a review. *IEEE Sensors Journal*, 19(23), pp. 10953–10971.

Deepa, N., Pham, Q.V., Nguyen, D.C., Bhattacharya, S., Prabadevi, B., Gadekallu, T.R., Maddikunta, P.K.R., Fang, F. and Pathirana, P.N., 2022. A survey on blockchain for big data: approaches, opportunities, and future directions. *Future Generation Computer Systems*, 131, pp. 209–226.

Demirkan, S., Demirkan, I. and McKee, A., 2020. Blockchain technology in the future of business cyber security and accounting. *Journal of Management Analytics*, 7(2), pp. 189–208.

Hasan, M.K., Alkhalifah, A., Islam, S., Babiker, N.B., Habib, A.A., Aman, A.H.M. and Hossain, M.A., 2022. Blockchain technology on smart grid, energy trading, and big data: security issues, challenges, and recommendations. *Wireless Communications and Mobile Computing*, 2022(1), p. 9065768.

Kaddoura, S. and Grati, R., 2021. Blockchain for healthcare and medical systems. In: *Enabling Blockchain Technology for Secure Networking and Communications*, pp. 249–270. IGI Global.

Lakkineni, S., Tawalbeh, L.A. and Alsmadi, I., 2023. Big data and blockchain for cybersecurity applications: challenges and solutions. In: *Computational Intelligence for Cybersecurity Management and Applications*, pp. 3–28. CRC Press.

Mora, O.B., Rivera, R., Larios, V.M., Beltrán-Ramírez, J.R., Maciel, R. and Ochoa, A., 2018. A use case in cybersecurity based in blockchain to deal with the security and privacy of citizens and smart cities cyberinfrastructure. In: *2018 IEEE International Smart Cities Conference (ISC2)*, pp. 1–4. IEEE.

Muheidat, F. and Tawalbeh, L.A., 2021. Artificial intelligence and blockchain for cybersecurity applications. In: *Artificial Intelligence and Blockchain for Future Cybersecurity Applications*, pp. 3–29. Cham: Springer International Publishing.

Prokofieva, M. and Miah, S.J., 2019. Blockchain in healthcare [Online]. *Australasian Journal of Information Systems*, 23.

Rahim, R., Patan, R., Manikandan, R. and Kumar, S.R., 2020. Introduction to blockchain and big data. In: *Blockchain, Big Data and Machine Learning*, pp. 1–23. CRC Press.

Rawat, D.B., Doku, R. and Garuba, M., 2019. Cybersecurity in big data era: from securing big data to data-driven security. *IEEE Transactions on Services Computing*, 14(6), pp. 2055–2072.

Salama, R. and Al-Turjman, F., 2022. AI in blockchain towards realizing cyber security. In: *2022 International Conference on Artificial Intelligence in Everything (AIE)*, pp. 471–475. IEEE.

Wang, L. and Jones, R., 2019. Big data, cybersecurity, and challenges in healthcare. In: *2019 SoutheastCon*, pp. 1–6. IEEE.

Wylde, V., Rawindaran, N., Lawrence, J., Balasubramanian, R., Prakash, E., Jayal, A., Khan, I., Hewage, C. and Platts, J., 2022. Cybersecurity, data privacy and blockchain: a review. *SN Computer Science*, 3(2), p. 127.

6

IoT-enabled Cloud-based Solutions for Big Data Analytics

LEARNING OBJECTIVES

- Analyze how IoT and Big Data Analytics work together, and why this combination is important for handling large volumes of data generated by connected devices.
- Explore how different IoT devices generate data and recognize the importance of energy-efficient and sustainably designed devices in reducing power consumption and environmental impact.
- Identify and assess the major challenges involved in processing IoT data, such as scalability, latency, and energy usage, and learn how these challenges can be addressed through sustainable resource-optimization techniques.
- Describe the role of cloud computing in supporting IoT-based big data analytics and reflect on its environmental impact, including energy consumption and carbon footprint.
- Integrate and apply sustainability-driven design principles to real-world IoT-cloud analytics use cases, balancing performance, cost, and ecological responsibility.

6.1 Introduction to IoT-enabled Big Data Analytics

The Internet of Things (IoT) has ushered in a new era of connectivity, where physical objects and systems are seamlessly intertwined with digital networks and computing resources. This paradigm shift has led to an unprecedented influx of data, often referred to as the "big data" phenomenon. However, harnessing the true potential of this data deluge requires robust and scalable solutions that can process, analyze, and derive meaningful insights from the vast and diverse data streams generated by IoT devices. Next, cloud computing is a transformative technology that provides virtually unlimited computing resources, robust storage capabilities, and advanced data processing and analytics tools. The integration of IoT and cloud-based approaches has unlocked a powerful synergy, enabling organizations to leverage the scalability and elasticity of the cloud to process and analyze IoT-generated data at scale. In this chapter, we will explore the intricacies of IoT-enabled cloud-based solutions for big data analytics, delving into the challenges, opportunities, and best practices that shape this dynamic field. We will examine the energy efficiency and sustainable design considerations for IoT devices, the challenges associated with processing and optimizing resource consumption for IoT data, and the role of cloud computing in enabling sustainable and efficient data handling and processing strategies.

The IoT has emerged as a disruptive force, revolutionizing the way we interact with the physical world. At its core, IoT refers to the interconnection of physical objects, devices, and systems through sensors, actuators, and communication technologies. These connected devices are capable of collecting, exchanging, and processing vast amounts of data, enabling new levels of automation, efficiency, and intelligence in various domains. Figure 6.1 shows the interconnection between AI, big data, IoT devices, and robotics. The rapid proliferation of IoT devices has given rise to the phenomenon of "big data," characterized by its massive volume, high velocity, and diverse variety. IoT devices generate continuous streams of data from multiple sources, including sensor readings, user interactions, and machine-to-machine communications. This data deluge presents both challenges and opportunities for organizations seeking to extract valuable insights and drive informed decision-making.

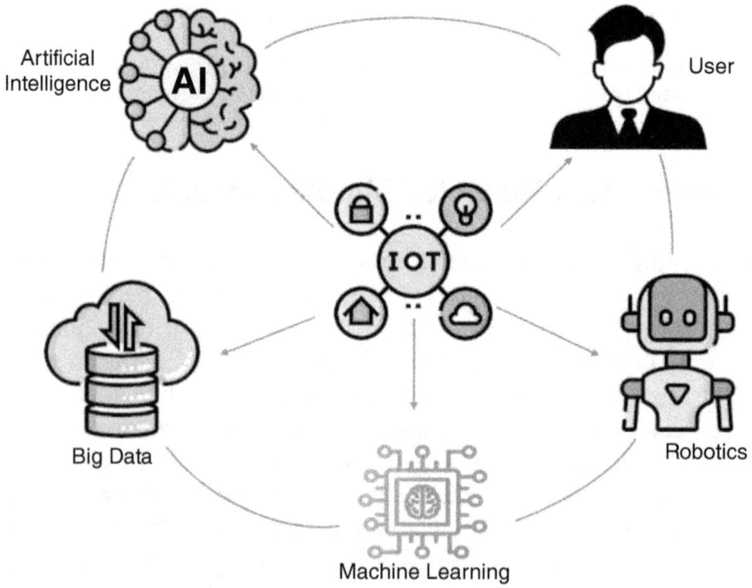

Figure 6.1 Internet of Things(IoT).

6.1.1 Motivation

The rapid growth of IoT devices in smart cities, the health-care industry, energy systems, and industrial automation has resulted in massive data generation. Although this data enables valuable insights, its efficient processing poses challenges related to scalability, energy consumption, and environmental sustainability. Conventional analytics methods often struggle with the volume and complexity of IoT data, leading to increased computational overhead. Cloud computing offers scalable resources for IoT big data analytics, but large-scale cloud infrastructures also raise environmental concerns. Therefore, there is a growing need for energy-aware and sustainable solutions that effectively integrate IoT and cloud technologies. This chapter is motivated by the need to address these challenges and present environmentally responsible approaches for IoT-enabled cloud-based big data analytics systems.

6.1.2 Chapter Contributions

This chapter makes the following key contributions:

- This chapter provides a clear overview of IoT-enabled big data analytics, highlighting data characteristics, processing requirements, and sustainability concerns. It examines IoT devices and data generation processes with a focus on energy efficiency and sustainable hardware design.
- Chapter identifies major challenges in IoT data processing and discusses optimization strategies aimed at reducing energy and resource consumption.
- It analyses the role of cloud computing in IoT big data analytics, emphasizing environmental impacts and sustainability challenges. Next, it presents green cloud computing solutions, including energy-aware resource allocation, virtualization, and renewable-energy-driven data centers.
- Further, it proposes integrated IoT-cloud approaches that support scalable, efficient, and sustainable data handling and analytics.

6.1.3 Organization of the Chapter

The remainder of the chapter is structured as follows: Section 6.2 examines IoT devices and data generation with a focus on energy efficiency and sustainable device design. The chapter further discusses key challenges in IoT data processing and strategies for optimizing resource consumption in Section 6.3. The role of cloud computing is explored by analyzing environmental impacts and green cloud solutions in Section 6.4. Finally, the integration of IoT and cloud-based approaches is presented with an architecture to advance sustainable big data handling and processing strategies in Section 6.5. Lastly, Section 6.6 provides the concluding remarks on the chapter.

6.2 IoT Devices and Data Generation: Examining Energy Efficiency and Sustainable Device Design

Figure 6.2 presents synergy between IoT and big data analytics, which is driven by several key factors mentioned as follows:

1. **Data Generation at Scale:** IoT devices are designed to continuously generate data, often in real time, leading to an unprecedented volume and velocity of data that requires robust processing and analysis capabilities.
2. **Heterogeneous Data Sources:** IoT systems comprise a diverse range of devices and sensors, generating data in various formats and structures, necessitating powerful data integration and management techniques.
3. **Real-time Processing and Analysis:** Many IoT applications require real-time or near-real-time processing and analysis of data to enable timely decision-making and automated responses.
4. **Distributed Computing and Storage:** The sheer scale and complexity of IoT data demand distributed computing and storage solutions to handle the computational and storage requirements effectively.
5. **Advanced Analytics Techniques:** IoT-enabled big data analytics leverages a wide range of advanced analytical techniques, including machine learning, deep learning, predictive analytics, and complex event processing, to uncover valuable insights from the data.

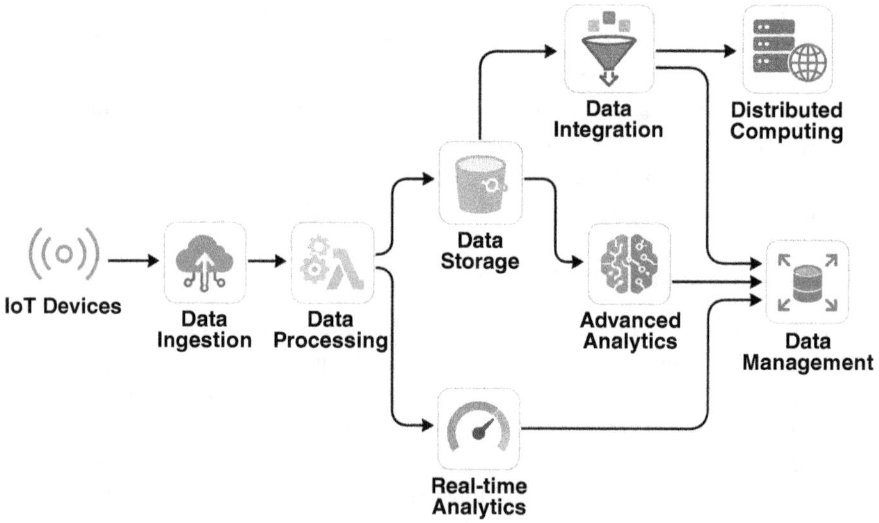

Figure 6.2 Synergy between IoT and big data analytics.

The convergence of IoT and big data analytics has the potential to revolutionize various industries, including manufacturing, health care, transportation, energy, and smart cities. For instance, in manufacturing, IoT sensors and connected machinery can generate real-time data on production processes, enabling predictive maintenance, optimized resource utilization, and quality control. In health care, wearable devices and remote monitoring systems can collect patient data, facilitating personalized care, early disease detection, and improved treatment outcomes. However, realizing the full potential of IoT-enabled big data analytics requires addressing several challenges, such as data privacy and security, scalability and performance considerations, energy efficiency and sustainability, and the need for skilled professionals with expertise in IoT, big data, and analytics. Next, Figure 6.3 examines energy efficiency and sustainable device design for IoT devices and data generation.

IoT devices are the fundamental building blocks of the IoT ecosystem, enabling the seamless integration of physical objects and systems with digital networks and computing resources. These devices come in various forms, ranging from simple sensors and actuators to complex systems and appliances, each designed to serve specific purposes and functionalities. As the backbone of IoT systems, these devices play a critical role in data generation, continuously sensing and capturing information from their surrounding environments. The data generated by IoT devices can be diverse, encompassing various formats and structures, such

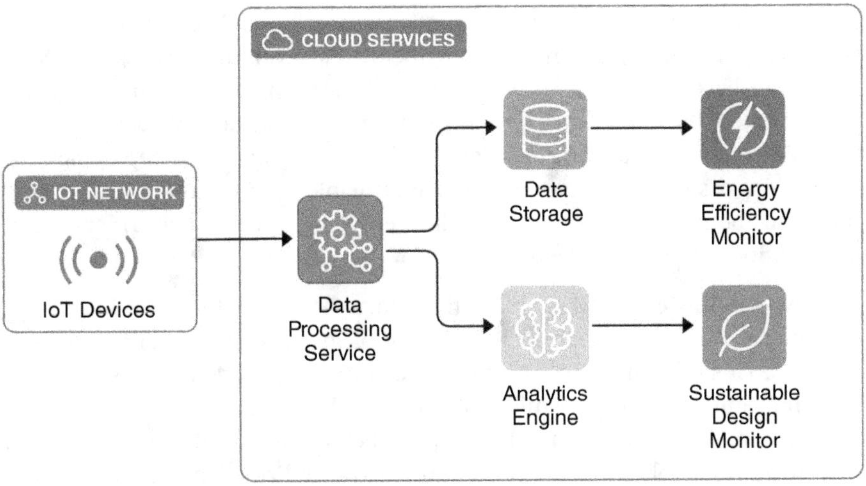

Figure 6.3 IoT devices and data generations.

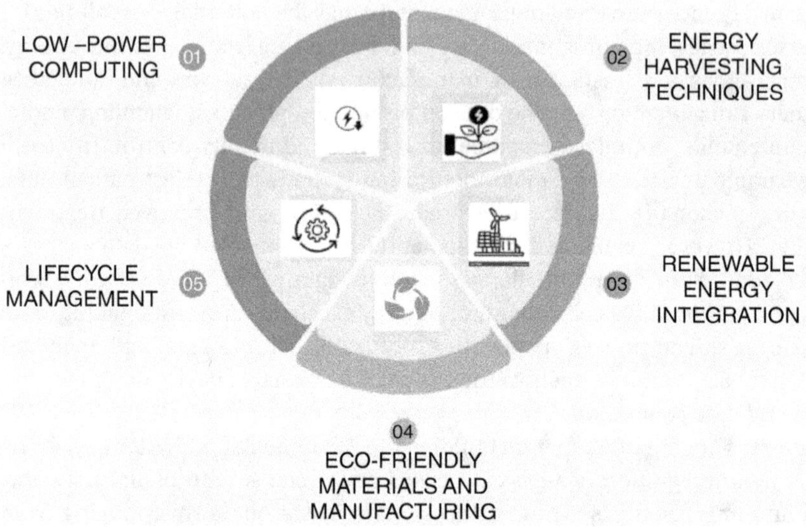

Figure 6.4 Energy efficiency and sustainable device design parameters.

as numerical readings, text, images, audio, and video. This heterogeneous data stream presents unique challenges for data processing, storage, and analysis. However, the proliferation of IoT devices has also raised concerns regarding their energy consumption and environmental impact. Many IoT devices are designed to operate continuously, often powered by batteries or embedded power sources, which can contribute to increased energy consumption and resource depletion. Additionally, the manufacturing, deployment, and eventual disposal of these devices can have significant environmental implications if not addressed properly. To address these challenges, energy efficiency and sustainable device design have emerged as critical considerations in the development and deployment of IoT devices, as shown in Figure 6.4. These principles aim to minimize the environmental footprint of IoT systems while ensuring optimal performance and functionality, as mentioned below:

- **Low-power Computing:** One of the primary strategies for achieving energy efficiency in IoT devices is the adoption of low-power computing technologies. This involves designing hardware and software components that consume minimal energy while still meeting the required performance and functionality specifications. Techniques such as energy-efficient processors, low-power wireless communication protocols, and power management algorithms can significantly reduce the energy consumption of IoT devices.

- **Energy Harvesting Techniques:** Another approach to sustainable IoT device design is the integration of energy harvesting techniques. These techniques involve harnessing ambient energy sources, such as solar, thermal, kinetic, or electromagnetic energy, to power IoT devices or supplement their existing power sources. By leveraging renewable energy sources, the reliance on traditional batteries or power grids can be reduced, contributing to a more sustainable and eco-friendly IoT ecosystem.
- **Renewable Energy Integration:** In addition to energy harvesting, the direct integration of renewable energy sources, such as solar panels or wind turbines, can provide a sustainable and reliable power supply for IoT devices, particularly in remote or off-grid locations.
- **Eco-friendly Materials and Manufacturing:** The design and manufacturing processes of IoT devices should also consider the use of environmentally friendly materials and sustainable manufacturing practices. This includes the selection of recyclable and biodegradable materials, as well as the implementation of energy-efficient and resource-efficient manufacturing processes.
- **Life Cycle Management:** A holistic approach to sustainable IoT device design must consider the entire life cycle of the devices, from manufacturing and deployment to maintenance and eventual disposal or recycling. Proper life cycle management practices can minimize the environmental impact of IoT devices and promote a circular economy approach.

By embracing energy efficiency and sustainable device design principles, organizations can not only reduce the environmental impact of their IoT systems but also potentially achieve cost savings through reduced energy consumption and resource utilization. Additionally, sustainable IoT devices can contribute to meeting regulatory requirements and corporate sustainability goals, while positioning organizations as environmentally responsible and forward-thinking.

6.3 Challenges in IoT Data Processing: Optimizing for Sustainable Resource Consumption

IoT has revolutionized the way data is generated, collected, and processed. With billions of connected devices continuously generating vast amounts of data, the challenges associated with processing and analyzing this data have become increasingly complex. Sustainable resource consumption is a critical consideration in IoT data processing, as it directly impacts the environmental footprint and operational costs of IoT systems.

The challenges in IoT data processing can be categorized into the following key areas:

- **Data Volume and Velocity:** IoT devices generate an unprecedented volume of data at high velocities, often in real time or near real time. This data deluge can overwhelm traditional data processing systems, leading to bottlenecks, latency issues, and inefficient resource utilization.
- **Data Heterogeneity:** IoT data comes in various formats and structures, including numerical readings, text, images, audio, and video. This heterogeneity poses challenges in data integration, normalization, and processing, requiring sophisticated techniques and specialized tools.
- **Distributed Data Sources:** IoT data is generated from numerous distributed sources, such as sensors, devices, and gateways, making data collection, aggregation, and processing more complex and resource-intensive.
- **Real-time Processing Requirements:** Many IoT applications demand real-time or near-real-time data processing and analysis to enable timely decision-making and automated responses. Ensuring low latency while optimizing resource consumption is a significant challenge.
- **Scalability and Fault Tolerance:** As the number of IoT devices and data sources continues to grow, data processing systems must be highly scalable and fault-tolerant to accommodate the increasing workloads and ensure reliable operation.

To address these challenges and optimize resource consumption in IoT data processing, several strategies and techniques can be employed:

- **Distributed and Parallel Processing:** By leveraging distributed and parallel processing frameworks, such as Apache Hadoop, Apache Spark, or Apache Kafka, IoT data can be processed in a distributed manner across multiple nodes, improving scalability and resource utilization.
- **In-network Data Aggregation:** Instead of transmitting raw data from IoT devices to centralized processing systems, in-network data aggregation techniques can be employed to perform preprocessing and aggregation at the edge, reducing the amount of data transmitted and minimizing resource consumption.
- **Edge Computing:** Edge computing architectures bring computational resources closer to the data sources, allowing for preprocessing, filtering, and aggregation of IoT data at the edge before transmitting it to centralized systems. This approach reduces bandwidth requirements and relieves the burden on central processing resources.
- **Data Compression and Filtering:** Employing data compression techniques and intelligent filtering algorithms can significantly reduce the volume of

data transmitted and stored, optimizing resource consumption while preserving the essential information.

- **Energy-efficient Computing:** Adopting energy-efficient computing technologies, such as low-power processors, energy-efficient storage solutions, and optimized cooling systems, can minimize the energy consumption and environmental impact of IoT data processing infrastructures.
- **Sustainable Data Center Operations:** Implementing sustainable practices in data center operations, such as leveraging renewable energy sources, optimizing cooling and airflow management, and implementing efficient power distribution and management systems, can contribute to reducing the environmental footprint of IoT data processing.

6.4 Cloud Computing in IoT Big Data Analytics: Environmental Impacts and Green Cloud Solutions

Cloud computing has emerged as a critical enabler for IoT big data analytics, providing scalable and on-demand computing resources, robust data storage capabilities, and powerful data processing and analysis tools. The convergence of IoT and cloud computing has unlocked new opportunities for organizations to leverage the power of big data analytics, enabling real-time insights, predictive maintenance, and data-driven decision-making. However, the rapid growth of cloud computing infrastructure and operations has also raised concerns regarding its environmental impact. The energy consumption, greenhouse gas emissions, and e-waste associated with data centers and cloud computing resources have become significant contributors to the overall environmental footprint of the technology industry.

The environmental impacts of cloud computing are as follows:

- **Energy Consumption:** Data centers that power cloud computing services are energy-intensive facilities, consuming vast amounts of electricity for computing, cooling, and power distribution. This energy consumption contributes to greenhouse gas emissions and depletes nonrenewable energy resources.
- **Greenhouse Gas Emissions:** The energy consumed by data centers is often generated from fossil fuel-based power plants, leading to significant greenhouse gas emissions, primarily in the form of carbon dioxide (CO_2). These emissions contribute to global warming and climate change.
- **Water Usage:** Data centers require significant amounts of water for cooling purposes, placing strain on local water resources, particularly in areas with water scarcity.

- **E-waste Generation:** The rapid technological advancements and frequent hardware upgrades in data centers result in the generation of substantial electronic waste (e-waste), which can have adverse environmental impacts if not properly managed and recycled.

To mitigate these environmental impacts and promote sustainable practices in cloud computing, various green cloud solutions and strategies have been developed:

- **Energy-efficient Data Center Design:** Implementing energy-efficient data center designs that optimize cooling systems, airflow management, and power distribution can significantly reduce energy consumption and associated greenhouse gas emissions.
- **Renewable Energy Integration:** Leveraging renewable energy sources, such as solar, wind, or hydroelectric power, to power data centers can substantially reduce the carbon footprint of cloud computing operations.
- **Virtualization and Resource Optimization:** Virtualization technologies and advanced resource optimization algorithms can maximize resource utilization, reducing the need for additional physical hardware and minimizing energy consumption and e-waste generation.
- **Sustainable Resource Management:** Adopting sustainable resource management practices, such as efficient water usage, e-waste recycling, and responsible procurement of materials, can further reduce the environmental impact of cloud computing operations.
- **Carbon Offsetting and Reforestation:** Cloud service providers can offset their carbon emissions by investing in reforestation projects, carbon capture and storage technologies, or purchasing carbon credits from verified offset projects.
- **Green Computing Certifications:** Pursuing green computing certifications, such as LEED (Leadership in Energy and Environmental Design) or Energy Star, can incentivize and recognize sustainable data center practices and environmental stewardship.

Cloud service providers and organizations leveraging cloud computing for IoT big data analytics play a crucial role in driving the adoption of green cloud solutions. By prioritizing sustainability, implementing energy-efficient practices, and embracing renewable energy sources, they can not only reduce their environmental footprint but also contribute to the overall effort of mitigating the impact of technology on the environment. As the demand for IoT big data analytics continues to grow, it is essential for stakeholders to collaborate and prioritize sustainable practices, ensuring that the benefits of cloud computing and IoT are realized without compromising environmental sustainability.

6.5 Integration of IoT and Cloud-based Approaches for Big Data Analytics: Advancing Sustainable Data Handling and Processing Strategies

The integration of IoT and cloud-based approaches has emerged as a powerful combination for enabling efficient and sustainable big data analytics solutions. By leveraging the strengths of both technologies, organizations can harness the power of IoT-generated data while minimizing the environmental impact and optimizing resource consumption. IoT devices generate vast amounts of data from various sources, including sensors, actuators, and connected devices. This data can provide valuable insights into operational processes, customer behavior, and environmental conditions, among others. However, processing and analyzing this data at the edge (where the IoT devices reside) can be resource-intensive and often impractical due to the limited computational and storage capabilities of IoT devices. Figure 6.5 illustrates a data pipeline architecture designed for integrating IoT and Cloud environments. It follows a logical flow from left to right, starting with data collection from various sources (IoT devices, databases, and web) into a landing zone. The data then undergoes sequential stages of ingestion, processing, and discovery to refine raw information into usable assets. Finally, the processed data supports advanced analytics based on different applications, enabling specific outcomes like real-time machine learning, sustainable reporting, and research access.

Cloud computing, on the other hand, offers virtually unlimited computing resources, scalable storage, and advanced data processing and analytics

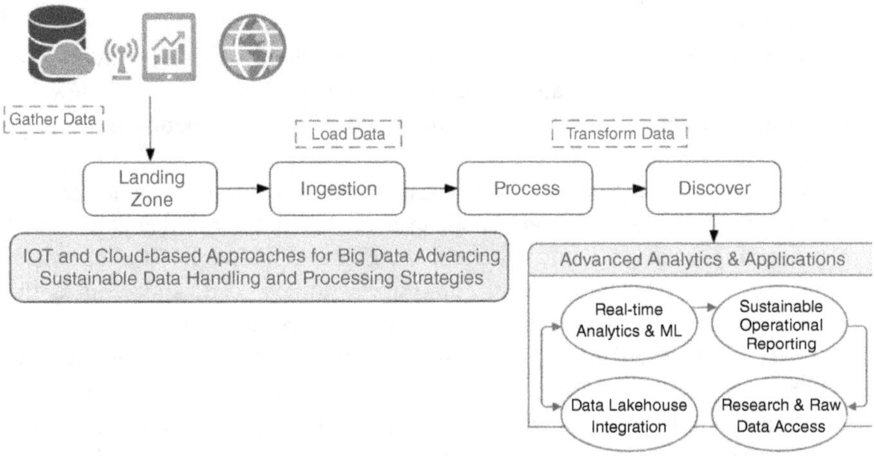

Figure 6.5 IoT-cloud-based big data handling and processing.

capabilities. By integrating IoT and cloud-based approaches, organizations can offload the data processing and analysis workloads from the edge to the cloud, ensuring efficient and sustainable data handling and processing. Strategies and best practices for the same are as follows:

- **Edge-cloud Collaboration:** Adopt an edge-cloud collaborative architecture where IoT devices perform preliminary data processing and filtering at the edge, transmitting only the relevant data to the cloud for further analysis and storage. This approach reduces bandwidth requirements, minimizes data transmission costs, and optimizes resource utilization.
- **Data Offloading Techniques:** Implement efficient data offloading techniques to transfer IoT data from the edge to the cloud in a secure and reliable manner. This can include techniques such as batch processing, data compression, and secure communication protocols.
- **Energy-aware Scheduling and Resource Allocation:** Develop energy-aware scheduling and resource allocation algorithms that consider the energy consumption and resource constraints of IoT devices. These algorithms can dynamically allocate workloads between the edge and cloud, optimizing energy efficiency and resource utilization.
- **Distributed Data Processing:** Leverage distributed data processing frameworks, such as Apache Spark or Apache Flink, to process and analyze IoT data in a distributed manner across multiple cloud computing nodes. This approach enhances scalability, fault tolerance, and resource utilization.
- **Containerization and Virtualization:** Adopt containerization and virtualization technologies to ensure efficient resource utilization in the cloud and enable seamless portability and scalability of IoT applications and analytics workloads.
- **Sustainable Cloud Infrastructures:** Utilize cloud service providers that prioritize sustainability and implement green practices, such as renewable energy sourcing, energy-efficient data centers, and responsible resource management.
- **Data Life Cycle Management:** Implement data life cycle management strategies that govern the entire life cycle of IoT data, from generation and processing to storage and eventual archiving or deletion. This approach ensures efficient data handling, minimizes storage costs, and reduces the environmental impact associated with unnecessary data retention.
- **Continuous Monitoring and Optimization:** Continuously monitor the performance, resource utilization, and energy consumption of the integrated IoT and cloud-based systems. Use this data to optimize processes, identify inefficiencies, and implement improvements for sustainable data handling and processing.

By integrating IoT and cloud-based approaches for big data analytics, organizations can unlock various benefits, including:

- **Scalability and Elasticity:** The cloud's virtually unlimited resources provide the scalability and elasticity required to handle the ever-increasing volumes of IoT data, ensuring efficient data processing and analysis.
- **Cost Optimization:** By leveraging the pay-as-you-go model of cloud computing, organizations can optimize their costs based on their actual resource requirements, avoiding overprovisioning or underutilization of resources.
- **Access to Advanced Analytics Tools:** Cloud platforms offer a wide range of advanced analytics tools, including machine learning, deep learning, and predictive modeling, enabling organizations to extract valuable insights from their IoT data.
- **Improved Sustainability:** By offloading resource-intensive workloads to the cloud and leveraging sustainable cloud infrastructures, organizations can reduce their overall environmental impact and contribute to a more sustainable future.

As the adoption of IoT and big data analytics continues to grow, the integration of cloud-based approaches becomes increasingly crucial for enabling sustainable data handling and processing strategies. By embracing this integration and adhering to best practices, organizations can unlock the full potential of IoT data while minimizing their environmental footprint and promoting responsible resource consumption.

6.6 Conclusion

As we conclude this chapter, it is evident that the integration of IoT and cloud-based approaches for big data analytics is not merely a technological advancement but a necessity for achieving sustainable and responsible data handling and processing strategies. By leveraging the strengths of both technologies, organizations can unlock the full potential of IoT data while minimizing their environmental impact and optimizing resource consumption. The journey toward sustainable IoT-enabled cloud-based solutions for big data analytics is a collaborative effort, requiring the participation and commitment of stakeholders across various domains. From device manufacturers to cloud service providers and from data engineers to environmental advocates, a collective effort is required to prioritize energy efficiency, embrace renewable energy sources, and implement sustainable practices throughout the entire data life cycle. Furthermore, continuous research and innovation in areas such as energy-aware scheduling algorithms, edge-cloud collaboration techniques, and advanced data processing frameworks will be crucial in addressing the ever-evolving challenges in this field. By fostering a culture of environmental stewardship and responsible resource management, we can pave the way for a future where technological advancements coexist harmoniously with our planet's finite resources.

In conclusion, the integration of IoT and cloud-based approaches for big data analytics represents a paradigm shift toward a more sustainable and responsible era of data-driven decision-making. By embracing the strategies and best practices outlined in this chapter, we can unlock the transformative potential of these technologies while contributing to a greener and more sustainable future for generations to come.

Practice Set

A Multiple Choice Questions (MCQ)

1 What is a key benefit of integrating IoT with cloud-based solutions for big data analytics?
 a Increased device costs
 b Enhanced data storage only
 c Sustainable and responsible data handling
 d Centralized data processing

2 What challenge is associated with processing IoT data?
 a Simplified device design
 b Optimizing for sustainable resource consumption
 c Decreased data volume
 d Reduced need for data security

3 What is a primary environmental concern in cloud computing for IoT data analytics?
 a High data redundancy
 b High energy consumption and environmental impact
 c Simplified data management
 d Decreased network speed

4 Which aspect of IoT device design is emphasized for sustainability?
 a Increased device complexity
 b High energy consumption
 c Energy efficiency and sustainable design
 d Limited device functionality

5 What is a significant focus of research in sustainable IoT-enabled cloud-based solutions?
   a Device aesthetics
   b Energy-aware scheduling algorithms
   c Centralized data storage
   d Increased data duplication

6 How can cloud-based solutions contribute to sustainable data handling?
   a By increasing data processing speed
   b By optimizing resource consumption and embracing renewable energy sources
   c By reducing the need for data analysis
   d By simplifying cloud service models

7 What role does edge-cloud collaboration play in IoT big data analytics?
   a Reducing data security
   b Addressing challenges in data processing and resource management
   c Simplifying device design
   d Enhancing device aesthetics

8 Which of the following is NOT a strategy for sustainable IoT-enabled cloud-based solutions?
   a Embracing renewable energy sources
   b Implementing energy-aware scheduling algorithms
   c Increasing data redundancy
   d Prioritizing energy efficiency

9 What is a crucial factor for minimizing the environmental impact of IoT and cloud-based analytics?
   a Centralized data processing
   b High device cost
   c Energy efficiency and responsible resource management
   d Increased data volume

10 Which practice is essential for fostering a culture of environmental stewardship in data analytics?
   a Ignoring environmental impacts
   b Embracing energy-efficient technologies and practices
   c Increasing device complexity
   d Centralizing data storage

B Fill-in-the-Blanks

11 The integration of IoT and cloud-based approaches for big data analytics helps achieve __________ and responsible data handling.

12 A key challenge in IoT data processing is optimizing for __________ resource consumption.

13 Cloud computing in IoT big data analytics raises concerns about __________ and environmental impact.

14 Energy-aware scheduling algorithms and edge-cloud collaboration techniques are examples of __________ in sustainable IoT solutions.

15 To minimize environmental impact, it is important to prioritize __________ efficiency and embrace renewable energy sources.

C Short Answer Questions

16 What are some benefits of integrating IoT with cloud-based solutions for big data analytics?

17 How does energy efficiency play a role in sustainable IoT device design?

18 Describe the environmental impacts associated with cloud computing in the context of big data analytics.

19 What are some of the strategies for sustainable data handling and processing in IoT and cloud-based solutions?

20 How can edge-cloud collaboration techniques address challenges in IoT data processing?

D Long Answer Questions

21 Discuss the significance of energy efficiency in IoT device design and its impact on sustainable big data analytics.

22 Analyze the environmental challenges posed by cloud computing in IoT big data analytics and propose strategies to mitigate these impacts.

23 Evaluate the role of edge-cloud collaboration in optimizing resource consumption and improving sustainability in IoT-enabled cloud-based solutions.

24 Examine the best practices for integrating IoT and cloud-based approaches to achieve sustainable data handling and processing.

25 Explore the future potential of IoT-enabled cloud-based solutions in promoting a greener and more sustainable data-driven era.

Further Readings

Awotunde, J.B., Jimoh, R.G., Ogundokun, R.O., Misra, S. and Abikoye, O.C., 2022. Big data analytics of IoT-based cloud system framework: smart healthcare monitoring systems. In: *Artificial Intelligence for Cloud and Edge Computing*, pp. 181–208. Cham: Springer International Publishing.

Bajaj, K., Sharma, B. and Singh, R., 2022. Implementation analysis of IoT-based offloading frameworks on cloud/edge computing for sensor generated big data. *Complex & Intelligent Systems*, 8(5), pp. 3641–3658.

Chakraborty, S., Bhatt, V. and Chakravorty, T., 2020. Big-data, IoT wearable and mHealth cloud platform integration triads—a logical way to patient-health monitoring. *International Journal of Engineering and Advanced Technology*, 9(3), pp. 388–394.

Feng, C., Adnan, M., Ahmad, A., Ullah, A. and Khan, H.U., 2020. Towards energy-efficient framework for IoT big data healthcare solutions. *Scientific Programming*, 2020(1), p. 7063681.

Hajjaji, Y., Boulila, W., Farah, I.R., Romdhani, I. and Hussain, A., 2021. Big data and IoT-based applications in smart environments: a systematic review. *Computer Science Review*, 39, p. 100318.

Kaddoura, S. and Grati, R., 2021. Blockchain for healthcare and medical systems. In: *Enabling Blockchain Technology for Secure Networking and Communications*, pp. 249–270. IGI Global.

Kahveci, S., Alkan, B., Mus'ab H. A., Ahmad, B. and Harrison, R., 2022. An end-to-end big data analytics platform for IoT-enabled smart factories: a case study of battery module assembly system for electric vehicles. *Journal of Manufacturing Systems*, 63, pp. 214–223.

Li, W., Chai, Y., Khan, F., Jan, S.R.U., Verma, S., Menon, V.G., Kavita, F. and Li, X., 2021. A comprehensive survey on machine learning-based big data analytics for IoT-enabled smart healthcare system. *Mobile Networks and Applications*, 26, pp. 234–252.

Lu, Y. and Xu, X., 2019. Cloud-based manufacturing equipment and big data analytics to enable on-demand manufacturing services. *Robotics and Computer-Integrated Manufacturing*, 57, pp. 92–102.

Mahmud, R., Koch, F.L. and Buyya, R., 2018. Cloud-fog interoperability in IoT-enabled healthcare solutions. In: *Proceedings of the 19th International Conference on Distributed Computing and Networking*, pp. 1–10. Association for Computing Machinery.

Prokofieva, M. and Miah, S.J., 2019. Blockchain in healthcare [Online]. *Australasian Journal of Information Systems*, 23.

Rani, S., Bhambri, P. and Kataria, A., 2023. Integration of IoT, big data, and cloud computing technologies: trend of the era. In: *Big Data, Cloud Computing and IoT*, pp. 1–21. Chapman and Hall/CRC.

Rehman, A., Haseeb, K., Saba, T., Lloret, J. and Tariq, U., 2021. Secured big data analytics for decision-oriented medical system using internet of things. *Electronics*, 10(11), p. 1273.

Sharma, S., Chang, V., Tim, U.S., Wong, J. and Gadia, S., 2019. Cloud and IoT-based emerging services systems. *Cluster Computing*, 22, pp. 71–91.

Sikarwar, R., Yadav, P. and Dubey, A., 2020. A survey on IOT enabled cloud platforms. In: *2020 IEEE 9th International Conference on Communication Systems and Network Technologies (CSNT)*, pp. 120–124. IEEE.

Taher, N.C., Mallat, I., Agoulmine, N. and El-Mawass, N., 2019. An IoT-cloud based solution for real-time and batch processing of big data: application in healthcare. In: *2019 3rd International Conference on Bio-engineering for Smart Technologies (BioSMART)*, pp. 1–8. IEEE.

Wazid, M., Das, A.K., Hussain, R., Succi, G. and Rodrigues, J.J., 2019. Authentication in cloud-driven IoT-based big data environment: survey and outlook. *Journal of Systems Architecture*, 97, pp. 185–196.

7

Emerging Trends in Big Data Analytics

LEARNING OBJECTIVES

- Understand emerging trends in big data analytics with a focus on sustainability, efficiency, and future-ready technologies.
- Analyze the role of edge computing and IoT analytics in enabling real-time, low-latency, and energy-efficient data processing.
- Explore the potential of quantum computing for solving complex big data analytics problems beyond classical computing limits.
- Examine the integration of blockchain with big data analytics for enhancing data security, transparency, and trust.
- Develop insights into explainable AI (XAI) techniques to improve the interpretability, transparency, and reliability of analytics outcomes.

7.1 Introduction

The explosive growth of data from Internet of Things (IoT) devices, enterprise platforms, social media, and intelligent systems has made big data analytics a central pillar of modern digital transformation. While conventional analytics frameworks have been effective in centralized settings, they are increasingly strained by today's requirements for real-time insights, scalability, security, and environmental responsibility. Despite significant advancements, existing big data systems still face several important limitations that need further research attention. Most current frameworks are designed primarily for high performance and scalability, often overlooking sustainability aspects such as energy efficiency and environmental impact, especially in large cloud-based infrastructures. Additionally, many systems remain heavily centralized, which makes real-time processing of massive IoT data inefficient due to higher latency and increased bandwidth consumption, highlighting the need for better edge-cloud integration. Another major gap lies in the lack of transparency, as deep learning–driven analytics often function as black boxes, making results difficult to interpret and trust. Furthermore, ensuring data security, integrity, and trust in decentralized and multisource data environments remains a challenge, as existing solutions provide limited support for secure and transparent data sharing mechanisms.

This shift has driven the emergence of new trends in big data analytics that combine advanced computing paradigms, decentralized architectures, and transparent artificial intelligence (AI) techniques to better address evolving technological and societal needs. From a technical perspective, the chapter highlights the transition from purely centralized analytics systems to hybrid edge-cloud and decentralized architectures. It discusses energy-aware algorithms, quantum-inspired and quantum-enhanced learning methods, and secure data workflows supported by distributed ledger technologies. Additionally, it emphasizes the integration of both intrinsic and it builds practical understanding of explainable AI (XAI), helping learners see how AI decisions can be made more understandable, reliable, and user-friendly.

7.1.1 Motivation

Today's data-driven applications demand more than just high accuracy; they require analytics solutions that are efficient, secure, and easy to trust. Rising energy consumption in data centers, strict latency requirements in time-sensitive applications, growing privacy concerns, and the "black-box" nature of deep learning models have highlighted the limitations of traditional approaches. Emerging technologies such as edge computing, quantum computing, blockchain, and XAI offer powerful solutions by enabling localized processing, faster computation, secure data sharing, and clearer model interpretations.

7.1.2 Research Objectives

- This chapter aims to explore key advancements shaping the future of big data analytics. Specifically, it focuses on understanding sustainable analytics techniques that reduce energy and resource usage.
- To analyze the effectiveness of edge computing and IoT-based analytics in supporting real-time, low-latency, and energy-efficient data processing architectures.
- To explore the applicability and performance potential of quantum computing techniques for addressing complex and large-scale big data analytics problems beyond the capabilities of classical systems.

- To examine the integration of blockchain technologies with big data analytics for improving data security, transparency, and trust in decentralized environments.
- To study XAI techniques and their role in enhancing the interpretability, transparency, and reliability of advanced analytics outcomes.

7.1.3 Chapter Organization

The rest of the chapter is organized as follows:

Section 7.2 discusses sustainable approaches for big data analytics, with an emphasis on green computing and efficient resource utilization. Next, Section 7.3 examines edge computing and IoT analytics for real-time and distributed data processing. Subsequent sections explore quantum computing-based analytics and blockchain-integrated big data frameworks. Further, the chapter highlights a detailed discussion on XAI and its role in enhancing interpretability and trust in next-generation big data analytics systems. At last, the chapter is concluded with the final thoughts.

7.2 Sustainable Approaches for Big Data Analytics

As the scale and complexity of big data analytics operations continue to grow, concerns about their environmental impact and energy consumption have become increasingly prevalent. The massive volumes of data being generated, processed, and stored require substantial computational resources and energy, contributing to greenhouse gas emissions and environmental degradation. Consequently, there is a growing emphasis on adopting sustainable approaches to big data analytics that aim to reduce the ecological footprint and promote responsible resource utilization.

1. **Green Computing and Energy-efficient Infrastructures:** One of the key aspects of sustainable big data analytics is the implementation of green computing practices and energy-efficient infrastructures. This involves adopting hardware and software solutions that prioritize energy efficiency and minimize power consumption.
   a. Low-power Processors: Utilizing energy-efficient processors, such as ARM-based or low-power x86 processors, can significantly reduce the energy consumption of big data analytics infrastructures without compromising performance.

   b. Solid-state Drives (SSDs): Replacing traditional hard disk drives with SSDs can substantially reduce energy consumption, as SSDs consume less power and generate less heat, reducing cooling requirements.
   c. Virtualization and Containerization: Implementing virtualization and containerization technologies can optimize resource utilization by consolidating multiple workloads onto fewer physical servers, reducing energy consumption and infrastructure costs.
   d. Efficient Cooling Systems: Implementing efficient cooling systems, such as liquid cooling or free cooling (using outside air for cooling), can significantly reduce the energy consumed by data center cooling infrastructures.
   e. Renewable Energy Sources: Leveraging renewable energy sources, such as solar, wind, or hydroelectric power, can further reduce the carbon footprint and environmental impact of big data analytics operations.
2. **Efficient Data Management and Processing:** Adopting efficient data management and processing practices can minimize the storage and computational requirements, thereby reducing energy consumption and operational costs associated with big data analytics.
   a. Data Deduplication: Implementing data deduplication techniques can eliminate redundant data copies, reducing the amount of storage required and minimizing the energy consumed by storage systems.
   b. Data Compression: Employing effective data compression algorithms can significantly reduce the storage footprint and bandwidth requirements for data transmission, resulting in energy savings.
   c. Intelligent Caching: Utilizing intelligent caching strategies can minimize redundant data processing by caching and reusing intermediate results, reducing computational workloads and associated energy consumption.
   d. In-memory Computing: Leveraging in-memory computing technologies, such as in-memory databases and data grids, can improve performance and reduce energy consumption by minimizing disk I/O operations.
   e. Efficient Algorithms and Frameworks: Adopting efficient algorithms and frameworks for big data processing, such as Apache Spark or Apache Flink, can optimize resource utilization and reduce computational overhead, leading to energy savings.
3. **Responsible Data Life Cycle Management:** Implementing responsible data life cycle management practices can help reduce the overall data footprint and associated environmental impact of big data analytics operations.
   a. Data Minimization: Adopting data minimization principles by only collecting and retaining data that is strictly necessary for the intended purpose can minimize storage and processing requirements, reducing energy consumption and costs.

   b. Data Retention Policies: Establishing and enforcing data retention policies that define the appropriate duration for storing and retaining data can prevent unnecessary data accumulation and facilitate timely data disposal.
   c. Secure Data Disposal: Implementing secure data disposal mechanisms, such as cryptographic erasure or physical destruction of storage media, can ensure that data is properly handled and disposed of at the end of its life cycle, reducing environmental impact and mitigating potential security risks.
4. **Collaborative and Distributed Analytics:** Fostering collaboration and adopting distributed analytics approaches can optimize resource utilization and reduce redundant data processing and storage, leading to more sustainable big data analytics operations.
   a. Shared Analytics Platforms: Developing shared analytics platforms and collaborative environments can enable organizations to share computational resources, data, and analytical models, reducing duplication of efforts and promoting resource efficiency.
   b. Distributed Data Processing: Implementing distributed data processing frameworks, such as Apache Hadoop or Apache Spark, can enable parallel processing of data across multiple nodes, improving scalability and resource utilization.
   c. Edge Computing and Fog Computing: Leveraging edge computing and fog computing architectures can bring data processing closer to the data sources, reducing the need for transmitting large volumes of data to centralized data centers and minimizing network bandwidth requirements.
   d. Federated Learning: Adopting federated learning approaches can enable collaborative model training and analytics across distributed data sources without requiring data consolidation, reducing data movement and associated energy costs.
5. **Monitoring and Optimization:** Continuous monitoring and optimization of big data analytics infrastructures and processes are essential for achieving sustainable operations and identifying opportunities for improvement.
   a. Energy Monitoring and Reporting: Implementing energy monitoring and reporting systems can provide insights into the energy consumption patterns of different components and workloads, enabling targeted optimization efforts.
   b. Workload Optimization: Optimizing workload scheduling and resource allocation can ensure efficient utilization of computational resources, reducing energy consumption and operational costs.

c. Capacity Planning and Right-sizing: Conducting regular capacity planning and right-sizing exercises can help organizations adjust their infrastructure to match actual workload demands, avoiding overprovisioning and unnecessary energy consumption.
d. Continuous Improvement: Adopting a culture of continuous improvement and encouraging the development and adoption of innovative, sustainable practices can drive ongoing optimization and reduction of the environmental impact of big data analytics operations.

While implementing sustainable approaches for big data analytics may require initial investments in infrastructure, software, and process changes, the long-term benefits include reduced operational costs, improved energy efficiency, and a lower environmental footprint. Moreover, embracing sustainability can enhance an organization's reputation, attract eco-conscious customers and employees, and contribute to broader societal goals of environmental stewardship and sustainability.

It is essential for organizations to adopt a holistic approach that considers the entire life cycle of their big data analytics operations, from data collection and processing to storage and disposal. Collaboration among stakeholders, including technology providers, researchers, policymakers, and end users, is crucial for driving the development and adoption of sustainable practices in big data analytics.

7.3 Edge Computing and IoT Analytics

The proliferation of IoT devices has led to a significant increase in the volume and velocity of data being generated at the edge of networks. These devices, ranging from sensors and wearables to industrial equipment and smart home appliances, continuously produce vast amounts of data that need to be processed, analyzed, and acted upon. Traditional approaches of transmitting all this data to centralized data centers for processing and analysis are becoming increasingly inefficient, resource-intensive, and prone to latency issues. Edge computing and IoT analytics have emerged as promising solutions to address these challenges by enabling data processing and analysis closer to the source, reducing network bandwidth requirements, enhancing privacy and security, and enabling real-time decision-making.

1. **Edge Analytics Frameworks:** Edge analytics frameworks are designed to process and analyze data directly on IoT devices or edge nodes, such as gateways or edge servers, without the need to transmit raw data to centralized data centers. These frameworks leverage the computational resources available at the edge to perform various analytics tasks, including data filtering, aggregation, and preprocessing.

   a. Lightweight Analytics Engines: Edge analytics frameworks often utilize lightweight analytics engines optimized for resource-constrained environments, such as TensorFlow Lite, Apache NiFi MiNiFi, or Apache Edgent. These engines can perform basic analytics tasks while minimizing computational overhead and energy consumption.
   b. Machine Learning (ML) on the Edge: Many edge analytics frameworks support deploying and running ML models directly on edge devices, enabling real-time inference and decision-making without the need for round-trip communication with centralized systems.
   c. Streaming Data Processing: Edge analytics frameworks often incorporate streaming data processing capabilities, allowing for real-time analysis of data streams generated by IoT devices and enabling immediate action or alerting based on predefined rules or conditions.
   d. Distributed Analytics: Some edge analytics frameworks support distributed analytics architectures, enabling coordination and collaboration among multiple edge nodes, load balancing, and fault tolerance.
2. **Distributed IoT Analytics:** While edge computing addresses many challenges associated with IoT data processing, there is often a need to combine edge and cloud resources in a distributed analytics architecture. This hybrid approach leverages the strengths of both environments, enabling efficient data processing, storage, and analysis while optimizing resource utilization and minimizing network traffic.
   a. Edge Preprocessing and Filtering: Edge nodes can perform data preprocessing tasks, such as cleaning, filtering, and aggregation, reducing the volume of data that needs to be transmitted to the cloud for further analysis.
   b. Cloud-based Analytics and Storage: After initial processing at the edge, relevant data can be transmitted to the cloud for more complex analytics, long-term storage, and integration with other data sources or enterprise systems.
   c. Bidirectional Data Flow: In addition to sending data from the edge to the cloud, a distributed IoT analytics architecture can enable bidirectional data flow, allowing cloud-based models, updates, or configurations to be pushed back to edge nodes for local execution.
   d. Orchestration and Management: Orchestration and management platforms are crucial for coordinating and managing the distributed analytics infrastructure, ensuring efficient resource allocation, load balancing, and seamless data flow between edge and cloud environments.
3. **Privacy and Security in IoT Analytics:** IoT devices often generate sensitive or personal data, raising concerns about privacy and security. Edge computing and IoT analytics architectures must incorporate robust privacy and security measures to protect data and ensure compliance with relevant regulations.

  a. Data Minimization and Anonymization: Implementing data minimization techniques and anonymizing sensitive data at the edge can reduce the risk of data breaches and enhance privacy protection.
  b. Secure Data Transmission: Employing secure data transmission protocols, such as Transport Layer Security (TLS) or Datagram Transport Layer Security (DTLS), can protect data in transit between edge nodes and cloud environments.
  c. Encryption and Access Control: Encrypting data at rest and in transit, combined with robust access control mechanisms, can prevent unauthorized access and ensure data confidentiality and integrity.
  d. Secure Hardware and Trusted Execution Environments: Utilizing secure hardware and trusted execution environments on edge devices can provide an isolated and protected environment for executing sensitive analytics workloads and handling sensitive data.
  e. Federated Learning and Privacy-preserving Analytics: Adopting federated learning approaches and privacy-preserving analytics techniques, such as differential privacy and secure multiparty computation, can enable collaborative model training and analytics while preserving data privacy.
4. **Edge-Cloud Collaboration:** For IoT analytics to be truly effective, there needs to be seamless collaboration between edge and cloud computing resources. This collaboration enables efficient data flow, resource allocation, and orchestration, optimizing the overall performance and scalability of IoT analytics solutions.
  a. Unified Data Management: Implementing unified data management platforms that can handle data ingestion, processing, and analysis across edge and cloud environments can simplify data governance and enable end-to-end visibility and control.
  b. Hybrid Cloud Integration: Integrating edge computing infrastructures with hybrid cloud environments can leverage the scalability and advanced analytics capabilities of public clouds while retaining control over sensitive data and workloads on private clouds or on-premises systems.
  c. Intelligent Workload Placement: Developing intelligent workload placement strategies that dynamically allocate analytics tasks between edge and cloud resources based on factors such as data volume, computational requirements, and latency constraints can optimize resource utilization and performance.
  d. Edge-cloud Orchestration: Deploying edge-cloud orchestration platforms can automate the deployment, scaling, and management of IoT analytics workloads across distributed edge and cloud environments, ensuring efficient resource allocation and load balancing.

By combining edge computing and IoT analytics with cloud resources, organizations can unlock the full potential of their IoT data, enabling real-time decision-making, reducing latency, improving privacy and security, and optimizing resource utilization. However, successful implementation requires careful consideration of factors such as network infrastructure, data governance, and integration with existing systems and processes. Collaboration among IoT device manufacturers, edge computing providers, cloud service providers, and analytics platform vendors is crucial for developing interoperable and scalable edge-cloud analytics solutions. Additionally, ongoing research and innovation in areas such as federated learning, privacy-preserving analytics, and edge hardware acceleration will further enhance the capabilities and adoption of edge computing and IoT analytics.

7.4 Quantum Computing-based Analytics

Quantum computing, a revolutionary computing paradigm that harnesses the principles of quantum mechanics, has the potential to transform various domains, including big data analytics. While still in its early stages, quantum computing offers significant advantages over classical computing approaches, particularly in solving certain types of complex problems more efficiently. The application of quantum computing to big data analytics is an emerging field with promising applications and the potential to unlock new frontiers in data processing, analysis, and decision-making.

1. **Quantum Algorithms for Big Data Analytics:** One of the key advantages of quantum computing lies in the development of quantum algorithms that can outperform classical algorithms for specific computational tasks. In the context of big data analytics, quantum algorithms can provide significant performance advantages for tasks such as optimization, ML, and data processing.
   a. Quantum Optimization Algorithms: Optimization problems are ubiquitous in various domains, such as logistics, finance, and manufacturing. Quantum algorithms like Grover's algorithm and the quantum approximate optimization algorithm can solve certain optimization problems exponentially faster than classical algorithms, enabling more efficient decision-making and resource allocation.
   b. Quantum ML: Quantum computing has the potential to enhance ML algorithms by providing more efficient ways to perform tasks like data encoding, model training, and inference. Quantum neural networks and quantum kernel methods can leverage quantum parallelism and quantum entanglement to process high-dimensional data and tackle complex learning tasks more efficiently.

   c. Quantum Data Processing: Certain data processing tasks, such as data searching, pattern recognition, and data compression, can benefit from quantum algorithms like Grover's algorithm and quantum Fourier transform, which can offer exponential speedups compared to classical approaches.
2. **Quantum-enhanced ML:** ML is a crucial component of big data analytics, enabling predictive modeling, pattern recognition, and decision support. Quantum computing can enhance ML algorithms and neural networks by leveraging quantum properties like superposition and entanglement.
   a. Quantum-enhanced Neural Networks: Quantum neural networks can leverage quantum parallelism and quantum entanglement to process high-dimensional data and tackle complex learning tasks more efficiently. These quantum neural networks can potentially achieve higher accuracy and faster convergence than classical neural networks for certain problems.
   b. Quantum Kernel Methods: Quantum kernel methods, such as quantum support vector machines and quantum kernel ridge regression, can leverage quantum computing to perform efficient kernel computations, enabling more accurate and scalable ML models for big data analytics.
   c. Quantum-assisted Feature Mapping: Quantum computing can be used to perform efficient feature mapping, transforming high-dimensional data into a feature space better suited for ML algorithms, potentially leading to improved model accuracy and performance.
3. **Quantum Simulation and Modeling:** Quantum computers can simulate and model complex quantum systems and phenomena more accurately than classical computers, providing insights and solutions that are difficult or impossible to achieve with classical computing resources. This capability has significant applications in various domains, including materials science, chemistry, and financial modeling.
   a. Quantum Chemistry Simulations: Quantum computers can simulate and model the behavior of molecules and chemical reactions with unprecedented accuracy, enabling researchers to design new materials, optimize chemical processes, and develop more effective drugs and catalysts.
   b. Quantum Materials Science: By simulating and modeling the quantum behavior of materials at the atomic level, quantum computers can aid in the design and development of new materials with tailored properties, such as improved strength, conductivity, or superconductivity.
   c. Quantum Finance and Risk Modeling: Quantum computing can be applied to financial modeling and risk analysis, enabling more accurate simulations of complex financial systems, portfolio optimization, and risk management strategies.

4. **Quantum-secure Data Analytics:** As quantum computing continues to advance, there is a growing concern about the security implications for classical cryptographic systems. Quantum-resistant cryptographic techniques and secure data analytics protocols will be essential to protect sensitive data and ensure privacy in the era of quantum computing.
   a. Post-quantum Cryptography: Developing and implementing quantum-resistant cryptographic algorithms, such as lattice-based cryptography and hash-based signatures, can ensure the long-term security of data and communications against potential quantum attacks.
   b. Quantum Key Distribution (QKD): QKD leverages quantum mechanics principles to enable secure key exchange between parties, providing provably secure communication channels for sensitive data analytics applications.
   c. Quantum-secure Data Processing: Developing quantum-secure data processing protocols and techniques, such as homomorphic encryption and secure multiparty computation, can enable collaborative data analytics while preserving data privacy and security in a post-quantum computing environment.
5. **Hybrid Quantum-classical Approaches:** While quantum computing holds immense potential for big data analytics, classical computing resources will continue to play a crucial role in the near future. Hybrid approaches that combine classical and quantum computing resources can leverage the strengths of both paradigms, enabling efficient and scalable big data analytics solutions.
   a. Quantum-classical Hybrid Algorithms: Developing hybrid algorithms that leverage both quantum and classical computing resources can enable more efficient problem-solving by offloading computationally intensive tasks to quantum computers while relying on classical computers for pre-processing and post-processing tasks.
   b. Quantum-classical Hybrid Architectures: Integrating quantum computing hardware with classical high-performance computing (HPC) systems can create powerful hybrid architectures capable of tackling large-scale data analytics challenges by leveraging the complementary strengths of both computing paradigms.
   c. Quantum-accelerated Analytics: Incorporating quantum accelerators or coprocessors into classical computing systems can provide a performance boost for specific analytics tasks, such as optimization, ML, and data processing, without requiring a full-scale quantum computer.

While quantum computing-based analytics holds immense promise, several challenges must be addressed to realize its full potential. These challenges include the development of large-scale, fault-tolerant quantum computers, the creation of efficient quantum algorithms and software stacks, and the integration of quantum computing resources with existing big data analytics infrastructures and workflows. Furthermore, addressing the skills gap and fostering interdisciplinary collaboration among quantum computing researchers, computer scientists, data analysts, and domain experts will be crucial for driving innovation and practical applications of quantum computing in big data analytics. Significant investments in research, development, and infrastructure are required to unlock the full potential of quantum computing-based analytics. Collaboration among academia, industry, and government entities will be essential to advance this field and position organizations to leverage the transformative capabilities of quantum computing in their big data analytics operations.

7.5 Blockchain and Big Data Analytics

Blockchain technology, with its decentralized, immutable, and transparent nature, has the potential to revolutionize the way data is managed, shared, and analyzed in the context of big data analytics. By providing a secure and trustworthy environment for data sharing and collaboration, blockchain can address some of the key challenges associated with big data analytics, such as data integrity, provenance, and governance.

1. **Decentralized Data Sharing and Collaboration:** One of the primary applications of blockchain technology in big data analytics is enabling secure and transparent data sharing among multiple parties. Traditional centralized data sharing models often face challenges related to trust, data ownership, and governance, limiting the potential for collaboration and data-driven insights.
   a. Decentralized Data Marketplaces: Blockchain-based decentralized data marketplaces can facilitate secure and transparent data exchange among various stakeholders. These platforms enable data owners to monetize their data assets while providing buyers with verifiable provenance and data quality assurance.
   b. Collaborative Analytics Platforms: Developing decentralized analytics platforms built on blockchain technology can enable secure and transparent collaborative analytics among multiple organizations or entities without relying on a central authority. These platforms leverage smart contracts and consensus mechanisms to ensure data integrity and governance.
   c. Data Sharing and Access Control: Blockchain-based access control mechanisms can provide granular control over data sharing and access permissions, ensuring that data is accessed and utilized only by authorized parties and for intended purposes.

2. **Data Provenance and Traceability:** Ensuring data provenance and traceability is crucial for maintaining data integrity and enabling trustworthy analytics. Blockchain technology can provide an immutable and auditable record of data transactions, enabling organizations to track the origin, transformations, and usage of data throughout its life cycle.
   a. Immutable Data Ledger: The blockchain's immutable ledger provides a tamper-proof record of data transactions, ensuring that data cannot be modified or deleted without leaving an auditable trail.
   b. Data Lineage and Audit Trail: By leveraging blockchain's transparency and traceability features, organizations can establish a comprehensive data lineage and audit trail, enabling them to track data provenance, understand data transformations, and ensure compliance with regulatory requirements.
   c. Data Integrity Verification: Cryptographic techniques, such as digital signatures and hash functions, can be used in conjunction with blockchain to verify the integrity of data and ensure that it has not been tampered with during transmission or storage.
3. **Secure Data Monetization:** Blockchain technology can facilitate secure and transparent data monetization by enabling data owners to monetize their data assets while ensuring data privacy, access control, and fair compensation.
   a. Data Ownership and Rights Management: Blockchain-based solutions can provide a secure and transparent mechanism for managing data ownership and rights, enabling data owners to retain control over their data assets and grant access or usage rights to interested parties.
   b. Micropayments and Data Monetization: Leveraging blockchain-based cryptocurrencies and smart contracts, data owners can securely monetize their data assets by enabling micropayments or revenue-sharing models based on data usage or access.
   c. Transparent Revenue Distribution: Smart contracts on the blockchain can automate the distribution of revenue or compensation among multiple parties involved in data sharing or collaborative analytics, ensuring transparency and fairness.
4. **Blockchain-based Consent Management:** In the era of data privacy regulations, such as the General Data Protection Regulation, managing and demonstrating user consent for data collection and usage has become a critical requirement. Blockchain technology can provide a secure and auditable framework for consent management.
   a. Decentralized Consent Ledger: A blockchain-based decentralized consent ledger can securely record and manage user consent for data collection, processing, and sharing, providing an immutable and transparent audit trail.

   b. User Control and Revocation: Blockchain-based consent management solutions can empower individuals by providing them with granular control over their personal data, including the ability to revoke consent or access permissions when desired.
   c. Compliance and Auditing: The transparent and auditable nature of blockchain can facilitate compliance with data privacy regulations by providing verifiable records of user consent and data usage, enabling efficient auditing and reporting processes.
5. **Decentralized Analytics Platforms:** Beyond enabling secure data sharing and collaboration, blockchain technology can serve as the foundation for developing decentralized analytics platforms that leverage the collective computational resources and data assets of multiple parties.
   a. Distributed Analytics and Computation: Decentralized analytics platforms built on blockchain can leverage distributed computing resources and data sources to perform collaborative analytics tasks, such as model training, data processing, and decision support.
   b. Incentive Mechanisms: Blockchain-based incentive mechanisms, such as tokenization and smart contracts, can incentivize participants to contribute computational resources, data assets, or domain expertise to the decentralized analytics platform, fostering a collaborative and self-sustaining ecosystem.
   c. Transparency and Auditability: The inherent transparency and auditability of blockchain can ensure that the decentralized analytics platform operates in a fair and transparent manner, building trust among participants and stakeholders.

While blockchain technology presents promising opportunities for big data analytics, several challenges must be addressed to enable widespread adoption and integration with existing analytics infrastructures and workflows.

1. **Scalability and Performance:** Existing blockchain platforms face scalability and performance limitations, which can hinder their ability to handle the high volume and velocity of data associated with big data analytics workloads. Ongoing research and development efforts are focused on improving blockchain scalability through techniques like sharding, off-chain computation, and layer-2 scaling solutions.
2. **Interoperability and Standards:** Ensuring interoperability and establishing industry-wide standards for blockchain-based data sharing and analytics solutions is crucial for enabling cross-platform collaboration and integration with existing systems and processes.

3. **Regulatory and Legal Considerations:** The adoption of blockchain technology in big data analytics may require addressing regulatory and legal considerations related to data governance, privacy, and compliance, particularly in industries with strict data protection regulations.
4. **Skills and Expertise:** Implementing and managing blockchain-based analytics solutions requires a combination of skills and expertise in blockchain technology, distributed systems, cryptography, and data analytics. Addressing the skills gap and fostering cross-disciplinary collaboration will be essential for successful adoption and implementation.
5. **Integration with Existing Analytics Infrastructures:** Integrating blockchain-based solutions with existing big data analytics infrastructures, including data processing frameworks, storage systems, and visualization tools, may require significant architectural changes and the development of custom integration layers or adapters.

Despite these challenges, the potential benefits of leveraging blockchain technology in big data analytics, such as enhanced data integrity, secure collaboration, and transparent data governance, make it a promising area for further research and innovation. Collaboration among technology providers, industry stakeholders, and regulatory bodies will be crucial in overcoming these challenges and unlocking the transformative potential of blockchain in the realm of big data analytics.

7.6 XAI-based to Enhanced Interpretability

As AI and ML models become increasingly complex and opaque, there is a growing need for XAI techniques to enhance the interpretability and transparency of these models in big data analytics applications. XAI aims to provide human-understandable explanations for the decisions and predictions made by AI systems, addressing concerns related to trust, accountability, and ethical considerations.

1. **Interpretable Machine Learning Models:** One approach to enhancing interpretability in big data analytics is to develop and deploy interpretable machine learning models that are inherently more transparent and explainable. These models strike a balance between predictive performance and interpretability, making them valuable in domains where explainability is critical, such as health care, finance, and regulatory compliance.

   a. Linear and Logistic Regression: Linear and logistic regression models are among the most interpretable models, as they provide a direct relationship between input features and the predicted output, enabling easy understanding of the model's decision-making process.
   b. Decision Trees and Rule-based Models: Decision trees and rule-based models, such as random forests and gradient boosting machines, represent knowledge in a hierarchical, human-readable format, making them easier to interpret and understand compared to more complex models like neural networks.
   c. Generalized Additive Models (GAMs): GAMs are a class of interpretable models that use a sum of smooth functions to model the relationship between input features and the target variable, providing insights into the individual contributions of each feature.
2. **Model Explanation Techniques:** For complex models like deep neural networks, where direct interpretability is challenging, model explanation techniques can provide post-hoc explanations for the model's predictions and decisions. These techniques aim to uncover the underlying reasoning and rationale behind the model's outputs, enabling better understanding and trust.
   a. SHAP (SHapley Additive exPlanations): SHAP is a game-theoretic approach that assigns an importance value (Shapley value) to each feature, indicating its contribution to the model's prediction. SHAP explanations can be presented in various forms, including feature importance plots and local explanations for individual predictions.
   b. LIME (Local Interpretable Model-agnostic Explanations): LIME is a model-agnostic technique that approximates the behavior of a complex model locally by fitting an interpretable surrogate model (e.g., linear regression or decision tree) in the vicinity of the instance being explained, providing local explanations for individual predictions.
   c. Counterfactual Explanations: Counterfactual explanations provide insights into how the model's prediction would change if certain input features were modified. These explanations can be particularly useful in scenarios where understanding the causal relationships between input features and the model's output is crucial.
3. **Interactive Visualization and Storytelling:** Effective communication and visualization of analytics results and insights are essential for enhancing interpretability and fostering trust in AI-driven decision-making. Interactive visualization and storytelling techniques can facilitate the effective translation of complex data patterns and model outputs into human-understandable narratives.

   a. Interactive Dashboards and Visualizations: Developing interactive dashboards and visualizations that allow users to explore and interact with data, model predictions, and explanations can enhance understanding and enable stakeholders to uncover insights and patterns that may not be immediately apparent.
   b. Narrative Visualization and Storytelling: Combining data visualization with narrative storytelling techniques can help convey complex analytical insights in a more accessible and engaging manner, facilitating better understanding and decision-making among nontechnical stakeholders.
   c. Collaborative Visualization and Exploration: Enabling collaborative visualization and exploration environments can foster human–AI collaboration, where domain experts and subject matter experts can interact with AI models, provide feedback, and gain insights into the model's decision-making process.
4. **Human–AI Collaboration:** Promoting human–AI collaboration is crucial for enhancing interpretability and ensuring that AI systems are aligned with human values, ethical principles, and domain-specific knowledge. By involving domain experts and subject matter experts in the analytics process, organizations can leverage the complementary strengths of human expertise and AI capabilities.
   a. Interactive Model Refinement: Developing interactive model refinement processes that allow domain experts to provide feedback, adjust model parameters, or refine decision boundaries can enhance the interpretability and alignment of AI models with real-world requirements and constraints.
   b. Human-in-the-Loop AI: Implementing human-in-the-loop AI systems, where human experts are actively involved in the decision-making process, can ensure that AI models are operating within acceptable boundaries and that their decisions are interpretable and aligned with human values and ethical considerations.
   c. Collective Intelligence and Crowdsourcing: Leveraging collective intelligence and crowdsourcing techniques can facilitate the integration of diverse human perspectives, domain knowledge, and real-world experiences into the development and refinement of interpretable AI models for big data analytics.
5. **Ethical AI and Responsible Analytics:** Incorporating XAI principles into the development and deployment of AI and ML models for big data analytics is essential for promoting ethical AI practices, ensuring transparency, and fostering responsible and trustworthy analytics applications.

a. Bias and Fairness Testing: Developing and implementing techniques for testing AI models for potential biases and unfair decisions can help mitigate the risks of discrimination and promote ethical and responsible analytics practices.
b. Regulatory Compliance and Auditing: XAI techniques can facilitate compliance with regulatory requirements and enable efficient auditing of AI-driven decisions, particularly in domains with strict accountability and transparency requirements, such as finance, health care, and public services.
c. Ethical AI Frameworks and Governance: Establishing ethical AI frameworks and governance models that incorporate XAI principles can help organizations navigate the ethical and societal implications of AI-driven analytics and ensure responsible development and deployment of these technologies.

While XAI techniques offer significant benefits in terms of enhancing interpretability and fostering trust in AI-driven analytics, several challenges must be addressed to enable their widespread adoption and effective implementation.

1. Trade-off between Accuracy and Interpretability: There is often a trade-off between the predictive performance of AI models and their interpretability, as more complex models tend to be more accurate but less interpretable. Balancing this trade-off requires careful consideration of the specific use case and the relative importance of accuracy versus interpretability.
2. Scalability and Computational Overhead: Some XAI techniques, particularly those involving model approximation or counterfactual analysis, can be computationally intensive, posing scalability challenges for big data analytics applications with large-scale datasets and complex models.
3. Human Factors and User Experience: Effective implementation of XAI techniques requires careful consideration of human factors and user experience design, ensuring that explanations and visualizations are intuitive, engaging, and tailored to the needs and domain knowledge of end users.
4. Evaluation and Benchmarking: Developing standardized evaluation metrics and benchmarks for assessing the quality and effectiveness of XAI techniques is crucial for enabling meaningful comparisons and driving progress in the field.
5. Integration with Existing Analytics Workflows: Integrating XAI techniques seamlessly into existing big data analytics workflows and infrastructures may require architectural changes, additional computational resources, and the development of custom interfaces or APIs.

Despite these challenges, the adoption of XAI techniques is becoming increasingly important as AI and ML models play a more significant role in critical decision-making processes across various domains. Addressing the need for interpretability and transparency in AI-driven analytics is essential for fostering trust, accountability, and responsible innovation. Collaboration among researchers, practitioners, policymakers, and end users is vital for driving the development and adoption of effective XAI techniques tailored to the specific requirements and constraints of big data analytics applications. Additionally, ongoing research and innovation in areas such as human–AI interaction, interactive visualization, and ethical AI governance will further enhance the interpretability and trustworthiness of AI-driven analytics solutions.

7.7 Conclusion

The field of big data analytics is rapidly evolving, driven by the relentless growth of data volumes, the emergence of new data sources, and the increasing demand for real-time insights and decision-making. As organizations navigate this data-driven landscape, embracing emerging trends and leveraging cutting-edge technologies will be crucial for unlocking the full potential of big data analytics. Adopting sustainable approaches to big data analytics is imperative to mitigate the environmental impact of data processing and storage operations, promote responsible resource utilization, and align with broader sustainability goals. Edge computing and IoT analytics enable real-time decision-making, reduce latency, and optimize resource utilization by bringing data processing closer to the source. The advent of quantum computing promises to revolutionize data analysis and simulations, offering exponential speedups and new capabilities for tackling complex computational problems. Meanwhile, the integration of blockchain technology fosters secure and trustworthy data sharing, ensures data provenance, and enables collaborative analytics across multiple stakeholders. Furthermore, the adoption of XAI techniques is becoming increasingly important as AI and machine learning models play a more significant role in critical decision-making processes. XAI enhances the interpretability and transparency of these models, fostering trust, accountability, and responsible innovation in big data analytics applications. While these emerging trends hold immense potential, their successful implementation and integration with existing big data analytics infrastructures and workflows present several challenges. Scalability, security, privacy, ethical considerations, and the development of skilled professionals are among the key issues that must be addressed through collaborative efforts among researchers, industry practitioners, policymakers, and stakeholders.

The future of big data analytics is undoubtedly intertwined with the ongoing evolution of these emerging trends and technologies. By embracing sustainable practices, leveraging edge computing and quantum computing capabilities, integrating blockchain for secure collaboration, and fostering interpretability through XAI, we can unlock new frontiers of innovation and progress toward more efficient, trustworthy, and responsible big data analytics solutions.

Practice Set

A Multiple Choice Questions (MCQ)

1 Which emerging trend in big data analytics focuses on reducing latency by processing data closer to its source?
a Quantum computing
b Edge computing
c Blockchain
d Explainable AI (XAI)

2 What is a key benefit of integrating quantum computing into big data analytics?
a Enhanced data storage
b Exponential speedups in data analysis
c Simplified data sharing
d Reduced data volume

3 How does blockchain technology contribute to big data analytics?
a By reducing data processing speed
b By ensuring data provenance and secure data sharing
c By increasing data redundancy
d By centralizing data storage

4 What is a primary goal of adopting sustainable approaches to big data analytics?
a Increasing data volume
b Mitigating environmental impact and promoting responsible resource utilization
c Simplifying data visualization
d Enhancing data redundancy

5 Which technology is crucial for enhancing the interpretability and transparency of AI models?
a Edge computing
b Quantum computing
c Blockchain
d Explainable AI (XAI)

6 What is a major challenge associated with integrating emerging trends into big data analytics?
- **a** Decreased data volume
- **b** Scalability, security, privacy, and ethical considerations
- **c** Reduced data complexity
- **d** Simplified data management

7 What role does edge computing play in IoT analytics?
- **a** Increasing data latency
- **b** Enhancing real-time decision-making and optimizing resource utilization
- **c** Centralizing data processing
- **d** Reducing device functionality

8 Which emerging technology promises to revolutionize data analysis with exponential speedups?
- **a** Blockchain
- **b** Quantum computing
- **c** Explainable AI (XAI)
- **d** Edge computing

9 What is a key benefit of using explainable AI (XAI) in big data analytics?
- **a** Increasing data storage capacity
- **b** Enhancing model interpretability and transparency
- **c** Simplifying data preprocessing
- **d** Centralizing data analysis

10 Which of the following is NOT a focus area for the integration of blockchain technology in big data analytics?
- **a** Secure data sharing
- **b** Data provenance
- **c** Centralized data management
- **d** Collaborative analytics

B Fill-in-the-Blanks

11 Adopting __________ approaches to big data analytics helps mitigate the environmental impact of data processing and storage operations.

12 The integration of __________ technology fosters secure and trustworthy data sharing and ensures data provenance.

13 Edge computing helps in optimizing resource utilization by bringing data processing closer to the ___________.

14 The use of ___________ computing promises exponential speedups and new capabilities for tackling complex computational problems.

15 Explainable AI (XAI) enhances the ___________ and transparency of AI models, fostering trust and accountability.

C Short Answer Questions

16 What are the benefits of integrating edge computing with IoT analytics?

17 How can quantum computing impact big data analytics?

18 Describe how blockchain technology enhances data security and collaboration in big data analytics.

19 What are some challenges associated with implementing sustainable approaches in big data analytics?

20 Explain the importance of explainable AI (XAI) in enhancing the interpretability of AI models.

D Long Answer Questions

21 Discuss the advantages and potential applications of edge computing in the context of IoT and big data analytics.

22 Analyze how quantum computing could transform big data analytics and address current limitations in data processing.

23 Evaluate the role of blockchain technology in ensuring data security and facilitating collaborative analytics in big data environments.

24 Examine the significance of adopting sustainable practices in big data analytics and how these practices can be implemented effectively.

25 Explore the impact of Explainable AI (XAI) on the transparency and trustworthiness of AI-driven big data analytics applications.

Further Readings

Amalina, F., Hashem, I.A.T., Azizul, Z.H., Fong, A.T., Firdaus, A., Imran, M. and Anuar, N.B., 2019. Blending big data analytics: review on challenges and a recent study. *IEEE Access*, 8, pp. 3629–3645.

Banerjee, A., Chakraborty, C., Kumar, A. and Biswas, D., 2020. Emerging trends in IoT and big data analytics for biomedical and health care technologies. In: *Handbook of Data Science Approaches for Biomedical Engineering*, pp. 121–152. Academic Press.

Basha, S.M., Rajput, D.S., Bhushan, S.B., Poluru, R.K., Patan, R., Manikandan, R., Kumar, A. and Manikandan, R., 2019. Recent trends in sustainable big data predictive analytics: past contributions and future roadmap. *International Journal on Emerging Technologies*, 10(2), pp. 50–59.

Cremin, C.J., Dash, S. and Huang, X., 2022. Big data: historic advances and emerging trends in biomedical research. *Current Research in Biotechnology*, 4, pp. 138–151.

Goyal, D., Goyal, R., Rekha, G., Malik, S. and Tyagi, A.K., 2020. Emerging trends and challenges in data science and big data analytics. In: *2020 International Conference on Emerging Trends in Information Technology and Engineering (ic-PETITE)*, pp. 1–8. IEEE.

Hariri, R.H., Fredericks, E.M. and Bowers, K.M., 2019. Uncertainty in big data analytics: survey, opportunities, and challenges. *Journal of Big Data*, 6(1), pp. 1–16.

Hasan, R., Palaniappan, S., Mahmood, S., Naidu, V.R., Agarwal, A., Singh, B., Sarker, K.U., Abbas, A. and Sattar, M.U., 2020. A review: emerging trends of big data in higher educational institutions. In: *Micro-Electronics and Telecommunication Engineering: Proceedings of 3rd ICMETE 2019*, pp. 289–297. Singapore: Springer. https://doi.org/10.1007/978-981-15-2329-8_29

Henriques, A.C.V., de Souza Meirelles, F. and da Cunha, M.A.V.C., 2020. Big data analytics: achievements, challenges, and research trends. *Independent Journal of Management & Production*, 11(4), pp. 1201–1222.

Iqbal, R., Doctor, F., More, B., Mahmud, S. and Yousuf, U., 2020. Big data analytics and computational intelligence for cyber–physical systems: recent trends and state of the art applications. *Future Generation Computer Systems*, 105, pp. 766–778.

Kaddoura, S. and Grati, R., 2021. Blockchain for healthcare and medical systems. In: *Enabling Blockchain Technology for Secure Networking and Communications*, pp. 249–270. IGI Global.

Maheshwari, S., Gautam, P. and Jaggi, C.K., 2021. Role of big data analytics in supply chain management: current trends and future perspectives. *International Journal of Production Research*, 59(6), pp. 1875–1900.

Mohamed, A., Najafabadi, M.K., Wah, Y.B., Zaman, E.A.K. and Maskat, R., 2020. The state of the art and taxonomy of big data analytics: view from new big data framework. *Artificial Intelligence Review*, 53, pp. 989–1037.

Mohammadpoor, M. and Torabi, F., 2020. Big data analytics in oil and gas industry: an emerging trend. *Petroleum*, 6(4), pp. 321–328.

Naga Rama Devi, G., 2018. Emerging trends in big data analytics—a study. In: *International Conference on Communications and Cyber Physical Engineering 2018*, pp. 563–570. Singapore: Springer Singapore.

Prokofieva, M. and Miah, S.J., 2019. Blockchain in healthcare [Online]. *Australasian Journal of Information Systems*, 23.

Rawat, K.S. and Sood, S.K., 2021. Emerging trends and global scope of big data analytics: a scientometric analysis. *Quality & Quantity*, 55(4), pp. 1371–1396.

Rehman, A., Naz, S. and Razzak, I., 2022. Leveraging big data analytics in healthcare enhancement: trends, challenges and opportunities. *Multimedia Systems*, 28(4), pp. 1339–1371.

Thakur, S. and Jha, S.K., 2023. Cloud computing and its emerging trends on big data analytics. In: *2023 4th International Conference on Electronics and Sustainable Communication Systems (ICESC)*, pp. 1159–1164. IEEE.

8

Data Governance, Compliance, and Sustainability

LEARNING OBJECTIVES

- Understand the principles and practices required to maintain data quality and ensure data integrity across large-scale data systems.
- Examine regulatory and legal frameworks governing big data usage, with emphasis on compliance, accountability, and ethical responsibility.
- Analyze auditing techniques and compliance monitoring mechanisms used to assess adherence to data governance and regulatory standards.
- Develop an understanding of incident response strategies and data breach management practices with a focus on long-term sustainability and risk mitigation.
- Recognize the importance of training and awareness programs in promoting the ethical and responsible use of big data among stakeholders.

8.1 Introduction

In the era of big data, where vast amounts of information are generated and processed daily, ensuring data governance, compliance, and sustainability has become a paramount concern. The convergence of cutting-edge technologies such as artificial intelligence, Internet of Things, and blockchain has revolutionized data management practices, but it has also introduced new challenges and risks. This chapter delves into the critical aspects of data governance, compliance, and sustainability, offering insights and best practices for organizations navigating the intricate landscape of big data analytics. Each terminology is discussed as follows:

Data governance plays a key role in helping organizations manage data responsibly and effectively. It involves setting clear guidelines on how data is collected, stored, shared, and maintained, while also defining who is accountable for each stage of the data life cycle. When governance practices are well established, data becomes more reliable and consistent, supporting informed decision-making and day-to-day operations. Strong governance also helps build confidence among stakeholders by ensuring that data is handled with care and transparency.

Compliance is closely tied to governance, as organizations must follow applicable laws, regulations, and ethical standards when working with data. Meeting these requirements is not just a legal obligation but also a matter of trust and credibility. Regular reviews, audits, and monitoring processes allow organizations to track how well they are meeting compliance expectations and to address issues before they escalate. As regulations continue to evolve, a proactive approach to compliance helps reduce risks and ensures that data practices remain aligned with current standards.

Sustainability in data governance focuses on maintaining responsible data practices over the long term. This includes managing data securely throughout its life cycle, preparing for potential incidents such as data breaches, and making thoughtful choices about infrastructure and resource use. Equally important is investing in training and awareness programs so that individuals understand their responsibilities and the ethical implications of data use. Together, these efforts support a balanced approach that encourages innovation while safeguarding data integrity, security, and societal trust. In the context of big data, data governance, regulatory compliance, and sustainability are feasible through well-defined policies, continuous monitoring mechanisms, secure life cycle management, and ongoing training that ensure responsible, compliant, and long-term use of large-scale data systems.

8.1.1 Motivation

The widespread use of big data has transformed how organizations analyze information and make decisions, but it has also raised concerns around data reliability, security, and ethical use. As regulatory expectations continue to tighten, managing data in a compliant and transparent manner has become increasingly important. In parallel, frequent data incidents and long-term operational demands highlight the need for sustainable data practices. These challenges create a strong motivation to examine governance, compliance, and sustainability together within big data environments.

8.1.2 Chapter Contributions

This chapter makes the following key contributions:

- The chapter explains key governance practices that support the responsible handling of large-scale data by outlining policies, roles, and accountability mechanisms that guide how data is collected, stored, accessed, and shared across complex big data environments.

- It reviews compliance requirements and regulatory considerations relevant to big data systems, focusing on legal obligations, data protection norms, and ethical guidelines that influence organizational data practices across different domains and jurisdictions.
- Next, it discusses approaches for monitoring, auditing, and managing data-related risks through continuous oversight, internal controls, and structured assessment methods that help identify vulnerabilities, ensure compliance, and reduce operational and security risks.
- Last, it emphasizes the importance of ethical awareness and capacity building for long-term data sustainability by highlighting the role of training programs, organizational culture, and stakeholder responsibility in promoting ethical decision-making and responsible use of big data over time.

8.1.3 Organization of the Chapter

The remainder of the chapter is structured as follows: Section 8.2 discusses data quality and integrity, and then Section 8.3 highlights the regulatory framework aspects. Next, Section 8.4 talks about auditing and compliance monitoring mechanisms. Further, the chapter highlights sustainable incident response and data breach management concepts in Section 8.5. Next, training and awareness programs for the ethical use of big data in Section 8.6. At last, the chapter is concluded with the final thoughts.

8.2 Ensuring Data Quality and Integrity

In the realm of big data analytics, data quality and integrity are foundational pillars upon which trustworthy and reliable insights are built. Poor data quality can lead to inaccurate analyses, flawed decision-making, and potentially devastating consequences for organizations. As the volume, velocity, and variety of data continue to increase, ensuring data quality and integrity becomes an even more significant challenge. Data quality encompasses a multitude of dimensions, including *accuracy, completeness, consistency, timeliness, and validity*. Each of these dimensions plays a crucial role in ensuring that the data being analyzed is fit for its intended purpose and can be relied upon for informed decision-making. These dimensions are discussed as follows:

1. **Accuracy:** Data accuracy refers to the extent to which the data correctly represents the real-world entities or phenomena it is intended to capture. Inaccurate data can lead to erroneous conclusions and poor decision-making, potentially resulting in financial losses, reputational damage, or even legal consequences.

2. **Completeness:** Incomplete data can lead to missing insights and an incomplete understanding of the problem or opportunity at hand. Ensuring data completeness involves identifying and addressing any gaps or missing values in the datasets, either through additional data collection or through appropriate data imputation techniques.
3. **Consistency:** Data consistency refers to the uniformity and coherence of data across different sources, systems, or formats. Inconsistent data can lead to conflicting information, making it challenging to reconcile and analyze effectively.
4. **Timeliness:** In many big data applications, the timeliness of data is critical. Outdated or stale data may fail to capture the current state of affairs, leading to decisions based on outdated information and potentially missed opportunities or risks.
5. **Validity:** Data validity refers to the extent to which the data adheres to defined rules, constraints, and formats. Invalid data can lead to errors and inconsistencies in downstream processing and analysis. Figure 8.1 illustrates the process of maintaining data quality and integrity.

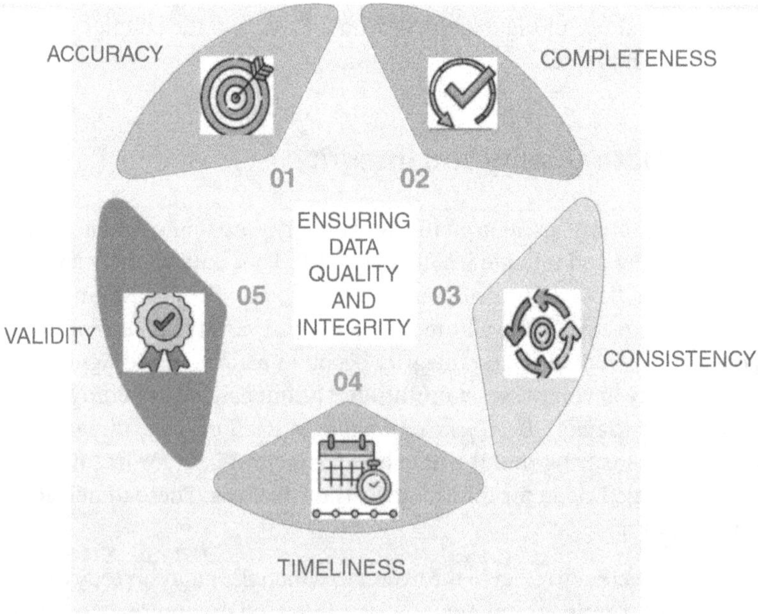

Figure 8.1 Data quality and integrity dimensions.

To ensure data quality and integrity, organizations must implement robust data governance frameworks that encompass a range of processes, tools, and best practices, which are highlighted as follows:

- **Data Profiling and Cleansing:** Data profiling involves analyzing and understanding the characteristics, patterns, and anomalies present in datasets. This process helps identify data quality issues, such as missing values, outliers, or inconsistencies. Once identified, data cleansing techniques can be applied to rectify these issues, ranging from manual data correction to automated data cleansing using advanced algorithms and machine learning techniques.
- **Data Quality Rules and Validation:** Organizations should establish comprehensive data quality rules and validation processes to ensure that data meets predefined quality standards. These rules can be implemented at various stages of the data life cycle, including data acquisition, transformation, and storage. Automated data validation tools can be employed to enforce these rules and flag any violations or anomalies for further investigation and remediation.
- **Data Stewardship and Ownership:** Effective data governance requires clear ownership and accountability for data quality. Organizations should establish data stewardship roles and responsibilities, ensuring that individuals or teams are assigned to manage and monitor the quality of specific data domains or assets.
- **Data Quality Metrics and Reporting:** Measuring and monitoring data quality is essential for continuous improvement. Organizations should define and track relevant data quality metrics, such as completeness rates, accuracy rates, or data freshness indicators. Regular data quality reports should be generated and reviewed, providing visibility into the state of data quality and enabling proactive identification and resolution of issues.
- **Data Quality Improvement Processes:** Data quality should be treated as an ongoing process rather than a one-time effort. Organizations should establish continuous improvement processes that incorporate feedback loops, root cause analysis, and corrective action plans. This iterative approach ensures that data quality issues are systematically identified, addressed, and prevented from recurring.

By prioritizing data quality and integrity through comprehensive governance frameworks, organizations can enhance the reliability and trustworthiness of their big data analytics initiatives. Accurate, complete, consistent, timely, and valid data serve as the foundation for informed decision-making, enabling organizations to maximize the value derived from their data assets while mitigating potential risks and adverse consequences.

8.3 Regulatory Framework Adherence

In the era of big data, where vast amounts of personal and sensitive information are collected, processed, and analyzed, regulatory frameworks have emerged as essential safeguards to protect individual privacy and ensure ethical data practices, as shown in Figure 8.2. Organizations operating in the realm of big data analytics must stay abreast of and adhere to these regulatory frameworks to mitigate legal and reputational risks, foster consumer trust, and maintain a sustainable data ecosystem.

Regulatory frameworks governing data privacy and protection are constantly evolving to keep pace with the rapid advancements in technology and the ever-increasing scope of data collection and processing. Some of the prominent regulatory frameworks that organizations must comply with include:

- **General Data Protection Regulation (GDPR):** Implemented by the European Union (EU), the GDPR is a comprehensive data protection regulation that aims to harmonize data privacy laws across the EU member states. It outlines strict guidelines for the collection, processing, and storage of personal data, with stringent requirements for obtaining explicit consent, ensuring data subject rights (such as the right to be forgotten), and implementing robust data protection measures.
- **California Consumer Privacy Act (CCPA):** In the United States, the CCPA is a landmark privacy law that grants California residents enhanced control over their personal data. It mandates organizations to disclose data collection and processing activities, provide mechanisms for consumers to access, delete, or opt out of the sale of their personal information, and implement reasonable security measures to protect consumer data.

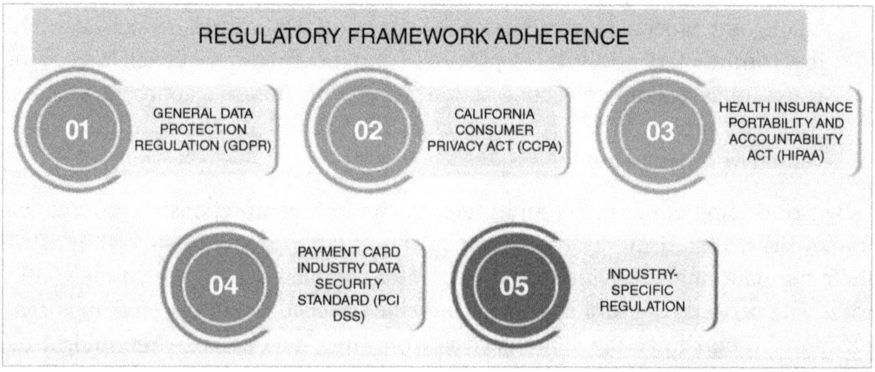

Figure 8.2 Regulatory framework for big data.

- **Health Insurance Portability and Accountability Act (HIPAA):** For organizations operating in the health-care sector, HIPAA sets standards for protecting sensitive patient health information. It establishes strict guidelines for data privacy and security, including regulations for data access, storage, transmission, and breach notification.
- **Payment Card Industry Data Security Standard (PCI DSS):** Organizations that handle payment card data, such as credit or debit card information, must comply with the PCI DSS. This standard outlines specific requirements for securing payment data, including encryption, access controls, and regular vulnerability testing.
- **Industry-specific Regulations:** Various industries, such as finance, telecommunications, and energy, may have their own sector-specific regulatory frameworks that organizations must adhere to when handling and processing data in those domains.

Achieving regulatory compliance requires a multifaceted approach that encompasses organizational policies, technical controls, and ongoing monitoring and auditing mechanisms.

- **Organizational Policies and Procedures:** Organizations should establish comprehensive data governance policies and procedures that align with the applicable regulatory frameworks. These policies should cover areas such as data collection and processing practices, data subject rights management, data retention and disposal, and incident response and breach notification processes.
- **Technical Controls:** Implementing robust technical controls is crucial for ensuring regulatory compliance. These controls may include data encryption, access controls, activity logging and monitoring, and secure data storage and transmission mechanisms.
- **Privacy by Design and Default:** Adopting a "privacy by design and default" approach ensures that data privacy and protection measures are embedded into the design and development of systems, products, and services from the outset rather than being an afterthought.
- **Data Protection Impact Assessments (DPIAs):** Conducting regular DPIAs can help organizations identify and mitigate potential privacy risks associated with their data processing activities. DPIAs should be performed for high-risk data processing operations or when introducing new technologies or processing methods.
- **Compliance Monitoring and Auditing:** Establishing robust compliance monitoring and auditing mechanisms is essential for ensuring ongoing adherence to regulatory requirements. This may involve implementing automated monitoring tools, conducting regular internal audits, and engaging external auditors to assess compliance levels and identify areas for improvement.

- **Training and Awareness Programs:** Cultivating a culture of regulatory compliance requires ongoing training and awareness programs for employees and stakeholders. These programs should cover the applicable regulatory frameworks, organizational policies and procedures, and the importance of adhering to data privacy and protection principles.

By prioritizing regulatory framework adherence, organizations can not only mitigate legal and financial risks but also foster consumer trust and maintain a sustainable data ecosystem. Demonstrating a commitment to data privacy and ethical data practices can provide a competitive advantage, enhance brand reputation, and position the organization as a responsible and trustworthy steward of personal and sensitive information.

8.4 Auditing and Compliance Monitoring Mechanisms

Figure 8.3 presents auditing and compliance monitoring mechanisms that are essential for ensuring ongoing adherence to established data governance policies, procedures, and regulatory requirements. These mechanisms provide visibility into data processing activities, enabling organizations to identify and address potential risks or noncompliance issues proactively, thereby maintaining a sustainable and trustworthy data ecosystem.

Auditing and compliance monitoring involve a range of processes, tools, and techniques designed to track, analyze, and report on data-related activities across the organization. These mechanisms serve as a critical line of defense against data

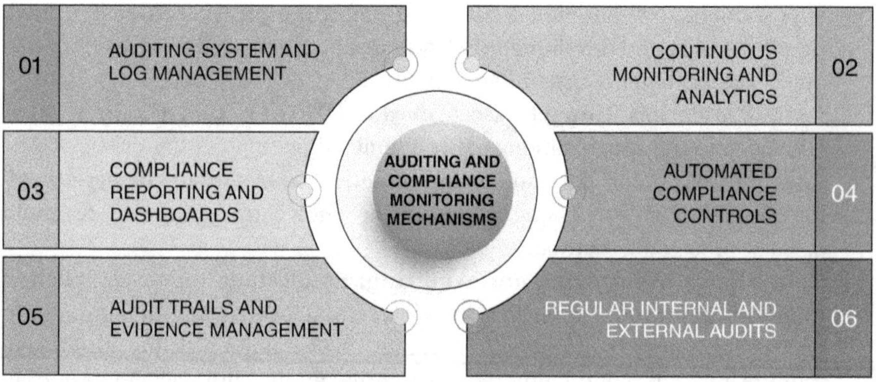

Figure 8.3 Auditing and compliance monitoring mechanism.

breaches, regulatory violations, and unethical data practices. These mechanisms are discussed in detail as follows:

1. **Auditing Systems and Log Management:** (a) Comprehensive auditing systems and log management solutions are crucial for capturing detailed information about data access, modification, and processing activities. (b) These systems should be designed to accommodate the scale and complexity of big data environments, ensuring efficient data collection, storage, and analysis. (c) Audit logs should capture relevant metadata, such as user identities, timestamps, data sources, and actions performed, providing a detailed audit trail for investigation and compliance purposes.
2. **Continuous Monitoring and Analytics:** (a) Continuous monitoring involves the real-time or near-real-time analysis of audit logs, system events, and data flows to detect potential anomalies, policy violations, or suspicious activities. (b) Advanced analytics and machine learning techniques can be employed to analyze audit logs and identify patterns indicative of noncompliance or potential threats. (c) Risk-based monitoring approaches can be implemented, prioritizing high-risk areas or critical data assets for enhanced scrutiny and analysis.
3. **Compliance Reporting and Dashboards:** (a) Effective compliance reporting and dashboarding solutions provide stakeholders with comprehensive visibility into the organization's compliance posture. (b) These solutions should present consolidated views of compliance metrics, audit findings, and remediation activities, enabling data-driven decision-making and risk management. (c) Customizable reporting templates and interactive dashboards can be tailored to meet the specific needs of different stakeholders, such as executives, data stewards, or auditors.
4. **Automated Compliance Controls:** (a) Automated compliance controls can be implemented to enforce data governance policies and regulatory requirements at various stages of the data life cycle. (b) These controls may include access restrictions, data masking or tokenization, data retention policies, and automated data quality checks. (c) By automating compliance controls, organizations can reduce the risk of human error, ensure consistent enforcement of policies, and streamline compliance processes.
5. **Audit Trails and Evidence Management:** (a) Maintaining comprehensive audit trails and evidence management systems is crucial for demonstrating compliance with regulatory requirements and supporting incident response and investigation efforts. (b) These systems should securely store and manage audit logs, system events, and other relevant evidence, ensuring data integrity and chain of custody. (c) Well-documented audit trails and evidence can be invaluable in the event of regulatory audits, legal proceedings, or data breach investigations.

6. **Regular Internal and External Audits:** (a) Conducting regular internal and external audits is essential for assessing the effectiveness of data governance, compliance, and sustainability measures. (b) Internal audits can be performed by dedicated teams or cross-functional audit committees to evaluate adherence to organizational policies and procedures. (c) External audits, conducted by independent third-party auditors, provide an objective assessment of the organization's compliance posture and can identify areas for improvement.

By implementing robust auditing and compliance monitoring mechanisms, organizations can proactively identify and mitigate potential risks, demonstrate adherence to regulatory requirements, and maintain a sustainable and trustworthy data ecosystem. These mechanisms not only help organizations avoid costly fines and legal consequences but also foster consumer trust and enhance their reputation as responsible stewards of data.

8.5 Sustainable Incident Response and Data Breach Management

Despite robust data governance and compliance measures, incidents such as data breaches or unauthorized access can still occur. In such scenarios, organizations must have a well-defined and sustainable incident response and data breach management strategy in place to minimize the impact, mitigate risks, and ensure compliance with legal and regulatory requirements. A sustainable incident response and data breach management strategy encompasses a range of processes, tools, and best practices designed to effectively detect, respond to, and recover from data-related incidents while promoting continuous improvement and adapting to evolving threats and regulatory landscapes. Figure 8.4 depicts the approach to sustainable incident response and data breach management mechanisms.

- **Incident Detection and Monitoring:** (a) Implementing advanced security monitoring and incident detection mechanisms is crucial for promptly identifying potential data breaches or unauthorized access attempts. (b) These mechanisms may include intrusion detection systems, security information and event management solutions, and real-time monitoring of network traffic and user activities. (c) Continuous monitoring and correlation of security events can facilitate early detection of potential threats and minimize the potential impact of a data breach.
- **Incident Response Planning and Procedures:** (a) Organizations should establish clear incident response plans and procedures that outline the

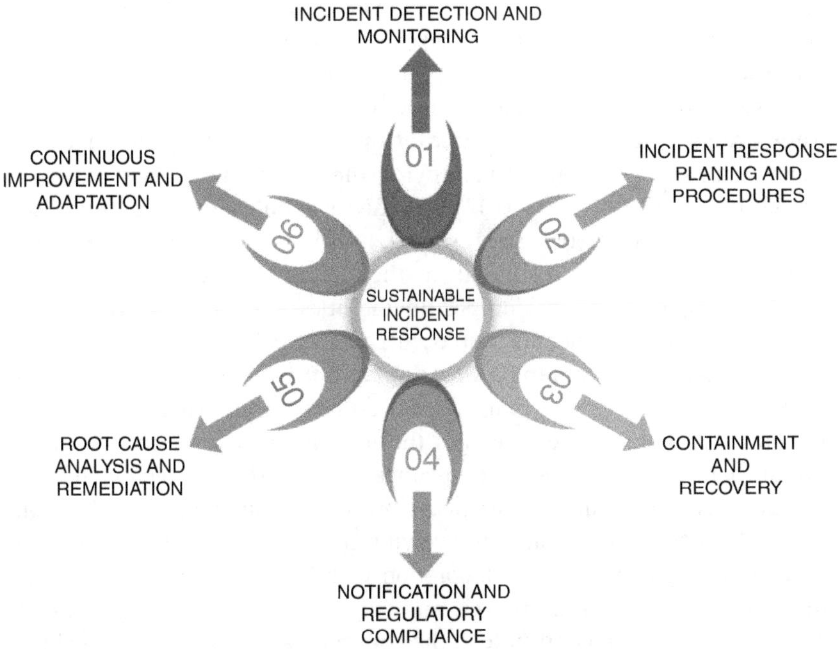

Figure 8.4 Sustainable incident response and data breach management.

specific steps to be taken in the event of a data breach or security incident. (b) These plans should define roles and responsibilities, communication channels, and escalation procedures to ensure a coordinated and efficient response. (c) Regular training and simulations can help ensure that incident response teams are prepared to respond effectively to various types of incidents.

- **Containment and Recovery:** (a) Implementing effective containment strategies is crucial for minimizing the spread of a data breach or security incident. (b) These strategies may involve isolating affected systems, disabling compromised accounts, or implementing temporary workarounds to limit further data exposure or system damage. (c) Recovery strategies should focus on restoring normal operations as quickly as possible, which may involve restoring data from backup systems or implementing alternative operational procedures.
- **Notification and Regulatory Compliance:** (a) Adhering to legal and regulatory requirements for notifying affected individuals, authorities, and relevant stakeholders in the event of a data breach is essential. (b) Organizations should maintain detailed documentation and evidence to

demonstrate compliance with notification obligations, as well as any remediation efforts undertaken. (c) Failure to comply with notification requirements can result in significant fines and legal consequences, as well as damage to the organization's reputation and consumer trust.

- **Root Cause Analysis and Remediation:** (a) Conducting thorough root cause analyses is crucial for identifying the underlying causes of a data breach or security incident. (b) This analysis should involve a multidisciplinary team with expertise in areas such as cybersecurity, data governance, and risk management. (c) Based on the findings, remediation measures should be implemented to address vulnerabilities, enhance security controls, and prevent similar incidents from occurring in the future.
- **Continuous Improvement and Adaptation:** (a) A sustainable incident response and data breach management strategy treats each incident as a learning opportunity and leverages the insights gained to strengthen the overall data governance and compliance framework. (b) Regular reviews and updates to incident response plans, procedures, and tools should be conducted to ensure alignment with evolving threats, regulatory changes, and industry best practices. (c) Collaboration with industry peers, participation in information-sharing initiatives, and staying abreast of emerging trends and technologies can contribute to the continuous improvement of incident response and data breach management capabilities.

By implementing a robust and sustainable incident response and data breach management strategy, organizations can effectively manage and mitigate the risks associated with data incidents while demonstrating their commitment to data protection, regulatory compliance, and responsible data stewardship. This proactive approach not only helps organizations minimize the potential damages and legal consequences of a data breach but also fosters consumer trust and maintains the organization's reputation as a responsible custodian of sensitive information.

8.6 Training and Awareness Programs for Ethical Use of Big Data

The ethical use of big data is a critical consideration that extends beyond technical implementations and legal compliance. Organizations must prioritize the development and implementation of comprehensive training and awareness programs to cultivate a culture of responsible data stewardship and ethical decision-making. Training and awareness programs should encompass various stakeholders, including data professionals, analysts, decision-makers, and general employees. These programs should aim to foster an understanding of the ethical implications of big data analytics, addressing topics such as data privacy, bias and fairness, transparency, and accountability. It is discussed in detail as follows:

- For data professionals and analysts, training should cover ethical principles and best practices for data collection, processing, and analysis. This includes understanding and mitigating potential biases in data sources, algorithms, and models, as well as recognizing and addressing ethical dilemmas that may arise during the data life cycle.
- Decision-makers and executives should receive training on the ethical implications of data-driven decision-making, highlighting the potential impacts on individuals, communities, and society at large. This training should also emphasize the importance of transparency and accountability in decision-making processes involving big data analytics.
- General employees should receive awareness training on data privacy, security, and ethical data handling practices. This training should cover topics such as the responsible use of data, the importance of data protection, and the potential consequences of data misuse or breaches.

Beyond formal training programs, organizations should foster an ongoing dialogue and encourage open discussions on ethical considerations surrounding big data analytics. This can be achieved through regular workshops, forums, or dedicated ethics committees that provide guidance and serve as a resource for addressing ethical concerns. Additionally, organizations should consider incorporating ethical principles and guidelines into their data governance frameworks, policies, and procedures. This can include establishing ethical review boards or incorporating ethical impact assessments as part of the big data analytics project life cycle.

By prioritizing training and awareness programs, organizations can cultivate a culture of ethical data stewardship, empowering individuals to make informed and responsible decisions when working with big data. This proactive approach not only mitigates risks but also fosters trust and accountability, ultimately contributing to the sustainable and responsible use of big data analytics.

8.7 Conclusion

In the dynamic landscape of big data analytics, where technological advancements intersect with ethical considerations, organizations must prioritize data governance, compliance, and sustainability. Ensuring data quality and integrity, adhering to regulatory frameworks, implementing auditing and compliance monitoring mechanisms, and establishing robust incident response and data breach management processes are imperative for mitigating risks and maintaining trust.

However, beyond technical and legal aspects, cultivating a culture of ethical data stewardship through comprehensive training and awareness programs is crucial. By equipping stakeholders with the knowledge and tools to navigate ethical dilemmas, organizations can foster responsible decision-making and contribute to the sustainable and responsible use of big data analytics. As the world becomes increasingly data-driven, the principles of data governance, compliance, and sustainability will continue to evolve, driven by technological advancements, regulatory changes, and societal expectations. Organizations that proactively embrace these principles and prioritize ethical practices will not only mitigate risks but also gain a competitive advantage by fostering trust, accountability, and responsible innovation.

The path forward requires a collaborative effort from all stakeholders, including policymakers, industry leaders, and the broader community. By working together and upholding the highest standards of data governance, compliance, and sustainability, we can unlock the transformative potential of big data analytics while preserving the ethical foundations of our data-driven society.

Practice Set

A Multiple Choice Questions (MCQ)

1 What is a primary focus of data governance in big data analytics?
- **a** Increasing data volume
- **b** Ensuring data quality and integrity
- **c** Simplifying data collection
- **d** Reducing data storage costs

2 Which regulatory framework aspect is essential for ensuring data compliance?
- **a** Data visualization techniques
- **b** Adherence to industry-specific regulations
- **c** Centralized data storage
- **d** Data compression methods

3 What is a key component of auditing and compliance monitoring mechanisms?
- **a** Data compression
- **b** Regular inspections and assessments
- **c** Enhanced data visualization
- **d** Increased data redundancy

4 What should organizations implement to manage data breaches sustainably?
  a High data redundancy
  b Robust incident response and data breach management processes
  c Simplified data collection methods
  d Centralized data processing

5 Why are training and awareness programs important in data governance?
  a To increase data storage capacity
  b To foster ethical data use and responsible decision-making
  c To simplify data analysis
  d To enhance data visualization

6 What does data quality and integrity ensure in big data analytics?
  a Increased data volume
  b Reliable and accurate data
  c Simplified data processing
  d Reduced data storage costs

7 Which mechanism helps ensure adherence to regulatory frameworks?
  a Data encryption
  b Auditing and compliance monitoring
  c Enhanced data visualization
  d Centralized data management

8 What is an important aspect of sustainable incident response?
  a Increasing data redundancy
  b Implementing effective data breach management processes
  c Simplifying data collection methods
  d Enhancing data visualization techniques

9 Which of the following is NOT a key element of ethical data stewardship?
  a Comprehensive training programs
  b Regular data audits
  c Ignoring regulatory compliance
  d Raising awareness of ethical dilemmas

10 What role do stakeholders play in data governance and compliance?
  a Ignoring ethical considerations
  b Collaborating to uphold data governance standards
  c Increasing data storage costs
  d Centralizing data management

B Fill-in-the-Blanks

11 Ensuring data __________ and integrity is crucial for mitigating risks in big data analytics.

12 Organizations must adhere to __________ frameworks to ensure compliance with industry regulations.

13 Robust incident response and data breach management processes are essential for __________ management.

14 Training and awareness programs are vital for promoting __________ data use and responsible decision-making.

15 A collaborative effort from stakeholders helps in upholding the highest standards of data __________ and compliance.

C Short Answer Questions

16 What are the key components of ensuring data quality and integrity in big data analytics?

17 How do auditing and compliance monitoring mechanisms contribute to regulatory adherence?

18 Describe the role of sustainable incident response in managing data breaches.

19 Why is it important to include training and awareness programs in data governance strategies?

20 What are the benefits of fostering a culture of ethical data stewardship in organizations?

D Long Answer Questions

21 Discuss the importance of data quality and integrity in maintaining trust and mitigating risks in big data analytics.

22 Analyze the role of regulatory frameworks in ensuring compliance and how organizations can effectively adhere to these regulations.

23 Evaluate the strategies for sustainable incident response and data breach management and their impact on data governance.

24 Examine the significance of training and awareness programs in promoting ethical use of big data and how they can be implemented effectively.

25 Explore the collaborative efforts required from various stakeholders to uphold high standards of data governance, compliance, and sustainability in a data-driven society.

Further Readings

Abraham, R., Schneider, J. and Vom Brocke, J., 2019. Data governance: a conceptual framework, structured review, and research agenda. *International Journal of Information Management*, 49, pp. 424–438.

Doyle, E., McGovern, D., McCarthy, S. and Perez-Alaniz, M., 2019. Compliance-innovation: a quality-based route to sustainability. *Journal of Cleaner Production*, 210, pp. 266–275.

Handoko, B.L., Riantono, I.E. and Gani, E., 2020. Importance and benefit of application of governance risk and compliance principle. *Systematic Reviews in Pharmacy*, 11(9), pp. 510–513.

Janssen, M., Brous, P., Estevez, E., Barbosa, L.S. and Janowski, T., 2020. Data governance: organizing data for trustworthy Artificial Intelligence. *Government Information Quarterly*, 37(3), p. 101493.

Johannsen, A., Kant, D. and Creutzburg, R., 2020. Measuring IT security, compliance and data governance within small and medium-sized IT enterprises. *Electronic Imaging*, 32, pp. 1–11.

Kaddoura, S. and Grati, R., 2021. Blockchain for healthcare and medical systems. In: *Enabling Blockchain Technology for Secure Networking and Communications*, pp. 249–270. IGI Global.

Kumari, A., Golyan, A., Shah, R. and Raval, N., 2024. Introduction to data analytics. In: A. Kumari (Ed.), *Recent Trends and Future Direction for Data Analytics*, pp. 1–14. IGI Global.

Kumari, A., Tanwar, S. and Kumar, N., 2024. Artificial neural network-driven federated learning for heart stroke prediction in healthcare 4.0 underlying 5G. *Concurrency and Computation: Practice and Experience*, 36(3), p. e7911.

Ladley, J., 2019. *Data Governance: How to Design, Deploy, and Sustain an Effective Data Governance Program*. Academic Press.

Makaš, A., 2023. Governance, risk and compliance frameworks applicability in the organizations. *International Journal of Science and Research Archive*, 10(2), pp. 716–724.

Makowicz, B., 2023. Compliance and integrity as core elements of governance in the educational sector in the digital age. In: *The Future of Responsible Management Education: University Leadership and the Digital Transformation Challenge*, pp. 153–171. Cham: Springer International Publishing.

Oguejiofor, B.B., Omotosho, A., Abioye, K.M., Alabi, A.M., Oguntoyinbo, F.N., Daraojimba, A.I. and Daraojimba, C., 2023. A review on data-driven regulatory compliance in Nigeria. *International Journal of Applied Research in Social Sciences*, 5(8), pp. 231–243.

Prokofieva, M. and Miah, S.J., 2019. Blockchain in healthcare [Online]. *Australasian Journal of Information Systems*, 23.

Solaimani, S., 2024. From compliance to capability: on the role of data and technology in environment, social, and governance. *Sustainability*, 16(14), p. 6061.

Vojvodic, M. and Hitz, C., 2019. Governance team leadership and business user participation: organizational practices for innovative customer engagement in data compliance project. *Central European Business Review*, 8(2), pp. 15–45.

Vojvodic, M. and Hitz, C., 2022. Relation of data governance, customer-centricity and data processing compliance. *Central European Business Review*, 11(5), pp. 109–148.

9

The Role of Big Data in Scientific Research

LEARNING OBJECTIVES

- Understand how big data and advanced analytics support scientific discovery across data-intensive research domains.
- Examine the role of large-scale datasets, including genomic data, in enabling deeper scientific analysis and insight.
- Explore the use of high-performance computing and scientific simulations for handling complex and computation-heavy research tasks.
- Recognize the importance of data sharing and collaboration in large, global scientific research initiatives.
- Analyze sustainability challenges in big data research, with emphasis on responsible data management and long-term research practices.

9.1 Introduction

Scientific research has entered a phase where data plays a central role in shaping discovery and innovation. Advances in data collection technologies, sensors, and digital platforms have enabled researchers to generate and access vast amounts of information across disciplines. From biological sciences and climate studies to physics and social research, the ability to analyze large datasets has expanded the scope and depth of scientific inquiry. As a result, research questions that were once limited by data availability or computational capacity can now be explored with greater precision. The increasing reliance on data-intensive methods has also transformed how research is conducted. Techniques such as genomic analysis, large-scale simulations, and predictive modeling depend heavily on advanced computing infrastructures and efficient data management practices. High-performance computing (HPC) has become essential for processing complex datasets and running simulations that support hypothesis testing and scientific validation. At the same time, collaboration among researchers and institutions has grown, with shared datasets and global research initiatives becoming more common. Despite these advances, the use of big data in scientific research raises important concerns related to sustainability, ethical responsibility, and long-term data stewardship. Managing computational resources efficiently, ensuring responsible data sharing, and maintaining research integrity are now integral parts of the scientific process. Addressing these challenges is essential to ensure that big data continues to support meaningful and responsible scientific progress.

With the exponential growth in data generation, researchers now have access to vast datasets that can be analyzed to uncover patterns, correlations, and trends that were previously unimaginable. This chapter delves into the transformative role of big data in scientific research, examining its impact on advancing scientific discovery, data-intensive research fields, genomic data analysis, HPC, data collaboration, sustainability considerations, and real-world case studies.

9.1.1 Motivation

The increasing use of large and complex datasets has changed the way scientific research is carried out across disciplines. Researchers now rely on data-intensive methods to explore complex problems that cannot be addressed through traditional approaches alone. At the same time, challenges related to computational demands, data sharing, and long-term sustainability have become more visible. These developments motivate a focused discussion on how big data, advanced computing, and collaborative research practices together support scientific discovery.

9.1.2 Chapter Contributions

This chapter makes the following key contributions:

- This chapter provides an overview of how big data enables data-driven scientific research across multiple domains. It highlights the growing role of large datasets in shaping modern scientific inquiry in genomic data analysis as well.
- It discusses the role of HPC and simulations in handling large-scale scientific workloads. These technologies allow researchers to tackle complex problems faster and more efficiently.
- Further, it examines collaborative research models and shared data infrastructures in global scientific projects. It reflects how cooperation and open data sharing are becoming central to major scientific advancements.
- The chapter provides case studies of how big data and computational methods are applied in real scientific projects. These cases illustrate both challenges and successful strategies in data-driven research.

9.1.3 Organization of the Chapter

The rest of the chapter is organized as follows:

Sections 9.2 and 9.3 highlight the advancing scientific discovery, data-intensive scientific research, and its growing importance. Next, Section 9.4 discusses key application areas, including genomic analysis. Section 9.5 presents the large-scale simulations architecture supported by HPC. The role of data collaboration in global research initiatives is examined in Section 9.6. Then, the chapter addresses sustainability issues and presents real-world case studies to illustrate practical applications of big data analytics. The last chapter concludes with final thoughts.

9.2 Advancing Scientific Discovery

Big data has emerged as a powerful catalyst for scientific discovery, empowering researchers to ask more profound questions and explore previously uncharted territories. By leveraging the immense volume, variety, and velocity of data, scientists can uncover intricate patterns, correlations, and insights that were previously inaccessible or computationally intractable. This data-driven approach has led to breakthroughs in fields ranging from particle physics and astronomy to biology and climate science. One of the key advantages of big data in scientific research is its ability to facilitate data-intensive exploration and hypothesis testing. Researchers can analyze vast datasets, simulate complex systems, and validate theoretical models with unprecedented accuracy and precision. This allows for more rigorous and comprehensive testing of scientific hypotheses, leading to more robust and reliable findings. Moreover, big data analytics enables the integration of diverse data sources, fostering interdisciplinary collaborations and the synthesis of knowledge across scientific domains. By combining and analyzing data from multiple disciplines, researchers can gain a more holistic understanding of complex phenomena and uncover previously unrecognized connections and relationships. For instance, in the field of biology, researchers can integrate genomic data with data from proteomics, metabolomics, and environmental factors to gain a systems-level understanding of biological processes and disease mechanisms. This integration of diverse data sources has the potential to revolutionize fields such as personalized medicine, drug discovery, and ecological studies.

Another significant advantage of big data in scientific discovery is its ability to uncover patterns and correlations that may be imperceptible to human observers or traditional analytical methods. Advanced machine learning algorithms and data mining techniques can sift through massive datasets, identifying subtle patterns and extracting valuable insights that would otherwise remain hidden. For example, in the field of astronomy, big data analytics has enabled researchers to analyze vast amounts of telescope data and identify previously undetected celestial objects, such as exoplanets or distant galaxies. Similarly, in particle physics, the analysis of massive datasets generated by particle accelerators has led to the discovery of new subatomic particles and insights into the fundamental nature of matter and energy. Furthermore, big data analytics plays a crucial role in scientific simulations and modeling, enabling researchers to recreate complex systems and phenomena in silico. By leveraging HPC resources and big data technologies, scientists can perform computationally intensive simulations, such as modeling molecular dynamics, simulating climate patterns, or reconstructing the evolution of the universe. These simulations generate massive amounts of data, which can be analyzed and interpreted using advanced data analytics techniques, leading to new insights and a deeper understanding of the underlying processes. However, it is important to note that the advancement of scientific discovery through big data is not without challenges. Data quality, bias, and reproducibility are critical considerations that must be addressed. Robust data management practices, standardization, and rigorous validation processes are essential to ensure the reliability and integrity of scientific findings derived from big data analysis.

Additionally, ethical considerations, such as data privacy and responsible data use, must be carefully navigated, particularly in fields involving sensitive personal data or data with potential societal implications.

9.3 Data-intensive Research Fields

Certain scientific disciplines have become particularly data-intensive, as shown in Figure 9.1. These fields are at the forefront of big data adoption and are leveraging advanced data analytics techniques to unravel complex phenomena and push the boundaries of scientific knowledge. The scientific disciplines are discussed as follows:

1. **Astronomy and Astrophysics:** Modern astronomical research is heavily reliant on vast amounts of data generated by telescopes, satellites, and other observational instruments. The advent of advanced telescopes and detectors, such as the Hubble Space Telescope, the James Webb Space Telescope, and the Atacama Large Millimeter/submillimeter Array, has led to an unprecedented deluge of data capturing intricate details of celestial bodies, galaxies, and cosmic phenomena. Astronomers and astrophysicists utilize big data analytics techniques to process and analyze these massive datasets, allowing them to study the formation and evolution of stars, galaxies, and the universe itself. Advanced algorithms and machine learning models are employed to identify patterns, classify celestial objects, and extract meaningful insights from the vast repositories of observational data.

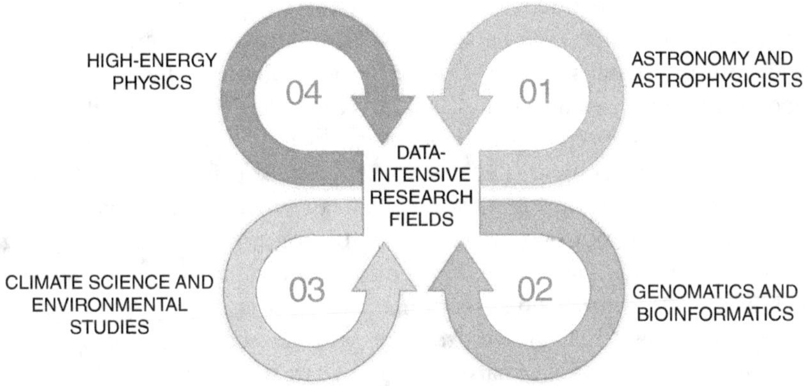

Figure 9.1 Research fields that are data-intensive.

2. **Genomics and Bioinformatics:** The field of genomics has been revolutionized by high-throughput sequencing technologies, which have enabled researchers to sequence entire genomes rapidly and cost-effectively. This has led to the generation of vast amounts of genomic data, encompassing DNA sequences, gene expressions, and other molecular information. Bioinformatics, which combines biology, computer science, and data analytics, plays a crucial role in analyzing and interpreting this deluge of genomic data. Advanced computational techniques, such as sequence alignment algorithms, gene expression analysis, and phylogenetic analysis, are employed to identify genetic variations, classify gene expressions, and uncover complex patterns and associations between genetic factors and phenotypic traits. The integration of genomic data with other omics data (such as transcriptomics, proteomics, and metabolomics) provides a comprehensive systems-level understanding of biological processes, diseases, and evolutionary mechanisms.
3. **Climate Science and Environmental Studies:** Climate science and environmental studies rely heavily on big data generated from a variety of sources, including Earth observation satellites, remote sensing devices, ground-based sensor networks, and weather monitoring stations. These data sources capture a wide range of environmental parameters, such as atmospheric conditions, weather patterns, ocean currents, and ecosystem dynamics. Big data analytics plays a crucial role in processing and analyzing this vast amount of environmental data. Climate scientists utilize advanced computational models and simulations to study climate patterns, predict future scenarios, and develop mitigation strategies for environmental challenges such as climate change, air pollution, and ecosystem degradation. Machine learning algorithms and data mining techniques are employed to identify patterns and correlations

within the massive datasets, enabling researchers to gain insights into complex environmental processes and their interactions with human activities.

4. **High-energy Physics:** The field of high-energy physics, which studies the fundamental particles and forces that govern the universe, generates massive amounts of data from particle accelerators and detectors. Facilities like the Large Hadron Collider (LHC) at CERN produce petabytes of data from particle collisions, capturing intricate details of subatomic interactions. Big data analytics and HPC resources are essential for processing and analyzing this deluge of data. Physicists employ advanced computational techniques, such as event reconstruction algorithms and particle tracking methods, to extract meaningful information from the vast datasets generated by these experiments. The analysis of particle collision data has led to groundbreaking discoveries, such as the detection of the Higgs boson particle, which has profound implications for our understanding of the fundamental building blocks of the universe.

These data-intensive research fields demand robust big data technologies, advanced analytical techniques, and substantial computational resources to extract meaningful insights from the vast amounts of data generated. Collaboration between domain experts, data scientists, and computational specialists is crucial for driving scientific discoveries and advancements in these fields. Furthermore, the integration of big data analytics with other emerging technologies, such as artificial intelligence (AI), Internet of Things (IoT), and HPC, is enabling new frontiers of data-driven research and facilitating interdisciplinary collaborations across scientific domains.

9.4 Genomic Data Analysis

The field of genomics has experienced a remarkable transformation with the advent of high-throughput sequencing technologies, enabling researchers to sequence entire genomes rapidly and cost-effectively. This technological advancement has led to an unprecedented deluge of genomic data, unlocking new frontiers in biological research and paving the way for groundbreaking discoveries in fields such as personalized medicine, disease prevention, and evolutionary studies. Genomic data analysis involves the study and interpretation of genetic information encoded in deoxyribonucleic acid (DNA) and ribonucleic acid (RNA) molecules. This data encompasses the complete set of genes and their sequences, as well as regulatory regions and other functional elements that govern the expression and regulation of these genes. The sheer volume and complexity of genomic data pose significant challenges, necessitating the development and application of advanced big data analytics techniques. Figure 9.2 illustrates the genomic data analysis pipeline in detail.

The figure illustrates the *genomic data analysis pipeline*, a structured workflow that converts raw biological samples into meaningful scientific and medical insights.

- **Data Generation:** The process starts with a variety of biological sources, including humans, plants, and microbes. DNA or RNA is extracted from these samples and processed through sequencing and alignment to create a comprehensive digital map of the genome.
- **Specialized Analysis:** From there, the workflow splits into two main paths. Variant discovery focuses on identifying mutations and genotypes within the DNA, while gene expression analysis uses RNA-SEQ to determine which genes are actively expressed under different conditions.

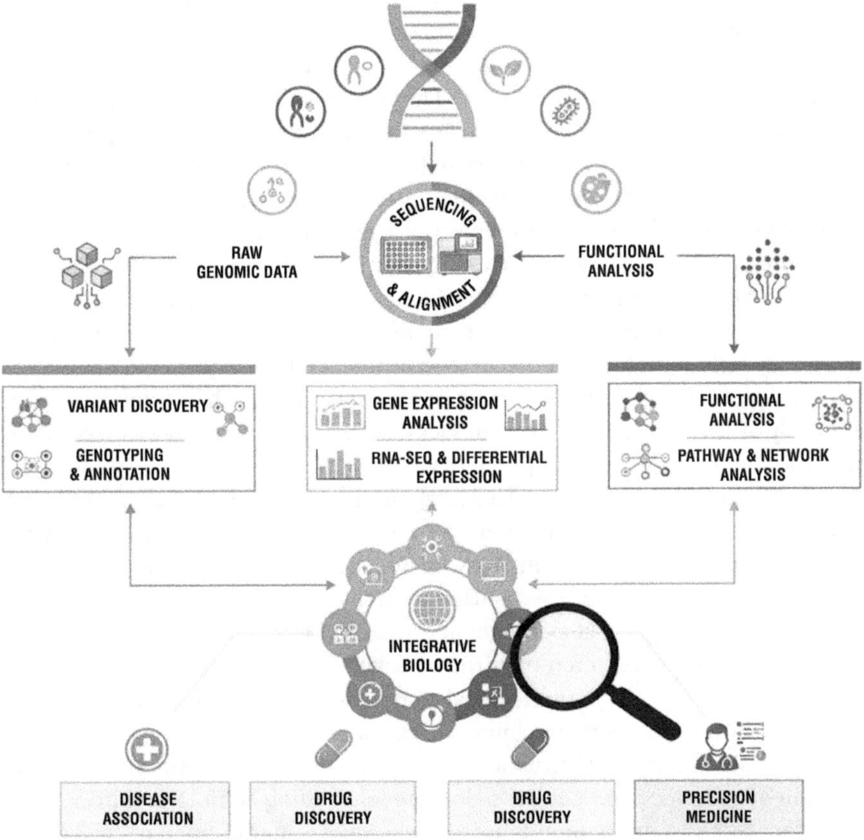

Figure 9.2 Genomic data analysis pipeline.

- **Biological Context:** The results are then interpreted through functional analysis, where variants are mapped to biological pathways and networks to understand their potential effects on health and disease.
- **Real-World Application:** Finally, the pipeline leads to integrative biology approaches, enabling discoveries in disease associations, drug development, and precision medicine that can be tailored to an individual's unique genetic makeup.

One of the primary goals of genomic data analysis is to identify genetic variations, such as single-nucleotide polymorphisms, insertions, deletions, and structural variations, and understand their implications for health, disease susceptibility, and evolutionary processes. By analyzing and comparing genomic data from different individuals, populations, or species, researchers can uncover patterns and associations between genetic variations and specific traits or phenotypes. Bioinformatics, a field that combines biology, computer science, and data analytics, plays a crucial role in genomic data analysis. Computational tools and algorithms are employed to process and analyze the vast amounts of genomic data generated by sequencing technologies. These tools include sequence alignment algorithms, which align and compare DNA or RNA sequences, gene prediction and annotation methods, and phylogenetic analysis techniques to study evolutionary relationships. Machine learning AI techniques have also become indispensable in genomic data analysis. These techniques can be used for tasks such as gene expression analysis, where machine learning models are trained to identify patterns and classify gene expression profiles based on genomic data. Additionally, deep learning algorithms have shown promise in tasks such as variant calling, where they can accurately identify genetic variations from sequencing data.

The integration of genomic data with other omics data, such as transcriptomics (the study of RNA transcripts), proteomics (the study of proteins), and metabolomics (the study of metabolites), provides a more comprehensive understanding of biological systems and processes. This integration enables researchers to study the intricate relationships between genotypes (genetic information) and phenotypes (observable traits), shedding light on the complex mechanisms underlying health, disease, and evolutionary processes. However, the analysis of genomic data presents unique challenges. Data storage and management are crucial, as genomic datasets can be massive, often requiring specialized data storage and processing infrastructures. Data privacy and ethical considerations are also paramount when working with sensitive genomic information, as genetic data can reveal personal and potentially sensitive information about individuals. Furthermore, the interpretation of genomic data requires a deep understanding of biological principles, statistical methods, and computational techniques. Interdisciplinary collaborations between geneticists, bioinformaticians, data scientists, and domain experts are essential for extracting meaningful insights from genomic data and translating these insights into practical applications.

In summary, genomic data analysis has revolutionized our understanding of the genetic underpinnings of life, enabling groundbreaking discoveries in fields such as personalized medicine, disease prevention, and evolutionary studies. By leveraging big data analytics techniques, bioinformatics tools, and interdisciplinary collaborations, researchers are unlocking the secrets encoded in our genomes, paving the way for a better understanding of biological processes and the development of more effective and targeted interventions.

9.5 HPC and Scientific Simulations

Much scientific research, particularly that involving complex simulations and modeling, requires immense computational power and HPC resources. HPC systems are designed to handle computationally intensive tasks that are beyond the capabilities of conventional computing systems, enabling researchers to tackle grand challenge problems and advance scientific discovery. In the context of big data analytics in scientific research, HPC plays a crucial role in processing and analyzing vast datasets, as well as performing complex simulations and modeling. The ability to process and analyze massive amounts of data often necessitates the use of supercomputers, distributed computing systems, and specialized hardware accelerators. Scientific simulations are computational models that represent and mimic real-world phenomena or systems, allowing researchers to study their behavior and dynamics under various conditions. These simulations can range from modeling molecular dynamics and chemical reactions at the atomic level to simulating the formation and evolution of galaxies on a cosmic scale.

Figure 9.3 presents a detailed architecture of an HPC system that comprises various stages in big data analysis: end users submit computational tasks through a user interface, which are managed by the job scheduler and distributed across multiple compute nodes equipped with CPUs/graphics processing units (GPUs) and memory. Data is accessed from high-speed storage through an interconnect network, and the processed results are retrieved and presented as output in the form of reports or documents. This workflow demonstrates how HPC systems handle large-scale data and complex computations efficiently. HPC systems enable researchers to perform computationally intensive simulations that would be impossible or impractical on traditional computing systems. For example, in the field of physics, simulations of particle collisions or the evolution of the universe require processing power on an unprecedented scale.

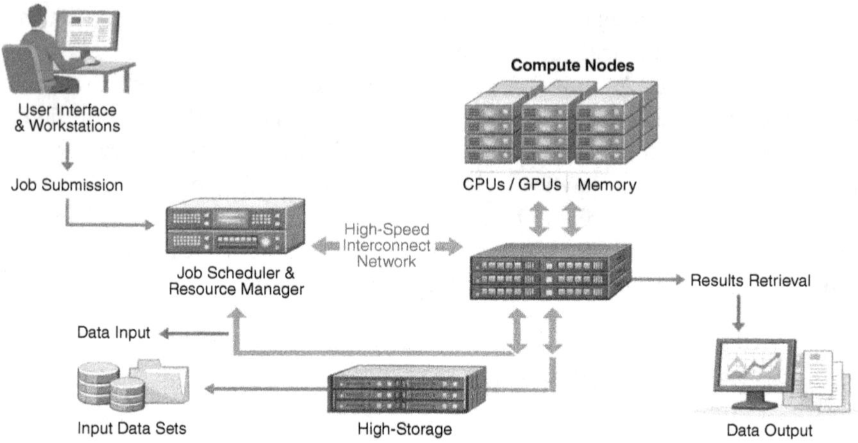

Figure 9.3 Architecture of the HPC system.

Similarly, in climate science, complex models that simulate atmospheric and oceanic processes demand significant computational resources to capture the intricate details and dynamics involved. It is useful for real-time data processing and analysis during simulations. This capability enables researchers to observe and analyze simulations as they unfold, facilitating adaptive simulations where parameters can be adjusted dynamically based on the insights gained from the analysis. This iterative process leads to more accurate and efficient modeling processes, as well as the potential for new discoveries and insights. HPC systems come in various architectures, ranging from traditional supercomputers with tightly coupled processors to distributed computing systems that harness the power of multiple interconnected nodes or clusters. Additionally, specialized hardware accelerators, such as GPUs and field-programmable gate arrays (FPGAs), are increasingly being employed to accelerate specific computational tasks in scientific simulations and data analysis. However, harnessing the full potential of HPC for big data analytics in scientific research presents several challenges. These include the complexity of programming and optimizing code for parallel and distributed computing environments, managing and analyzing the vast amounts of data generated by simulations, and addressing issues related to data movement and storage.

To address these challenges, researchers often rely on advanced software tools and libraries designed specifically for HPC environments. These tools enable efficient parallelization of computational tasks, facilitate data management and movement, and provide optimized algorithms and libraries for various scientific domains. Furthermore, the increasing adoption of cloud computing and the availability of HPC resources as a service have made HPC more accessible to researchers, enabling collaborations and the sharing of computational resources across institutions and geographic boundaries. In summary, HPC and scientific simulations are essential components of big data analytics in scientific research. HPC systems provide the computational power necessary to process and analyze massive datasets, while simulations enable researchers to model and study complex phenomena across various scientific domains. The integration of big data analytics with HPC systems facilitates real-time data processing, adaptive simulations, and the potential for groundbreaking discoveries. As computational demands continue to grow, the role of HPC and advanced simulation techniques will become increasingly pivotal in driving scientific progress and unlocking new frontiers of knowledge.

9.6 Data Collaboration in Global Scientific Projects

Scientific research has increasingly become a collaborative endeavor, with researchers from diverse institutions and geographical locations working together on global projects. Big data plays a pivotal role in facilitating this collaboration by enabling the sharing, integration, and analysis of data from multiple sources across the globe. Large-scale scientific projects, such as the Human Genome Project, the International Space Station, the Square Kilometer Array (SKA), and the Intergovernmental Panel on Climate Change (IPCC), involve researchers from around the world contributing data and expertise. These global initiatives aim to tackle complex scientific challenges that require a collective effort and the integration of diverse perspectives, resources, and datasets.

Effective data management, standardization, and interoperability are crucial for seamless collaboration and knowledge sharing across these global projects. Big data technologies, including distributed data storage systems, cloud computing platforms, and secure data transfer protocols, enable researchers to access and analyze data from remote locations, transcending geographical boundaries. One of the key challenges in global scientific collaborations is the heterogeneity of data sources and formats. Different research groups may use varying data collection methods, instruments, and data formats, making it difficult to integrate and analyze data from multiple sources. To address this challenge, collaborative efforts focus on establishing common data standards, metadata protocols, and data harmonization techniques. For example, in the field of genomics, the Global Alliance for Genomics and Health has developed standards and frameworks for responsible genomic data sharing and interoperability, enabling researchers from different institutions and countries to contribute and access genomic data securely.

Collaborative data analysis tools and virtual research environments provide platforms for researchers to share data, collaborate on analyses, and disseminate their findings. These tools often incorporate features such as secure data repositories, collaborative workspaces, and analytical pipelines tailored to specific scientific domains. For instance, the European Open Science Cloud initiative aims to create a virtual environment for researchers to access and process publicly funded research data across various disciplines, fostering cross-border and interdisciplinary collaboration. However, data collaboration in global scientific projects also presents challenges related to data governance, privacy, and intellectual property rights. Establishing robust data governance frameworks, adhering to ethical guidelines, and ensuring data security and sovereignty are essential for fostering trust and enabling effective global collaboration. Issues such as data ownership, access rights, and benefit-sharing agreements must be carefully navigated, particularly when dealing with sensitive data or research involving indigenous communities or vulnerable populations. International guidelines and frameworks, such as the Findable, Accessible, Interoperable, and Reusable principles and the Global Code of Conduct for Research in Resource-Poor Settings, provide guidance on responsible data sharing and ethical practices in global research collaborations. Furthermore, legal and regulatory considerations, such as data protection laws and export control regulations, must be addressed to ensure compliance and facilitate cross-border data sharing and analysis.

In summary, data collaboration in global scientific projects is crucial for advancing scientific discovery and addressing complex challenges that transcend geographical boundaries. By leveraging big data technologies, establishing common data standards, and fostering collaborative platforms and virtual research environments, researchers can seamlessly share, integrate, and analyze data from diverse sources. However, effective global collaboration requires addressing challenges related to data governance, privacy, ethics, and legal frameworks, ultimately enabling responsible and equitable collaboration in the pursuit of scientific knowledge.

9.7 Sustainability Considerations in Big Data Research

As the volume of data generated in scientific research continues to grow exponentially, sustainability considerations have become increasingly important. The storage, processing, and analysis of massive datasets associated with big data research can have significant environmental impacts, necessitating a conscious effort to mitigate these effects and ensure the long-term viability of data-intensive research. Figure 9.4 illustrates sustainability consideration in big data research. The energy consumption and carbon footprint associated with big data storage and processing are major sustainability concerns. Data centers, HPC facilities,

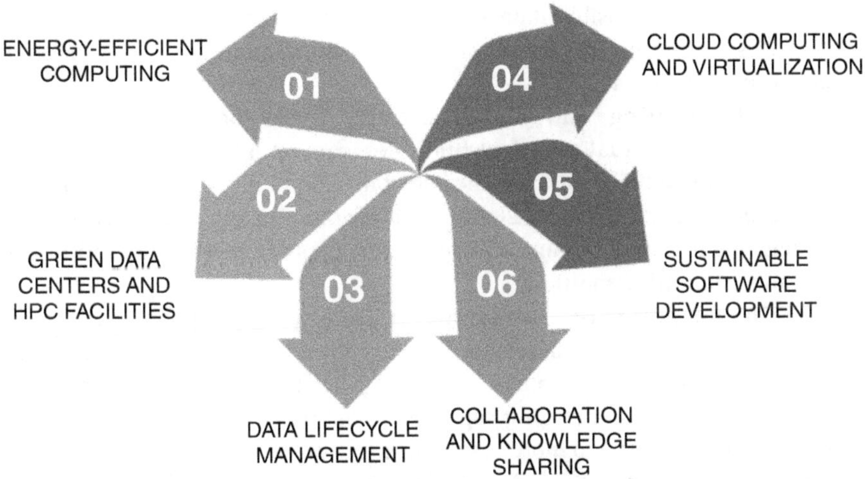

Figure 9.4 Sustainability consideration in big data research.

and cloud computing infrastructures required for big data research consume substantial amounts of energy for powering servers, cooling systems, and supporting infrastructure. This energy consumption not only has direct environmental implications but also contributes to greenhouse gas emissions and climate change. Furthermore, the rapid growth of data volumes necessitates the continuous expansion of storage and computing infrastructure, which can strain natural resources and contribute to electronic waste (e-waste) if not managed responsibly.

To address these sustainability challenges, organizations and research institutions are exploring and implementing various sustainable practices and technologies:

1. **Energy-efficient Computing:** Leveraging energy-efficient hardware, such as low-power processors, accelerators (e.g., GPUs, FPGAs), and specialized energy-optimized chips, can significantly reduce the energy consumption of big data analytics and HPC systems. Additionally, techniques like dynamic voltage and frequency scaling and power-aware scheduling can further optimize energy usage.
2. **Green Data Centers and HPC Facilities:** Implementing sustainable data center designs, utilizing renewable energy sources (e.g., solar, wind), and optimizing cooling systems through efficient heat management and free-air cooling can contribute to reducing the carbon footprint of large-scale data storage and processing facilities.
3. **Data Life Cycle Management:** Adopting effective data life cycle management strategies, including data compression, deduplication, and archiving, can reduce storage requirements and associated energy costs.

Additionally, responsible data retention policies and secure data deletion practices can minimize unnecessary data accumulation and the associated environmental impact.

4. **Cloud Computing and Virtualization:** Leveraging cloud computing resources and virtualization technologies can optimize resource utilization and reduce the need for dedicated computing infrastructure, leading to improved energy efficiency. Cloud providers often employ advanced energy management techniques and leverage economies of scale to offer more sustainable computing solutions.
5. **Sustainable Software Development:** Developing energy-efficient software algorithms and codes optimized for specific hardware architectures can significantly reduce computational overhead and energy consumption. Techniques like code profiling, algorithmic optimizations, and parallel computing can contribute to more sustainable software solutions.
6. **Collaboration and Knowledge Sharing:** Fostering collaboration and knowledge sharing among researchers, organizations, and industry partners can accelerate the development and adoption of sustainable practices in big data research. Shared best practices, open-source solutions, and collaborative efforts can drive innovation and promote environmental responsibility.

In addition to technological solutions, sustainability considerations in big data research involve addressing broader societal and ethical implications. Researchers must carefully evaluate the potential environmental impacts of their research projects, weighing the scientific benefits against the associated environmental costs. Engaging with stakeholders, policymakers, and the public can help shape responsible and sustainable big data research practices. Furthermore, educational and awareness programs play a crucial role in promoting sustainability in the scientific community. Training researchers, data scientists, and IT professionals on sustainable computing practices, energy-efficient techniques, and responsible data management can foster a culture of environmental consciousness in big data research.

By embracing sustainable practices and technologies, scientific research organizations can not only mitigate the environmental impacts of big data research but also contribute to the broader global efforts toward a more sustainable future. Striking a balance between scientific progress and environmental responsibility is essential for ensuring the long-term viability and ethical conduct of data-intensive research.

9.8 Real-world Case Studies

To illustrate the profound impact of big data in scientific research, it is valuable to explore real-world case studies that demonstrate the transformative power of data-driven approaches across diverse scientific domains. These case studies showcase how the integration of big data analytics, advanced computational resources, and interdisciplinary collaborations has led to groundbreaking discoveries and advancements in our understanding of the natural world, which is discussed as follows:

Case Study I

The Higgs Boson Discovery: The LHC at CERN (European Council for Nuclear Research), one of the largest and most complex scientific instruments ever built, has been at the forefront of big data research in particle physics. LHC produces millions of collisions every second in each detector, generating approximately *one petabyte of data per second*. None of today's computing systems is capable of recording such rates, so sophisticated selection systems are used for a first fast electronic preselection, only passing one out of 10 000 events. To analyze this deluge of data, CERN employed state-of-the-art big data technologies, distributed computing systems, and advanced data analytics techniques. Hence, the Worldwide LHC Computing Grid (WLCG) was introduced by CERN to provide global computing resources for the storage, distribution, and analysis of the data generated by the LHC. WLCG combines about 1.4 million computer cores and 1.5 exabytes of storage from over 170 sites in 42 countries.

This massive distributed computing infrastructure provides more than 12 000 physicists around the world with near real-time access to LHC data, and the power to process it. The collaborative effort of thousands of researchers from around the world, working together to analyze the LHC data, led to the historic discovery of the Higgs boson particle in 2012. This discovery not only confirmed a key prediction of the Standard Model of particle physics but also provided crucial insights into the fundamental building blocks of the universe and the nature of mass.

Case Study II

The Human Genome Project: The Human Genome Project, an international collaborative effort spanning over a decade, aimed to sequence the entire human genome and map all the genes within it. This ambitious project generated vast amounts of genomic data, necessitating the development of sophisticated *bioinformatics* tools and big data analytics techniques. By leveraging HPC resources, distributed data storage systems, and advanced algorithms for sequence alignment and analysis, researchers were able to process and interpret the deluge of genomic data. Today, we can sequence a genome in under 24 hours, directly leading to the *Precision Medicine* as well. The successful completion of the project in 2003 not only provided a comprehensive map of the human genome but also paved the way for groundbreaking advances in fields such as personalized medicine, genetic disease research, and evolutionary biology.

Case Study III

Climate Change Modeling and Prediction: Climate science is a data-intensive field that relies heavily on big data analytics to study and model the complex interactions between various environmental factors, such as atmospheric conditions, ocean currents, and land-use patterns. The IPCC has played a pivotal role in coordinating and synthesizing climate data from various sources to assess the scientific evidence for climate change and its potential impacts. By utilizing advanced computational models, simulations, and machine learning techniques, climate scientists can process and analyze massive datasets from Earth observation satellites, weather stations, and environmental monitoring systems. These analyses have provided critical insights into climate patterns, enabling researchers to predict future climate scenarios, assess the impacts of human activities, and develop mitigation strategies to address the challenges of climate change.

Case Study IV

The SKA Project: The SKA is an ambitious international project aimed at building the world's largest radio telescope, with an unprecedented collecting area of 1 square kilometer. This groundbreaking telescope will generate an unprecedented amount of data, estimated to be in the exabyte range (1 quintillion bytes) per day. To handle and process this massive data deluge, the SKA project is developing cutting-edge big data technologies, including HPC facilities, distributed data storage systems, and advanced data analytics pipelines. By leveraging these technologies, astronomers and astrophysicists will be able to study the formation and evolution of galaxies, detect faint radio signals from the early universe, and potentially uncover new insights into the nature of dark matter and dark energy.

These real-world case studies exemplify the transformative power of big data in scientific research, showcasing how data-driven approaches have led to groundbreaking discoveries and advancements across various disciplines. From unraveling the mysteries of the universe to decoding the human genome and from modeling complex climate systems to pushing the boundaries of astronomical observations, big data analytics has become an indispensable tool for scientific exploration and knowledge generation. As data continues to grow in volume, velocity, and complexity, the role of big data in scientific research will become increasingly pivotal. Collaboration among researchers, data scientists, and computational experts, coupled with continued advancements in data technologies and analytical techniques, will be key to unlocking new frontiers of scientific discovery and driving progress in our understanding of the natural world.

9.9 Conclusion

Big data technologies have revolutionized scientific research by enabling researchers to process and analyze vast amounts of data from various sources. This data-driven approach has accelerated scientific discoveries, fostered interdisciplinary collaborations, and opened new avenues for exploring complex phenomena across diverse fields. The role of big data in scientific research is multifaceted, ranging from genomic data analysis to HPC simulations and global data collaborations. As we continue to generate and collect more data, it becomes increasingly important to develop efficient and sustainable methods for data management, analysis, and interpretation. By leveraging the power of big data analytics, AI, and emerging technologies like the IoT and blockchain, researchers can gain deeper insights, uncover hidden patterns, and drive innovation in their respective domains. Ultimately, the responsible and ethical application of big data in scientific research holds the potential to address pressing global challenges and advance human knowledge.

Practice Set

A Multiple Choice Questions (MCQ)

1 How has big data technology transformed scientific research?
   a By reducing data collection methods
   b By enabling the processing and analysis of vast amounts of data
   c By simplifying laboratory experiments
   d By limiting data sources

2 What is one significant application of big data in genomic research?
   a Enhancing laboratory equipment
   b Analyzing large-scale genomic data
   c Simplifying scientific simulations
   d Reducing data redundancy

3 Which technology is crucial for conducting large-scale scientific simulations?
   a High-performance computing (HPC)
   b Blockchain
   c Explainable AI (XAI)
   d Edge computing

4 What role does data collaboration play in global scientific projects?
   a It centralizes data processing.
   b It fosters interdisciplinary research and shared insights.
   c It reduces the need for data security.
   d It limits data access.

5 What is a key consideration for sustainability in big data research?
   a Increasing data collection rates
   b Developing efficient and sustainable data management methods
   c Centralizing data storage
   d Reducing data analysis complexity

6 Which field benefits significantly from high-performance computing (HPC) for simulations?
   a Genomic data analysis
   b Environmental sustainability
   c Scientific simulations
   d Data visualization

7 How does big data facilitate advancements in scientific discovery?
   a By limiting data sources
   b By uncovering hidden patterns and insights
   c By reducing computational power
   d By simplifying data collection

8 What is one benefit of leveraging artificial intelligence in scientific research?
   a Reducing data volume
   b Enhancing data analysis and pattern recognition
   c Simplifying data management
   d Increasing data redundancy

9 What is the importance of interdisciplinary collaboration in big data research?
   a It centralized data management.
   b It promotes shared insights and diverse perspectives.

c It limits data access.
d It simplifies data collection methods.

10 Which emerging technology can enhance data management and interpretation in scientific research?
a Blockchain
b Traditional data processing methods
c Simplified data storage
d Centralized data analysis

B Fill-in-the-Blanks

11 Big data technologies have accelerated scientific discoveries by enabling the analysis of __________ amounts of data from various sources.

12 In scientific research, __________ computing is crucial for conducting large-scale simulations.

13 Efficient and sustainable methods for data __________ and interpretation are essential for managing the growing volume of research data.

14 Data collaboration in global scientific projects fosters __________ research and shared insights.

15 The responsible application of big data in research can address pressing __________ challenges and advance human knowledge.

C Short Answer Questions

16 How has big data technology accelerated advancements in scientific discovery?

17 What are some key benefits of high-performance computing (HPC) in scientific simulations?

18 Describe the role of big data in genomic data analysis and its impact on research.

19 Why is interdisciplinary collaboration important in global scientific projects involving big data?

20 What are some sustainability considerations when managing and analyzing big data in scientific research?

D Long Answer Questions

21 Discuss the impact of big data technologies on scientific research and discovery, highlighting specific fields where they have made significant contributions.

22 Analyze the role of high-performance computing (HPC) in enhancing scientific simulations and the challenges associated with its implementation.

23 Evaluate the importance of data collaboration in global scientific projects and how it contributes to advancing research across different domains.

24 Examine the sustainability considerations in big data research and propose strategies for developing efficient and environmentally responsible data management practices.

25 Explore how emerging technologies like artificial intelligence, IoT, and blockchain are shaping the future of scientific research and their potential benefits and challenges.

Further Readings

Brady, H.E., 2019. The challenge of big data and data science. *Annual Review of Political Science*, 22(1), pp. 297–323.

CERN Accelerating science., 2013. Animation shows LHC data processing. https://home.web.cern.ch/news/news/computing/animation-shows-lhc-data-processing.

Daniel, B.K., 2019. Big data and data science: a critical review of issues for educational research. *British Journal of Educational Technology*, 50(1), pp. 101–113.

Favaretto, M., De Clercq, E., Schneble, C.O. and Elger, B.S., 2020. What is your definition of Big Data? Researchers' understanding of the phenomenon of the decade. *PLoS One*, 15(2), p. e0228987.

Gupta, D. and Rani, R., 2019. A study of big data evolution and research challenges. *Journal of Information Science*, 45(3), pp. 322–340.

Haig, B.D., 2020. Big data science: a philosophy of science perspective. In: *Big Data in Psychological Research*, pp. 15–33. American Psychological Association.

Halwani, M.A., Amirkiaee, S.Y., Evangelopoulos, N. and Prybutok, V., 2022. Job qualifications study for data science and big data professions. *Information Technology & People*, 35(2), pp. 510–525.

Hassani, H., Huang, X. and Silva, E., 2019. Big data and climate change. *Big Data and Cognitive Computing*, 3(1), p. 12. https://doi.org/10.3390/bdcc3010012.

Hosseini, M., Wieczorek, M. and Gordijn, B., 2022. Ethical issues in social science research employing big data. *Science and Engineering Ethics*, 28(3), p. 29.

International Centre for Radio Astronomy Research., 2026. Square Kilometre Array. www.icrar.org/our-research/ska/.

Kaddoura, S. and Grati, R., 2021. Blockchain for healthcare and medical systems. In: *Enabling Blockchain Technology for Secure Networking and Communications*, pp. 249–270. IGI Global.

Kumar, P. and Kumari, A., 2024. *Blockchain for Biomedical Research and Healthcare*. Springer.

Leonelli, S., 2020. Scientific research and big data. In: *The Stanford Encyclopedia of Philosophy* (Winter 2025 Edition), Edward N. Zalta & Uri Nodelman (eds.), https://plato.stanford.edu/archives/win2025/entries/science-big-data/

Li, Z., Huang, Q., Carbone, G. J. and Hu, F., 2017. A high performance query analytical framework for supporting data-intensive climate studies. *Computers, Environment and Urban Systems*, 62, pp. 210–221.

National Human Genome Research Institute., 2024. Human Genome Project Fact Sheet. https://www.genome.gov/about-genomics/educational-resources/fact-sheets/human-genome-project.

Nazir, S., Khan, S., Khan, H.U., Ali, S., Garcia-Magarino, I., Atan, R.B. and Nawaz, M., 2020. A comprehensive analysis of healthcare big data management, analytics and scientific programming. *IEEE Access*, 8, pp. 95714–95733.

Parekh, H., Kumari, A., Yadav, D., Tanwar, S. and Kumar, P., 2024. Neural network-based cyber threats detection and mitigation framework in aerial communication systems underlying 6G. In: *2024 Eighth International Conference on Parallel, Distributed and Grid Computing (PDGC)*, pp. 651–657. IEEE.

Prokofieva, M. and Miah, S.J., 2019. Blockchain in healthcare [Online]. *Australasian Journal of Information Systems*, 23.

Raban, D.R. and Gordon, A., 2020. The evolution of data science and big data research: a bibliometric analysis. *Scientometrics*, 122(3), pp. 1563–1581.

Rawat, R. and Yadav, R., 2021. Big data: big data analysis, issues and challenges and technologies. In: *IOP Conference Series: Materials Science and Engineering*, Vol. 1022, No. 1, p. 012014. IOP Publishing.

Saez-Rodriguez, J., Rinschen, M.M., Floege, J. and Kramann, R., 2019. Big science and big data in nephrology. *Kidney International*, 95(6), pp. 1326–1337.

Schembera, B. and Durán, J.M., 2020. Dark data as the new challenge for big data science and the introduction of the scientific data officer. *Philosophy & Technology*, 33, pp. 93–115.

Succi, S. and Coveney, P.V., 2019. Big data: the end of the scientific method?. *Philosophical Transactions of the Royal Society A*, 377(2142), p. 20180145.
The University of Chicago., 2022. Scientists announced the discovery of the Higgs boson 10 years ago. What's next? https://news.uchicago.edu/story/scientists-announced-discovery-higgs-boson-10-years-ago-whats-next.

10

Future Perspectives

LEARNING OBJECTIVES

- Understand emerging trends in big data management, including innovative storage, processing, and analytical techniques, and their implications for future research and applications.
- Explore the role of generative AI in analyzing complex datasets to support sustainable development goals and societal advancement. Examine how advanced AI-driven analytics can enhance decision-making, optimize resource use, and address real-world challenges in social, economic, and environmental contexts.
- Develop awareness of the ethical, practical, and technological considerations in deploying generative AI for long-term societal benefits.

10.1 Introduction

The fields of big data, artificial intelligence (AI), the Internet of Things (IoT), and blockchain are rapidly evolving and converging, opening up new frontiers for big data management and analytics. As we look ahead, several emerging trends and technologies are poised to reshape the landscape, offering both opportunities and challenges. The rapid growth of big data and advancements in AI are shaping the way individuals, organizations, and societies make decisions. As datasets become larger and more complex, traditional methods of data management and analysis are no longer sufficient. Emerging technologies, including real-time analytics, cloud computing, and intelligent data frameworks, are enabling more efficient handling of information and supporting informed decision-making across multiple sectors. At the same time, generative AI (Gen AI) is opening new possibilities for extracting insights from complex datasets and addressing real-world challenges. From optimizing resource allocation to supporting sustainable development initiatives, AI-driven analytics is becoming an essential tool for creating solutions that balance technological progress with social and environmental responsibility. This chapter explores the future of data management and the transformative potential of Gen AI, such as ChatGPT, Gemini, and Grok. It highlights both opportunities and challenges, emphasizing responsible use, ethical considerations, and strategies for leveraging advanced technologies to promote sustainable growth and societal well-being.

10.1.1 Motivation

The growing complexity and volume of data, along with rapid advances in AI, are transforming the way societies function and make decisions. Traditional methods of managing and analyzing data are no longer enough to keep pace with modern challenges. At the same time, there is a growing need to harness these technologies responsibly to support sustainable development, optimize resource use, and address societal issues. These factors make it crucial to explore emerging data management trends and the role of Gen AI in shaping a future that is both technologically advanced and socially responsible.

10.1.2 Chapter Contribution

- Highlights emerging trends in big data management, including cloud-based systems, real-time analytics, and intelligent frameworks that improve the efficiency and reliability of handling large datasets.
- Explores how Gen AI can analyze complex data to support sustainable development, enhance decision-making, and optimize resource allocation.
- Provides insights into future directions for leveraging technology to create resilient, data-informed systems that balance innovation with responsibility.

10.1.3 Organization of the Chapter

In this chapter, the next section highlights the emerging data management trends. Then, the chapter examines the applications of Gen AI for sustainable development, highlighting practical examples and strategies. Ethical and societal considerations are discussed next, followed by a discussion on challenges, opportunities, and future perspectives. The chapter concludes with a forward-looking view on building responsible, AI-driven, and data-informed systems for sustainable growth.

10.2 Emerging Data Management Trends

Figure 10.1 presents the latest trends in big data management. The exponential growth of data, driven by the proliferation of devices, sensors, and digital interactions, has challenged traditional data management approaches, necessitating the development of new strategies and technologies.

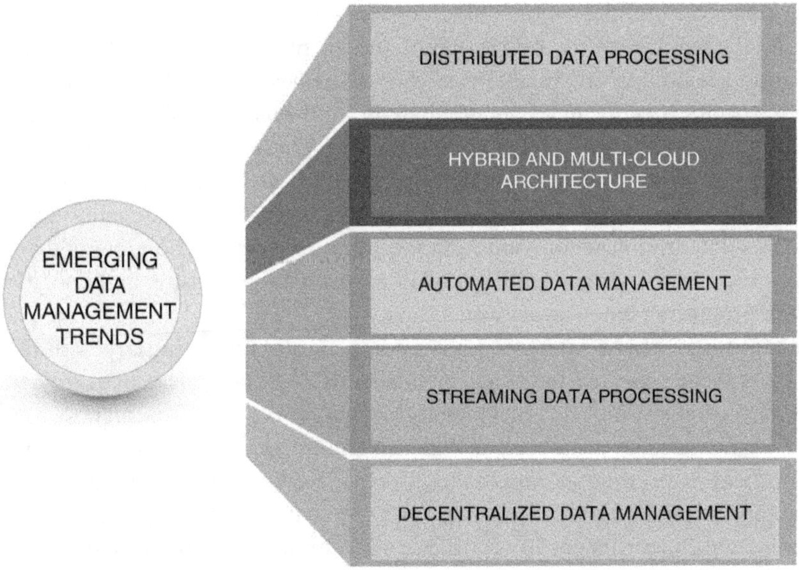

Figure 10.1 Latest trends in data management.

Several emerging trends are shaping the future of data management, addressing the complexities of big data and enabling more efficient, scalable, and secure data processing and analytics. It is discussed as follows:

1. **Distributed Data Processing:** The rise of edge computing and the IoT has led to a shift toward distributed data processing architectures. With IoT devices generating massive amounts of data at the edge, it becomes increasingly impractical to transmit all data to a centralized location for processing. Distributed data processing frameworks, such as Apache Spark, Hadoop, and Kafka, enable data processing and analytics to occur closer to the data source, reducing latency and improving real-time decision-making capabilities. Edge computing devices, equipped with processing power and storage capabilities, can preprocess and filter data locally, transmitting only relevant data to centralized systems. This approach not only reduces network bandwidth requirements but also addresses data privacy and security concerns by minimizing the need to transmit sensitive data over the network.
2. **Hybrid and Multicloud Architectures:** Organizations are increasingly adopting hybrid and multicloud architectures to leverage the scalability, flexibility, and cost-effectiveness of cloud computing while maintaining control over sensitive data and meeting regulatory compliance requirements. Hybrid cloud architectures combine on-premises infrastructure with public cloud resources, allowing organizations to keep critical data and

workloads on-premises while offloading less sensitive workloads to the cloud. Multicloud architectures, on the other hand, involve the use of multiple cloud providers, enabling organizations to choose the best-suited cloud services for their specific needs, avoid vendor lock-in, and ensure business continuity through redundancy and failover mechanisms. These architectures introduce challenges in data integration, data governance, and data security, as data may reside in multiple locations and environments. Emerging technologies, such as federated learning and secure multiparty computation, are addressing these challenges by enabling collaborative data processing and analytics while preserving data privacy and security.

3. **Automated Data Management:** The complexity of managing large volumes of diverse data has led to the development of automated data management solutions that leverage AI and machine learning (ML) techniques. These solutions can automate tasks such as data integration, data quality management, metadata management, and data governance, improving efficiency and reducing human error. Automated data integration tools can identify and resolve data inconsistencies, conflicts, and duplicates across disparate data sources, ensuring data consistency and accuracy. Data quality management solutions leverage ML algorithms to detect and correct data quality issues, such as missing values, outliers, and inconsistencies, improving the reliability and trustworthiness of data. Metadata management tools use AI and natural language processing techniques to automatically extract and organize metadata from data sources, enhancing data discoverability, understanding, and governance. Additionally, automated data governance solutions can enforce data policies, monitor data usage, and ensure compliance with relevant regulations and standards.
4. **Streaming Data Processing:** As real-time data streams from IoT devices, social media, and other sources become more prevalent, there is a growing need for efficient streaming data processing frameworks that can handle high-velocity data and support real-time analytics and decision-making. Traditional batch processing approaches are inadequate for dealing with continuously generated data streams, as they introduce latency and potential data loss. Streaming data processing frameworks, such as Apache Kafka, Apache Flink, and Apache Spark Streaming, enable the continuous ingestion, processing, and analysis of data streams in real time or near real time. These frameworks leverage techniques like windowing, event-time processing, and stateful operations to process and analyze data as it arrives, enabling timely insights and actions. Streaming data processing is particularly valuable in scenarios such as fraud detection, network monitoring, predictive maintenance, and real-time decision support systems, where timely responses and actions are critical.

5. **Decentralized Data Management:** The emergence of blockchain technology and decentralized data management platforms is enabling secure, transparent, and tamper-proof data sharing and collaboration among multiple parties. Blockchain-based data management solutions address issues of trust, data ownership, and data provenance by providing an immutable and distributed ledger for recording and verifying data transactions. Decentralized data management platforms, built on blockchain technology, allow participants to share and access data securely without relying on a central authority. These platforms leverage cryptographic techniques, such as digital signatures and consensus algorithms, to ensure data integrity, authenticity, and non-repudiation. In addition to enabling secure data sharing, decentralized data management platforms can facilitate data monetization by providing a transparent and auditable mechanism for data owners to sell or license their data to interested parties.

These emerging trends are driving the development of new data management solutions and architectures that can effectively handle the complexities of big data, while ensuring data quality, security, and compliance. As data continues to grow in volume, velocity, and variety, organizations that embrace these trends will be better positioned to extract value from their data assets and gain a competitive advantage. However, it is important to note that the adoption of these emerging trends may require significant investments in infrastructure, skills, and cultural shifts within organizations. Effective data governance, change management, and collaboration between technical and business stakeholders are crucial for the successful implementation and integration of these data management trends.

10.3 Generative AI-based Analytics for Sustainable Development of Society

Gen AI, a subset of AI focused on creating new data such as text, images, audio, and video, has the potential to revolutionize analytics and drive sustainable development across various sectors. By leveraging the power of *deep learning and neural networks*, generative AI models can extract insights from vast amounts of data and generate new, synthetic data that can be used for training AI systems, simulating scenarios, and testing hypotheses. Gen AI is now widely used across many fields, from content creation and marketing to scientific research, health care, and design. By simulating scenarios, generating insights, or automating creative tasks, it provides a powerful way to innovate and solve problems that were previously difficult or time-consuming. Some of the popular Gen AI tools are discussed as follows:

10.3.1 Popular Generative AI Tools

- **ChatGPT/GPT-4 (OpenAI):** For generating text, answering questions, summarizing content, and holding natural conversations.
- **DALL·E, MidJourney, Stable Diffusion:** For creating images from textual descriptions, enabling creative design and visualization.
- **Codex/GitHub Copilot:** For generating code and assisting software development projects.
- **Lumen5/Jasper:** For producing marketing content, blogs, and social media posts efficiently.
- **DeepMind AlphaFold:** For predicting protein structures, showing how generative AI can advance scientific discovery.

Gen AI offers a wide range of techniques and tools that are highly useful for analyzing complex datasets. Large language models, such as GPT-4 and LLaMA, enable the generation and interpretation of text-based data, while transformer architectures provide the foundation for attention-based learning, allowing models to focus on the most relevant information. For synthetic data generation, methods like variational autoencoders and generative adversarial networks can create realistic datasets that mimic real-world patterns, which is useful for training models or testing hypotheses. Techniques such as embedding vectors and feature extraction allow high-dimensional data to be represented in a compact numerical form, supporting downstream analysis. Gen AI also facilitates dimensionality reduction, predictive simulations, and anomaly detection, enabling researchers to identify trends, forecast outcomes, and spot unusual patterns in data. Additionally, metrics like perplexity, BLEU scores, and Frechet inception distance help assess the quality of AI-generated outputs, ensuring that synthetic data or predictions are reliable. The applications of generative AI-based analytics for sustainable development are vast and far-reaching, with significant implications for addressing pressing societal challenges and promoting environmental, economic, and social sustainability.

1. **Environmental Monitoring and Conservation:** Generative AI models can be trained on environmental data, such as satellite imagery, sensor data, climate models, and historical records, to generate synthetic data for simulating environmental scenarios and predicting the impact of various factors on ecosystems, biodiversity, and natural resources. For example, generative AI models can be used to simulate the effects of climate change on different regions, enabling stakeholders to evaluate the potential consequences and develop effective mitigation and adaptation strategies. Additionally, these models can aid in identifying areas at risk of deforestation, habitat loss, or natural disasters, allowing for proactive conservation efforts and resource management.

2. **Sustainable Agriculture and Food Security:** Agriculture is a critical sector for ensuring food security and promoting sustainable development. Generative AI can play a vital role in optimizing agricultural practices, improving crop yields, and reducing waste by analyzing historical data on crop yields, weather patterns, soil conditions, and other relevant factors. By generating synthetic data, generative AI models can simulate various scenarios and identify potential risks, such as pest outbreaks, drought conditions, or soil degradation. This information can guide farmers and agricultural organizations in developing effective strategies for sustainable farming practices, crop rotation, and efficient resource utilization. Furthermore, generative AI can aid in the development of precision agriculture techniques, enabling targeted and optimized application of inputs (e.g., fertilizers, pesticides) based on localized conditions, minimizing waste and environmental impact.
3. **Sustainable Energy and Infrastructure:** The transition toward sustainable energy sources and infrastructure is crucial for mitigating the impact of climate change and promoting environmental sustainability. Generative AI can be leveraged to simulate and optimize energy systems, such as renewable energy sources (e.g., solar, wind, hydroelectric) and smart grids, by generating synthetic data to evaluate different scenarios and identify potential bottlenecks or inefficiencies. By analyzing historical data on energy demand, weather patterns, and grid performance, generative AI models can generate synthetic data to test and optimize the design and operation of energy systems, ensuring reliable and efficient energy distribution while minimizing environmental impact. Additionally, generative AI can aid in the design and planning of sustainable infrastructure projects, such as transportation networks, buildings, and urban planning, by generating synthetic data for testing and evaluating different designs and scenarios, considering factors like energy efficiency, resource utilization, and environmental impact.
4. **Health Care and Medical Research:** Generative AI has the potential to accelerate medical research and improve health-care outcomes by generating synthetic patient data for training AI models, simulating clinical trials, and exploring new drug discoveries or treatment options. This approach can lead to more personalized and effective health-care solutions while minimizing the need for extensive real-world trials, which can be time-consuming, costly, and pose ethical concerns. Generative AI models can be trained on existing patient data, such as electronic health records, imaging data, and genetic information, to generate synthetic data that preserves the statistical properties and patterns of the original data while protecting individual privacy and data confidentiality. This synthetic data can be used to train AI models for various medical applications, such as disease diagnosis, treatment planning, and drug development, without compromising patient privacy or requiring access

to sensitive real-world data. Moreover, generative AI can simulate virtual clinical trials by generating synthetic patient cohorts and simulating different treatment scenarios, enabling researchers to evaluate the efficacy and safety of new drugs or therapies in a controlled and ethical manner.

5. **Education and Skill Development:** Education and skill development are critical enablers of sustainable development, empowering individuals and communities to participate in and contribute to economic, social, and environmental progress. Generative AI can be leveraged to create personalized learning experiences by generating synthetic data tailored to individual learners' needs, preferences, and learning styles. By analyzing data on student performance, learning behaviors, and educational content, generative AI models can generate customized learning materials, interactive simulations, and adaptive assessments to enhance the learning experience and promote effective knowledge acquisition and skill development. Additionally, generative AI can be used to create virtual learning environments and simulations, allowing learners to practice and develop skills in realistic, immersive scenarios without the need for physical resources or potential risks associated with real-world training. Furthermore, generative AI can aid in the development of intelligent tutoring systems and personalized learning assistants, providing real-time feedback, guidance, and support to learners based on their individual progress and areas of strength or weakness.

While generative AI holds immense potential for driving sustainable development, it is crucial to address ethical considerations, such as data privacy, bias mitigation, and responsible AI governance. Collaboration between researchers, policymakers, and stakeholders is essential to ensure that the benefits of generative AI are maximized while mitigating potential risks and unintended consequences. Ethical Considerations and Responsible AI Governance: As generative AI becomes more prevalent in various domains, it is essential to address ethical considerations and establish responsible AI governance frameworks to mitigate potential risks and ensure the responsible and trustworthy development and deployment of these technologies.

1. **Data Privacy and Security:** Generative AI models often rely on large datasets for training, raising concerns about data privacy and the potential misuse of sensitive information. It is crucial to implement robust data governance practices, anonymization techniques, and secure data handling protocols to protect individual privacy and ensure compliance with relevant regulations, such as the General Data Protection Regulation.
2. **Bias Mitigation:** Generative AI models can perpetuate and amplify existing biases present in the training data, leading to unfair or discriminatory outcomes. Proactive measures, such as bias detection and mitigation techniques,

should be employed to ensure fairness, accountability, and transparency in the development and deployment of generative AI systems.

3. **Accountability and Transparency:** As generative AI models become more complex and opaque, it is crucial to establish mechanisms for accountability and transparency. Explainable AI techniques can help stakeholders understand the decision-making processes and outputs of generative AI systems, enabling trust and responsible deployment.
4. **Ethical Governance and Oversight:** Comprehensive ethical governance frameworks and oversight mechanisms should be developed to ensure the responsible development and deployment of generative AI technologies. These frameworks should involve interdisciplinary collaboration among researchers, policymakers, industry leaders, and civil society organizations to address ethical concerns, establish guidelines, and promote responsible innovation.
5. **Validation and Testing:** Rigorous validation and testing procedures should be implemented to assess the performance, reliability, and potential risks of generative AI systems before deployment in real-world scenarios. This includes evaluating the models' robustness, fairness, and potential for unintended consequences or misuse.

By addressing these ethical considerations and implementing responsible AI governance practices, we can harness the transformative potential of generative AI for sustainable development while mitigating potential risks and ensuring the responsible and trustworthy deployment of these technologies.

10.4 Conclusion

The evolution of big data technologies and analytics, influenced by advancements in AI, IoT, and blockchain, is setting the stage for transformative changes across various sectors. Emerging data management trends, such as decentralized data architectures, edge computing, hybrid cloud strategies, and AI-driven data management, are redefining how organizations handle and utilize data. These trends not only enhance operational efficiency but also ensure greater security, compliance, and flexibility. Generative AI, in particular, holds immense promise for fostering sustainable development. Its ability to generate new data and models can revolutionize health care, drive environmental sustainability, enhance smart city infrastructure, and transform education and skill development. However, the potential benefits of generative AI come with ethical and social challenges that must be addressed to ensure responsible and equitable use. As we look to the future, it is clear that a synergistic approach, combining emerging technologies and ethical frameworks, will be crucial. By embracing these advancements thoughtfully and collaboratively, we can harness the power of big data technologies and analytics to create a more sustainable and prosperous society. The journey ahead promises to be both challenging and rewarding, demanding continuous innovation and vigilance to maximize the positive impact of these groundbreaking developments.

Practice Set

A Multiple Choice Questions (MCQ)

1 Which emerging data management trend focuses on decentralizing data storage and processing?
- **a** Hybrid cloud strategies
- **b** Edge computing
- **c** Decentralized data architectures
- **d** AI-driven data management

2 What is a key benefit of edge computing in data management?
- **a** Centralizing data processing
- **b** Reducing data latency
- **c** Increasing data volume
- **d** Simplifying data visualization

3 How can generative AI contribute to environmental sustainability?
- **a** By generating new data models for predicting environmental changes
- **b** By centralizing data management
- **c** By reducing data collection methods
- **d** By increasing data storage costs

4 What is an essential consideration when implementing generative AI in health care?
- **a** Data encryption
- **b** Ethical and social challenges
- **c** Simplified data collection
- **d** Increased data redundancy

5 Which trend involves using a combination of on-premises and cloud-based solutions?
- **a** Decentralized data architectures
- **b** Hybrid cloud strategies
- **c** Edge computing
- **d** AI-driven data management

6 What role does AI-driven data management play in organizations?
- **a** Enhancing operational efficiency and flexibility
- **b** Simplifying data collection methods
- **c** Increasing data volume
- **d** Centralizing data storage

7 Which emerging technology can enhance smart city infrastructure?
- **a** Blockchain
- **b** Generative AI
- **c** Traditional data processing
- **d** Edge computing

8 What is a key challenge associated with the use of generative AI?
- **a** Data storage capacity
- **b** Ethical and social issues
- **c** Simplified data processing
- **d** Increased data redundancy

9 What aspect of hybrid cloud strategies offers operational flexibility?
- **a** Centralized data management
- **b** Combining on-premises and cloud solutions
- **c** Reducing data latency
- **d** Simplifying data collection

10 Why is a synergistic approach important for future data management?
- **a** It combines emerging technologies with ethical frameworks
- **b** It reduces data volume
- **c** It centralizes data storage
- **d** It simplifies data analysis

B Fill-in-the-Blanks

11 Emerging data management trends, such as decentralized data architectures and __________ computing, are redefining how organizations handle data.

12 Generative AI has the potential to revolutionize health care, drive environmental __________, and transform education.

13 One of the main challenges associated with generative AI is addressing __________ and social issues.

14 Hybrid cloud strategies involve a combination of __________ and cloud-based solutions.

15 To maximize the positive impact of technological advancements, a __________ approach combining emerging technologies and ethical frameworks is crucial.

C Short Answer Questions

16 Describe how decentralized data architectures contribute to data management.

17 What are the benefits of adopting edge computing in data handling?

18 How can generative AI impact environmental sustainability?

19 What ethical and social challenges must be addressed when using generative AI in various sectors?

20 Explain the concept of hybrid cloud strategies and their advantages for organizations.

D Long Answer Questions

21 Discuss the transformative potential of emerging data management trends, such as decentralized architectures, edge computing, and AI-driven data management. How do these trends enhance operational efficiency and security?

22 Analyze the role of generative AI in advancing sustainable development across sectors like health care, smart cities, and education. What are the key benefits and challenges associated with its application?

23 Evaluate the importance of a synergistic approach in combining emerging technologies with ethical frameworks. How can organizations effectively balance innovation with responsibility?

24 Examine the impact of hybrid cloud strategies on operational flexibility and resource management. What factors should organizations consider when implementing these strategies?

25 Explore the future perspectives of big data technologies and analytics. How can thoughtful and collaborative adoption of these technologies lead to a more sustainable and prosperous society?

Further Readings

Ahir, S., Telavane, D. and Thomas, R., 2020. The impact of artificial intelligence, blockchain, big data and evolving technologies in coronavirus disease-2019 (COVID-19) curtailment. In: *2020 International Conference on Smart Electronics and Communication (ICOSEC)*, pp. 113–120. IEEE.

Al Habsi, T.A.S. and Dattana, V., 2021. A study on future perspectives of healthcare data analytics using Internet of Things. *Sparklinglight Transactions on Artificial Intelligence and Quantum Computing (STAIQC)*, 1(1), pp. 1–10.

Deepa, N., Pham, Q.V., Nguyen, D.C., Bhattacharya, S., Prabadevi, B., Gadekallu, T.R., Maddikunta, P.K.R., Fang, F. and Pathirana, P.N., 2022. A survey on blockchain for big data: approaches, opportunities, and future directions. *Future Generation Computer Systems*, 131, pp. 209–226.

Garcia, A.R., 2020. AI, IoT, Big data, and technologies in digital economy with blockchain at sustainable work satisfaction to smart mankind: access to 6th dimension of human rights. *Smart Governance for Cities: Perspectives and Experiences*, pp. 83–131. Springer.

Gill, S.S., Tuli, S., Xu, M., Singh, I., Singh, K.V., Lindsay, D., Tuli, S., Smirnova, D., Singh, M., Jain, U. and Pervaiz, H., 2019. Transformative effects of IoT, Blockchain and Artificial Intelligence on cloud computing: evolution, vision, trends and open challenges. *Internet of Things*, 8, p. 100118.

Hibti, M., Baïna, K. and Benatallah, B., 2019. Towards Swarm Intelligence architectural patterns: an IoT-Big Data-AI-Blockchain convergence perspective. In: *Proceedings of the 4th International Conference on Big Data and Internet of Things*, pp. 1–8. Association for Computing Machinery.

Himeur, Y., Elnour, M., Fadli, F., Meskin, N., Petri, I., Rezgui, Y., Bensaali, F. and Amira, A., 2023. AI-big data analytics for building automation and management systems: a survey, actual challenges and future perspectives. *Artificial Intelligence Review*, 56(6), pp. 4929–5021.

Kaddoura, S. and Grati, R., 2021. Blockchain for healthcare and medical systems. In: *Enabling Blockchain Technology for Secure Networking and Communications*, pp. 249–270. IGI Global.

Karatas, M., Eriskin, L., Deveci, M., Pamucar, D. and Garg, H., 2022. Big Data for Healthcare Industry 4.0: applications, challenges and future perspectives. *Expert Systems with Applications*, 200, p. 116912.

Kaur, I., Kumar, Y. and Sandhu, A.K., 2021. A comprehensive survey of AI, blockchain technology and big data applications in medical field and global health. In: *2021 International Conference on Technological Advancements and Innovations (ICTAI)*, pp. 593–598. IEEE.

Kumari, A., Tanwar, S., Tyagi, S. and Kumar, N., 2019. Fog data analytics: a taxonomy and process model. *Journal of Network and Computer Applications*, 128, pp. 90–104.

Kumari, A., Tanwar, S., Tyagi, S. and Kumar, N., 2019. Verification and validation techniques for streaming big data analytics in internet of things environment. *IET Networks*, 8(3), 155–163.

Kumari, A., Tanwar, S., Tyagi, S. and Kumar, N., 2020. Blockchain-based massive data dissemination handling in IIoT environment. *IEEE Network*, 35(1), pp. 318–325.

Kumari, A., Tanwar, S., Tyagi, S., Kumar, N., Parizi, R. M. and Choo, K. K. R., 2019. Multimedia big data computing and Internet of Things applications: a taxonomy and process model. *Journal of Network and Computer Applications*, 124, pp. 169–195.

Logeswaran, K., Savitha, S., Suresh, P., Prasanna Kumar, K.R., Gunasekar, M., Rajadevi, R., Dharani, M.K. and Jayasurya, A.S., 2024. Unifying technologies in Industry 4.0: harnessing the synergy of Internet of Things, Big Data, Augmented Reality/Virtual Reality, and Blockchain technologies. In: *Topics in Artificial Intelligence Applied to Industry 4.0*, pp. 127–147. Wiley.

Marengo, A., 2024. Navigating the nexus of AI and IoT: a comprehensive review of data analytics and privacy paradigms. *Internet of Things*, 27, p. 101318.

Prokofieva, M. and Miah, S.J., 2019. Blockchain in healthcare [Online]. *Australasian Journal of Information Systems*, 23.

Rejeb, A., Rejeb, K., Appolloni, A., Jagtap, S., Iranmanesh, M., Alghamdi, S., Alhasawi, Y. and Kayikci, Y., 2024. Unleashing the power of internet of things and blockchain: a comprehensive analysis and future directions. *Internet of Things and Cyber-Physical Systems*, 4, pp. 1–18.

Siripurapu, S., Darimireddy, N.K., Chehri, A., Sridhar, B. and Paramkusam, A.V., 2023. Technological advancements and elucidation gadgets for healthcare applications: an exhaustive methodological review-Part-I (AI, big data, block chain, open-source technologies, and cloud computing). *Electronics*, 12(3), p. 750.

Tyagi, A.K., 2021. Analysis of security and privacy aspects of blockchain technologies from Smart Era' perspective: the challenges and a way forward to future. In: *Recent Trends in Blockchain for Information Systems Security and Privacy*, pp. 141–157. CRC Press.

Tyagi, A.K., Aswathy, S.U. and Abraham, A., 2020. Integrating blockchain technology and artificial intelligence: synergies perspectives challenges and research directions. *Journal of Information Assurance and Security*, 15(5), p. 1554.

Index

www.ingramcontent.com/pod-product-compliance
Lightning Source LLC
LaVergne TN
LVHW011304051126
851579LV00058B/19